Prostitutes and Their Rescuers

Youth in a Globalizing World

Series Editors

Vincenzo Cicchelli, *Ceped, Université de Paris/*IRD
Sylvie Octobre, DEPS – DOC, *Ministère de la culture and Centre
Max Weber,* ENS *Lyon/*CNRS *(France)*

VOLUME 20

The titles published in this series are listed at *brill.com/ygw*

Prostitutes and Their Rescuers

Sociological Dynamics and Public Controversies in French Prostitution

By

Lilian Mathieu

With a Foreword by

Phil Hubbard

BRILL

LEIDEN | BOSTON

Cover illustration: Photo by Raphael Wild on Unsplash.

This book has received the support of the GIS Institut du Genre, the Vice-présidence à la recherche of the Ecole normale supérieure de Lyon and the Centre Max Weber.

Translated by A.D.T. International.

The Library of Congress Cataloging-in-Publication Data is available online at https://catalog.loc.gov
LC record available at https://lccn.loc.gov/2023001636

Typeface for the Latin, Greek, and Cyrillic scripts: "Brill". See and download: brill.com/brill-typeface

ISSN 2212-9383
ISBN 978-90-04-54005-7 (hardback)
ISBN 978-90-04-54153-5 (e-book)

Printed by Printforce, United Kingdom

Contents

Foreword

Few sociological subjects excite so much passion – and anger – as prostitution. Having studied in the field for thirty or so years, I know only too well how academic discussions can quickly deteriorate as audiences split into different ideological factions. In much of the urban West, radical feminists who refuse to recognize sex work as a legitimate form of work have become a more vocal contingent in recent times. However, there has clearly always been an abolitionist movement that regards prostitution as an inherently criminal, and perhaps even evil, profession. Against this, there is also a pro-sex work movement that recognizes that while sex working might not be the safest or most desirable form of work, it is among the most lucrative jobs that can be taken by women (and men) who lack other options, and on this basis, needs to be recognized and protected like other (legitimate) forms of working. Though both lobbies might agree on their overall aims – decent wages for women, the end of patriarchal relations, and the reduction of sexual violence – they hold almost antithetical attitudes towards prostitution. The encounters between different factions often produce much heat, but seldom progress our understanding of the matter at hand or offer much hope for reconciliation.

In the twenty-first century, these debates have become more centralized within government and policy circles, with the penalization of the purchase of sexual services having replaced the criminalization of the selling of sex as the default model for regulation (the so-called Swedish or Nordic model). Throughout much of Europe, we have therefore seen a perverse tendency towards a more open acceptance of commercial sexuality (on the Internet in particular), but an increasingly censorious attitude towards those men who purchase sexual services. Such policy fits with the radical feminist take on sex work which sees clients and pimps as exploiters and seemingly allows sex workers to sell services free from risk of punishment. But as Lilian Mathieu shows in this book, these policies have converse impacts: it is sex workers who are effectively punished, because their work has become harder, not easier, with clients seeking to evade arrest by seeking the services of prostitutes in more dangerous spaces. Prostitution is becoming less visible in our major cities – whether Paris or Lyon, or for that matter London, Amsterdam and Brussels – but while that might encourage us to think that the issue has gone away, or that sex work has simply migrated online (into the worlds of Camming and Internet pornography) this clearly doesn't tell the whole story. Sex work is sometimes underground and on the margins, perhaps, but it persists nonetheless. As long as there is economic necessity, there is supply, and as long as there are clients with unfulfilled sexual desires, there remains demand. Policy and regulation will never remove or destroy prostitution, it seems, but simply change its dominant forms and visibilities.

How then should the academics position themselves in this debate? This is not an easy question to answer, especially for male researchers whose motives and positionality can be lazily imputed by other parties, whether abolitionists or decriminalizers. But in this book Lilian Mathieu gives us the answer: by pursuing work, which is not dogmatic or mired in ideology, but which begins with grounded ethnography, describing the varied lives of prostitute women, men and trans workers in so much as they exist within a united field of social action. As he usefully notes, there is not one chosen identity within the sex working community, which cannot really be described as a chosen community at all: rather it is an identity which sex workers take on, and which reflects their relegation and subordination within social systems. Indeed, the fact that he talks of prostitutes rather than sex workers is no mere ideological device or slippage of language, but a deliberate and careful description of the way that the prostitute persists as a discredited identity, subject to symbolic violence of various kinds that often informs and encourages real, physical violence. Mathieu's work on the attitudes of residents to local sex working women is particularly revealing in this respect, and helps trace how stereotypes of clients, pimps and prostitutes enter into the realms of social action, with often devastating impacts on the workers who are displaced in the name of neighborhood well-being and community morality.

Much has been written about sex work and prostitution policy in the twenty-first century – perhaps even too much? But what we lack is the type of grounded, empirical but theoretically informed work which Lilian Mathieu offers in this timely and detailed summary of his research on sex work in France in the twenty-first century. Unlike some writing on the subject, which offers abstraction and high-level theorization, here the theoretical concepts – derived from Boltanski, Bourdieu, Castel, Goffman and others – are used as guiding devices that help us make sense of the complexity of the world, not make it more complex or abstract. What Lilian Mathieu presents cannot be considered as a purely objective summary of the lives of sex workers – how could it be? – but it is an account that does not let its conclusions be informed by dogma or ideology and follows the principles of good sociology throughout (it is analytically rigorous, ethically sensitive and pays important attention to questions of class, ethnicity, gender and sexuality as they intersect in the field). As such, this book needs to be read as more than an expose of the worlds of sex workers in France. It is a sociologically-informed and detailed explanation as to how policy and law impacts on sex workers, pimps and clients, and how this creates particular risks of violence that are contrary to the aims of those who make these laws. It is to be hoped it reaches a wide audience and is carefully read before it is pigeonholed as either pro- or anti-sex work, as the issues it discusses are too important to be clouded by entrenched ideology.

Professor Phil Hubbard
King's College London
July 2022

Introduction

Prostitutes and Their Rescuers, Avatars of an Interdependence

The title of this book might suggest that it addresses two distinct entities in parallel – people involved in prostitution on one side, and people who want to rescue them on the other. Certainly, these two groups appear to be radically distinct, belonging to social worlds that could not be further apart. The overwhelming majority of prostitutes come from the most disadvantaged strata of society and are subject to an accumulation of obstacles and vulnerabilities, starting with the stigma that makes happen them as sexual deviants. Meanwhile, their rescuers – whether they are social workers, police officers, activists, magistrates, politicians or intellectuals – belong to the most integrated segments of our societies. Generally able to draw on above-average economic and cultural resources, they also benefit from a positive image: working, as they aim to do, for the good of the weakest and most unfortunate is highly gratifying on a symbolic level. Prostitutes and their rescuers appear to fit into a series of opposing pairs – exclusion/integration, deviance/normality, marginality/norm, illegitimacy/legitimacy, passivity/determination, disorder/order, confusion/rationality etc. – and to require different analysis frameworks: the sociology of deviance for the former; the study of social movements and public policy for the latter.

However, this is not the perspective adopted here, and from this relational viewpoint the key word in the title could be the "and" that links prostitutes with their rescuers. This book is based on the presupposition of a close interdependence between the two groups. Regardless of their status and their intentions, rescuers need prostitutes in order to maintain their position, sometimes even going so far as to invent them when the kinds of prostitutes they are looking for are in short supply, as we will see with the fight against human trafficking. Prostitutes, meanwhile, have to deal with the activities and activism of those concerned about what happens to them. The rescuers' public statements, the analyses they publish, the decisions they adopt, the policies they promote or implement, etc., inevitably have consequences for how prostitutes perceive and carry out their activity. A simple example will make this clear: defining prostitution as sexist violence, as a whole activist movement has done, leads logically to the criminalization of the guilty parties, in this case the clients; this then affects prostitutes directly by depriving them of a proportion of their income while also pushing their activity further underground.

This perspective is certainly not original. The most fruitful developments in the sociology of deviance (Goffman 1963; Becker 1963) adopt precisely this relational approach, which requires marginality to be seen in relation to dominant norms. According to a now-famous formulation, it is "normal people" who produce deviance by labelling certain behaviors as such and submitting those who adopt them to different treatments, usually unfavorable or degrading (Garfinkel 1956). From this viewpoint, no conduct is deviant in itself; it is its social stigmatization that makes it become so. What might at first glance appear to be a tautology – deviance is whatever is considered and treated as deviant – has demonstrated its sociological value by illuminating both the restrictive force and the relativity of social norms. Since the seminal work of Goffman and Becker, many significant changes have affected the definitions of what is "normal" and "deviant" in our societies, particularly in terms of sexual morality. Once the very definition of sexual deviance, homosexuality can now be expressed publicly, while behavior that was once seen as trivial, such as street harassment, has become a public problem.

Prostitution is another practice whose definition, and the social reactions it causes, have evolved radically over recent decades – though without eliminating its status as external to the dominant norms. In other words, while prostitution is still considered a deviant behavior, this is no longer for the same reasons as before. One major evolution involves a transfer of stigma from the person selling sexual services to the person buying them. While prostitutes were treated for centuries as "women of ill repute", entirely devoted to vice and immorality, the turn of the twenty-first century has seen society's view of them turned on its head. Rather than being condemned and punished – or at least subject to strict control – prostitutes are now considered above all as victims who need to be rescued. This change has only been possible because those who argued for this victim status were no longer in a minority. They managed, after a long and arduous struggle, to achieve almost universal agreement for their positions at political level.

However, the fact that prostitutes are no longer as violently ostracized as in the past does not mean they have stopped being seen as remote from what Goffman called the "world of normals". Quite the opposite: considering them as victims means assigning to them a series of distinctive characteristics, such as experience of sexual violence, oppression by pimps, exposure to mental or physical illness, character traits such as an unusual degree of credulity, a flawed relationship with money, and a distorted experience of sexuality etc. Previously defined by their active contribution to social depravity, prostitutes nowadays tend to be distinguished by their passiveness in relation to the different forms of suffering to which they are subjected. They are no less fundamentally different from what "normal" women are, or should be.

Similarly, prostitution is still disapproved of, no longer because it constitutes a form of extramarital, multiple-partner sex for purposes other than reproduction, but instead because it represents patriarchal exploitation of women's bodies. The moral disapproval no longer affects those who earn a living from paid-for sexual services, but those who abuse their fundamental vulnerability by taking advantage of their bodies, either sexually (clients) or monetarily (pimps). What could be called a transfer of culpability naturally has concrete consequences: aware of the (still fairly recent) rejection of their practices, clients become more discreet about a form of consumption that new generations of men are tending to abandon. Once an activity that used to be relatively frequent (particularly as a first sexual experience) and publicly accepted, visiting prostitutes has become a shameful secret of male sexuality (Bajos and Bozon 2008). This has affected concrete forms of prostitution through both specific public policies (mainly penal and social) and more diffuse sociological transformations, such as changing levels of tolerance for the presence of prostitutes within urban spaces.

These changes are addressed here from the viewpoint of the situation in France. This is justified by the historical importance of France in how prostitution has been viewed and managed. What quickly came to be known in other countries as the "French system" – administrative regulation of the sex trade requiring prostitutes to register with their municipality and undergo regular health checks, with imprisonment for anyone seeking to escape these obligations – was designed and put in place in the wake of the French Revolution (Corbin 1996; Plumauzille 2016). These restrictive measures, from which clients were entirely exempt, were intended both to prevent venereal disease and to enforce morality in public spaces (via brothels, dedicated establishments for the purpose). They spread internationally during the nineteenth century. This regulatory framework directly inspired a whole imaginary world of prostitution, illustrated by a series of cultural representations – especially literary and pictorial (Houbre 2015) – that are still influential today. France is one of the countries that maintained its regulationist system the longest, despite its clear failure to achieve its goals. Eliminating it took two attempts – brothels were prohibited in 1946 (though only in mainland France) and health checks were abolished in 1960 (Brunet 1990).

France is also the country that has seen the most full-throated expression of the collective voices of prostitutes themselves, in spring 1975. The hundred or so women who occupied the church of Saint-Nizier in Lyon on the morning of 2 June 1975 to protest against police harassment had no idea they would become a foundational reference for all future activist movements of prostitutes around the world (Mathieu 2001; 2003). This was the first time that some of society's most ostracized and despised women had dared to confront repression and publicly express a set of demands. It was also the first time they had demanded the right to be consulted about the policies (penal, social, fiscal, family etc.) that affected them. Finally, it was also the first time they had claimed the power to express themselves directly, rather than through the obligatory intermediary of spokespeople from outside their group.

The results of the protest were varied and sometimes disappointing on all these levels, but it revealed tensions and fault lines that remain particularly sensitive even today. One example is the capacity of prostitutes to have their legitimate collective voice heard – and, above all, acknowledged. This question relates firstly to how the authority to speak in the name of the group can be delegated to representatives. The conditions for this are difficult to establish, given the population's level of cultural and economic disadvantage, indefinite contours and rarely converging interests (Bourdieu 1992b).[1] Above all, it concerns the nature of their claims and the ability of a group subject to multiple vulnerabilities and insecurities to identify the locus of what the sociology of social movements would call their *collective good* (Olson 1965). Does it lie in the recognition and institutionalization of what some consider to be their trade, or should it be directed more towards the abandonment of an activity seen as intrinsically oppressive?

This duality can be recognized as the fundamental split in the debates which, in France and many other countries, currently pit proponents of "sex work"[2] against advocates for the abolition of prostitution. The French version of this opposition has a number of distinctive features, however, which are largely dependent on the state of activism on the subject. Though French feminism, which was particularly dynamic at the time, gave active support to the church occupations, it became increasingly doubtful about the positions it should adopt with regard to prostitution, hesitating between condemning an activity considered fundamentally sexist and unconditionally supporting the demands of the prostitutes (Mignard 1976; Mathieu 2014b). This hesitation has now become a deep internal division within the French women's movement, feeding virulent disagreements between so-called "sex-positive" feminism supporting "sex work" and allies of abolitionism.

---

1 The adversaries of the "sex work" movement continually highlight its leaders' lack of representativeness, in that they come from the most privileged sections of the prostitution space (such as "escorts" who are graduates with French nationality).
2 The expression "sex work" ("*travail du sexe*") has strongly militant connotations in France, and its use suggests support for demands for recognition of the sale of sexual services as a "trade". This is why I do not use it, and prefer the more common, neutral term "prostitution".

The abolitionist movement has itself evolved significantly in recent years, in both its composition and its demands (Mathieu 2014a). French abolitionism emerged in the late nineteenth century on a similar basis to its British counterpart – originating among the progressive Protestant middle class – and focused its efforts on the abolition of the regulationist model. Its first significant evolution occurred immediately after the Second World War with the integration of left-wing Catholic currents. Through the organization the *Mouvement du Nid* ("Nest Movement"), which was to become central, these schools of thought claimed a dominant position in social outreach work targeting prostitutes, on one hand, and a role as legitimate spokespeople for what should be seen as the "collective good" of prostitutes, i.e. the complete and permanent abandonment of their activity, on the other.

This predominance of Catholic abolitionism, constructed over the 1960s and 1970s, was challenged by the AIDS epidemic. Fearing a return to the mandatory health checks it had historically been constructed to oppose, abolitionist social work withdrew from the field of prevention[3] and left the space open for new players promoting a participatory approach to public health. Associations sprang up to carry out preventive initiatives under the banner of "community health", drawing on the knowledge and abilities of prostitutes themselves and considering them as professionals with health-related skills that could be put to good use with their clients and their peers (Mathieu 2000). Whereas abolitionist social work sees prostitution as intrinsically negative, with rehabilitation as the only alternative, community health sees it as an activity that needs to be de-stigmatized and decriminalized in order to enable the full social reintegration of its practitioners.

Arising from the AIDS-prevention associations, new activist organizations emerged at the very end of the 1990s to demand recognition for prostitution, such as *Les Putes* (the "Whores") and the *Syndicat du travail du sexe* (STRASS, the Union of Sex Workers). Their mobilization and the radicalism of their opposition to abolitionism (Deschamps 2005) might not have been so significant if prostitution had not at the same time undergone an unprecedented politicization, illustrated by a series of laws being drafted: a new crime of human trafficking and the restoration of the offence of soliciting in 2003, followed by the criminalization of clients and the introduction of "paths out of prostitution" in 2016 – all of which were promoted and adopted for the greater good of prostitutes, unanimously seen as victims, despite protests from prostitutes

---

3   During the 1980s, abolitionists were heard to argue that giving up prostitution was the best
    protection against HIV.

themselves, who feared that these benevolent intentions would expose them to still greater insecurity and vulnerability.

This book – and especially its last four chapters – examines these activist movements, controversies and public policies in detail, putting them in context and studying their protagonists, all of whom (abolitionists, feminists, sex work activists, politicians, intellectuals etc.), despite their differences, claim to defend the collective good of prostitutes and can thus be encapsulated under the name of "rescuers". But again, this depiction is not enough on its own, and we must also capture the evolutions in the world of prostitution itself, to the extent that they support – or, conversely, are caused by – the dynamics of the controversies and the changing policies put in place. The first three chapters of the book thus focus more specifically on the changes, but also the continuities and stable elements, that are specific to the world of prostitution.

A brief description of my trajectory as a sociologist, specializing for thirty years or so in studying the different facets of prostitution, will provide context for the data on which this book is based and clarify the methodology by which they were collected. In this case, the conditions under which the research was undertaken are inseparable from the time when it was carried out. This does not mean that the validity of the knowledge generated is limited to its specific context and the location where it was gathered and developed; on the contrary, it constitutes a resource for comparison with similar data (especially international) so that general lessons can be learned.

I began working on prostitution in 1991, when I was still a student. That year, I was invited by Daniel Welzer-Lang, one of my teachers at the University of Lyon 2 and a specialist in the study of sexuality and social attitudes to sex, to join a team he was putting together to carry out research into "new territories of prostitution in Lyon". The research had been commissioned by the *Amicale du Nid* ("Friends of the Nest"), an abolitionist social work association, which was concerned about the disappearance of its target group of "traditional" prostitutes, working the alleys of the old city center, and the emergence of new segments in the sex market (transgender prostitutes, drug-addicted "occasional" prostitutes, massage parlors etc.), which it could only access with difficulty. The research received funding from the *Agence française de lutte contre le sida* (the French Agency for the Fight against AIDS), a semi-public organization of the time working to develop an HIV prevention policy, which the French government had been late to put in place. Changes within the world of prostitution and new public policies were thus woven together in this first research project, conducted mostly through individual interviews with prostitutes and by shadowing social workers in the streets. A joint publication set out the main results (Welzer-Lang, Barbosa and Mathieu 1994).

My work continued with a political science thesis at the University of Paris X-Nanterre on the subject of activism by prostitutes (Mathieu 2001; 2003). The goal was to study how collective action was possible among a population as stigmatized and disadvantaged (particularly in terms of gender, protest traditions and resources) as prostitutes. Comparing the church occupation movement in 1975, the establishment of the International Committee for Prostitutes' Rights in 1980 and the creation of community health associations, the thesis – produced on the basis of interviews and archival research – showed that these activist movements could only emerge because prostitutes had received support for their cause from outside their group. Depending on the situation, this support came from abolitionist activists, feminists or public health workers; their sincere conviction that they were contributing to prostitutes' collective good did not prevent them from exercising an inevitable influence on the forms and priorities of the prostitutes' advocacy. In other words, the research demonstrated a form of political dependence on the part of prostitutes, while also opening up knowledge about the space of debates relating to the status of prostitution.

My study of community health associations, which I had already begun to address in the thesis, continued in the early 2000s. This time the goal was no longer to examine their activist aspects, but to study their concrete practices in terms of health and safety for street prostitutes. Conducted through ethnographic observation over several months in Lyon (with the *Cabiria* association) and Marseille (with the *Autres regards* association),[4] this research enabled me to complete (and sometimes qualify or revise) the data collected during the research into new territories of prostitution in Lyon. Over the course of very long informal discussions, both at the associations' premises and in camper vans operating at night in the areas where prostitutes worked, I was able to collect very rich information about the backgrounds, living conditions, practices, difficulties, hopes etc. of the people I met. These data were often all the richer for being collected "on the spot", when prostitutes were taking a break from their work and talking about their immediate experience of competition, insecurity, their low levels of earnings etc. Included as an afterword to this book, a chapter on methodology describes in more detail not only the system for collecting data that I put in place at the time, but also how ethnography stimulated my "sociological imagination" and led me to formalize theoretically some of my empirical observations.

---

4   I was also able to carry out more occasional observations in Paris with the associations PASTT (Prevention, Action and Health for Transvestites and Transsexuals) and *Le Bus des femmes* (Women's Bus).

The data collected during this phase of my work mostly inform the first three chapters of the book, which deal with the structures and hierarchies within the world of prostitution, the role of violence and the social vulnerability of prostitutes respectively. These chapters are based on articles published shortly after the data were collected, and therefore, although I have tried to bring them up to date, they are now remote in time. Comparing them with more recent knowledge, relating to the state of prostitution closer to the present, does not appear to me to invalidate the analyses I propose; on the contrary, it attests to the stability – despite all the undeniable changes – and the ascendancy of certain fundamental logics in what I call the *prostitution space*. This applies, for example, to competition between prostitutes, which is currently all the more acute in that clients, now threatened with sanctions, are increasingly scarce and able to haggle for lower prices and unprotected practices. As the recruitment of prostitutes has become more international, the fact that this competition increasingly involves national or "ethnic" criteria only confirms the lack of cohesion in what I call, following Pollak (1988), a "destiny group". The same applies to the omnipresent insecurity, covered in the second chapter, in which prostitutes work, continuously exposed to attacks, extortion and rape. This exposure to violence has not been diminished by the now dominant view of prostitutes as "victims"; on the contrary, by insisting on their fundamental vulnerability, abolitionist and feminist narratives have unfortunately reinforced aggressors' feelings of impunity. Finally, recent measures such as the introduction of "paths out of prostitution", described in detail in Chapter 5, rather than lessening the distance between the practice of prostitution and social protection, have accentuated it, making the boundary between exclusion and integration, examined in the third chapter, even more definite and difficult to cross.

I continued my study of the social movements around prostitution by addressing the history and contemporary activity of French abolitionism. This was particularly relevant in that the movement regained its strength from the late 1990s onwards, despite the fact that the development of the fight against AIDS over the decade had led to abolitionism appearing stuck in the past. Its recommendations – based on social reintegration and abstinence – could only be seen as anachronistic in comparison with a viewpoint arguing for sexual modernity on the basis of recognizing and integrating formerly deviant practices. The closeness between community health associations and a group as dynamic at the time as *Act Up*, which spearheaded the renewed gay rights movement and the criticism of stigmatizing viewpoints (with regard to the gay and lesbian communities, but also drug addicts, migrants, prisoners and, of course, prostitutes), demonstrated this reversal of the power balance. However, this proved to be temporary, and the early 2000s saw a revival of abolitionism. The last four chapters examine several of the reasons that help to explain this. For example, AIDS was fading into the background of political concerns due to therapeutic advances, leading to a withdrawal of public support for AIDS associations; the majority sections of French feminism were converted to abolitionism; the schema of human trafficking was revived following the arrival of large numbers of migrant prostitutes; and prostitution arrived on the political agenda due to its crossover with the themes of immigration and delinquency, which became routine in France following the first electoral successes of the far right.

A study of the activist abolitionist press from the 1930s to the present provided a historical perspective on the shifting composition and positions of the abolitionist movement. What could be described as its recent conservative radicalization, leading it to promote increasingly repressive measures,[5] depends on both the growing influence of its most intransigent tendencies and the replacement of a generation rooted in social Catholicism – known in France as "cathos de gauche" or left-wing Catholics – with new members who have been socialized and politicized in a different religious climate. From this viewpoint, the hardening positions of the central *Mouvement du Nid* association could be seen as a new expression of the "taking back control" of the Catholic church by its conservative wing under the papacy of John Paul II following the progressive initiatives encouraged by the Second Vatican Council.[6]

However, this repressive tendency is not specific to the abolitionist movement, or even to the Catholic world. It affected the political field more generally, and social issues were generally perceived as calling for coercive responses (Wacquant 2004). The ascendancy of "zero tolerance" theories and the influence of ideologues of insecurity spread to the field of prostitution in a way that was all the more striking in that its leading voices came from the left of the political spectrum.[7] From this perspective, Chapters 4 and 5 show how the policy of criminalizing clients gave the Socialist Party (PS), its primary advocate, an opportunity to mark itself out from the coercive approach previously

---

5 This process is reminiscent of the one observed by Joseph Gusfield (1963) in his classic study of the American temperance movement. See Mathieu (2022) for an attempt to apply Gusfield's perspective to contemporary French abolitionism.

6 This process can be seen in other sectors and organizations. One example is the parallel shift, though much less confrontational and more focused on negotiation, in the CFDT (French Democratic Workers' Confederation) trade union, which also arose from social Catholicism.

7 This observation, as we shall see, applies not only to political parties but also to social movements – mostly feminists and alter-globalists – that are also rooted in the French left, or at least claim to be.

espoused by the right (via the criminalization of soliciting) while retaining a predominantly repressive framework. Whether the policy criminalizes the prostitute for soliciting or the client for using the service, it is still the police who are responsible for enforcing it, rather than social workers.

One of the key features of these new policies on prostitution is their territorial focus, sensitive to both the national and local levels. They all aim to remove unwanted prostitutes from either the national territory (by deporting illegal immigrants) or the urban space (by suppressing soliciting first, and then clients since 2016). From this perspective, the analyses in this book only confirm the observations of geographers in other contexts about the moralization of heritage-worthy spaces destined for gentrification (e.g. Hubbard 2004a; 2004b). The advantage of in-depth knowledge of a specific local situation acquired over long research (the city of Lyon in this case) is obvious here. As an observer of the evolutions of prostitution in Lyon since the beginning of the 1990s, I have seen how urban transformation and municipal policies have led to a rapid shift in the areas used by prostitutes. Competing with other European cities, promoting tourism, encouraging settlement among the more privileged social classes and aiming to make the most of its historic architectural heritage, Lyon has seen prostitution dwindle in the city center and move to increasingly remote (and unsafe) peripheral areas due to successive police operations.

Conducted through interviews with politicians and activists, the examination of a variety of documents (books and opinion columns by intellectuals, official reports, statements in the media etc.), observations of meetings and other public events, participation in institutional discussions,[8] monitoring parliamentary debates etc., this aspect of the research covers fifteen years (from 2002 to 2017) of protests, controversies and decisions that have transformed the field of opinion about prostitution and significantly affected the people most closely involved. The abolitionist and feminist "framing" of prostitution as a sexist form of slavery is now predominant, even though it is vigorously disputed by minority voices within feminism and a movement of "sex workers" spearheaded by STRASS. It seems that opinions and options with regard to prostitution have never been as polarized as they are now, at a time when the policies introduced in 2016 (criminalizing clients, paths out of prostitution, increased public awareness) seem to be having little impact on the collective good of prostitutes. Voluntary organizations on the ground have

---

8   Recognized as a specialist on the issue, I have been interviewed several times by institutional working groups (primarily the French National Assembly, the Senate and the National Consultative Committee on Human Rights) preparing or evaluating public policy on the subject.

reported increased exposure to aggression, more acute economic insecurity and vulnerability to police repression (particularly with regard to residency rights) in recent years.

The most recent research, entitled *Proscrim* and led by the sociologist Mathilde Darley between 2014 and 2018, focused specifically on this issue of how repressive institutions (the police and the legal system) have contributed to shaping prostitution. It was based on observing trials for pimping and human trafficking, monitoring police work and interviews with magistrates, police officers and associations. Its results, set out in Chapters 6 and 7, emphasize the interweaving of representations of what prostitutes and pimps are (and especially the ways these representations are distilled by abolitionists), the professional practices of specific "rescuers" – police officers and magistrates – and the concrete working conditions of both prostitutes and those who organize or exploit their activity. As these two chapters underline, it would be sociologically costly to oppose and separate the ways that "rescuers" see prostitution, with their varying degrees of realism and fantasy, and the "reality" of its concrete practice. The two are closely interdependent and influence each other mutually in the social construction of the sex trade.

The conclusion of the book aims to summarize the contribution of this approach, as described over the seven chapters, emphasizing the relevance of the French situation. Though it focuses on a specific country and a specific historical context, the book intends to add to the global intelligibility of prostitution, which requires it to be situated in comparison with other locations and contexts. In other words, its primary goal is for its observations and analyses to be discussed. If they are criticized or refuted through empirical fact and theoretical argument, the author's intentions will still have been fulfilled.[9]

---

9   This volume consists of updated and revised versions of texts previously published in French in a variety of journals and collective works, with references provided at the beginning of each chapter. I would like to thank the journals and publishers who have given permission for their translation and publication, as well as to Sylvie Octobre and Vincenzo Cicchelli for their help in ensuring the consistency of the book as a whole.

CHAPTER 1

The Prostitution Space

The sociology of deviance, which traditionally encompasses the study of prostitution, faces serious difficulties when it has to consider both the "collective coherence" of the populations it is interested in and the specific nature of the logics and dynamics affecting them.[1] Some of the analysis frameworks most widely-used in this area often prove insufficient to capture the specifically collective dimension of marginal worlds, either because they adopt a perspective centered on the deviant individual alone – as in certain approaches that seek psychological causes, or models postulating a rationality behind deviant behavior – or, from the viewpoint of labelling theory, by focusing on the labelling processes that contribute to the emergence of a status of offender against dominant norms. While this last approach has demonstrated its relevance in many areas,[2] it still tends to neglect the specific features of deviant behavior and the individuals that adopt it (Cusson 1992: 396; Scull 1988: 669), focusing instead on the "agencies of social control" (Cicourel 1995) that contribute to establishing this status. The approach in terms of "subculture", as it has been deployed in particular by several representatives of interactionism, doubtless constitutes one of the most significant contributions to understanding this question. By setting themselves the goal of addressing "the deviants' way of life, from their own viewpoint" (Becker 1963: 174) and developing a diversified conceptual system for the purpose – career, lifestyle, morality, trade etc. – the authors who have adopted this perspective have successfully highlighted several characteristics specific to marginal or stigmatized groups, which provide a foundation for the collective identity of the individuals belonging to them.

---

1   An initial version of this chapter appeared under the title "L'espace de la prostitution : éléments empiriques et perspectives en sociologie de la déviance" ("The prostitution space: empirical aspects and perspectives in the sociology of deviance"), *Sociétés contemporaines,* no. 38, 2000: 99-116.

2   In the field of prostitution, it should be noted that several historians (Corbin 1996; Walkowitz 1980), without claiming any allegiance to labelling theory, have nonetheless aligned themselves with the approach by describing how the regulationist system – requiring young women living from the sale of sexual services in the nineteenth century to submit to restrictive regulations (recording, listing in official registers, mandatory health checks etc.) – contributed to causing these women to permanently internalize the degraded status of a prostitute and isolating them from their original social background.

© LILIAN MATHIEU, 2023 | DOI:10.1163/9789004541535_003

Nevertheless, this approach is marked by a tendency to give deviant worlds a coherence and homogeneity that may be excessive.

One of the goals of this chapter is to outline approaches to analyzing this problem by proposing the empirical elements for an understanding of the world of prostitution as a *social space*. This concept appears well suited to accounting for both the way of life of the collectives of individuals sharing the same deviant status and the specific circumstances in which they are, in a way, "trapped" and that guide their conduct, representations or relationships with their condition or their peers. Considering the world of prostitution – and also, no doubt, the worlds of drug addiction, crime etc. – as a social space avoids presupposing a high level of cohesion and homogeneity within these deviant worlds by attributing to their members a uniformly shared "subculture" and a common feeling of identity, but incorporates their essential heterogeneity (including their internal segmentation[3] and hierarchical organization), the blurred nature of their borders and the dynamics that contribute to their organization or evolution. In other words, the aim is to take seriously the fact that marginal groups have a clear sense of collective existence – including in the eyes of their members – but that this sense is actually extremely fluid, informal and unstable. Neither collections of atomized individuals nor homogeneous, coherent communities, deviant social spaces can be considered as *configurations of interdependence* (Elias 1984), that mutually unite, with varying degrees of tightness or looseness, individuals who, though subject to a process akin to stigmatization leading to specific modes of identity management (Goffman 1963), have differing characteristics and occupy differing social positions. However, in order to construct the notion of the prostitution space, we will need to refine this concept of configurations of interdependence, calling on theoretical frameworks that are rarely used in the sociology of deviance – which actually enables us to better delimit the scope of their validity and relevance.

1   Prostitution as a Space of Interdependence

What initially strikes any observer examining the world of prostitution are the low levels of cohesion and unity inherent in its internal differentiation.

---

3   To a certain degree – i.e. to the extent that prostitution does not constitute a recognized profession – the notion of segmentation as applied to prostitution can be compared to the idea proposed by Bucher and Strauss, that *segments* are "groups that emerge within a profession" (1961: 326).

The world of prostitution appears to be made up of multiple "subunits", whose mutual relationships are based above all on aggravated hostility and competitiveness. This disjointed aspect of the world of prostitution seems to be intensified by the many principles of classification both female and male prostitutes use to distinguish themselves from each other: sexual identity (women, boys, transgender etc.), place of work (street, apartment, underground brothel etc.), type of services offered to clients, relationship to drugs, dependence on a pimp or independence, acceptance or rejection of the status of prostitute etc. Consequently, studying this world of blurred boundaries, which seems not to be truly bound together by any common principle, requires us to arm ourselves with conceptual instruments able to encompass both its internal heterogeneity and its mode of existence within the social world.

It is this requirement that is addressed by the notion of the prostitution space, which allows us to approach the world of prostitution as a space of relative interdependence and mutual self-reference between providers of sexual services. This space – from which we should not necessarily exclude clients and pimps[4] – presents itself as a network of mutually related positions, i.e. positions that are defined in relational terms rather than as a set of stable categories for which a typology could be established. Each one is defined by a set of relevant properties enabling it to be situated relative to the others and individually characterizing its occupants. In terms of the definitions they impose on the individuals occupying them, they all depend on their situation within the structure of the space, i.e. the structure of the distribution of efficient resources (or "capitals") within this space. This structure is constantly shifting, because the prostitution space is continually being disturbed by conflicts between its different occupants, with one of the primary elements at stake being the preservation or improvement of their respective positions.

Outlined in this way, the notion of the prostitution space is related to and inspired by the concept of the *field* developed by Pierre Bourdieu. However, there are several reasons for rejecting the idea of a "prostitution field" here. First of all, the low level of unification and the very significant heteronomy of the prostitution world – and particularly its high degree of subordination to the police and legal system, as well as the lack of control of the people grouped under the category of "prostitute" over the conditions by which they are assigned to it – prevents its being seen as an autonomous and clearly

---

4   It should be noted that drawing a clear distinction between prostitutes and pimps would not be appropriate – without wishing to pre-empt the subject of Chapter 6, exploitative relationships between prostitutes are not unusual, such as situations when one prostitute requires her colleagues to pay her a fee for working in a section of the street she claims as her property.

differentiated field. The prostitution space does not have the degree of objectivation specific to properly constituted fields and is extremely vulnerable to
external influences. Moreover, although the limits of the space, like those of
a field, are certainly an issue debated between prostitutes trying to establish
boundaries and impose a definition of the legitimate practice of prostitution
that is as favorable to them as possible, these attempts at delimitation are –
as we will see later – heavily outweighed by the official definitions and much
more effective practices of the legal world, the police and even the health and
social work sector.

The low level of objectivation of the social relationships within the prostitution space also leads us to reject the idea, associated with the field concept, of
a central, structuring and unifying stake or interest. It appears difficult to relate
the set of practices or representations current within the prostitution world
to such generating principles as would be constituted by the pursuit of a specific kind of capital or the intervention of a "prostitutional *illusio*", especially as
the agents within this space often find themselves there against their will (due
either to the absence of any alternative seen as plausible, or to coercion from
pimps). Moreover, the conditions for a minimum agreement on what the field
and its relevant stakes are, described by Bourdieu (1984: 115) as an "objective
complicity (…) underlying all the antagonisms", which leads all the agents in
a given field to share the belief that its specific social game is worth playing,
are far from being met in the case of prostitution. We would be hard pressed
to find a minimal belief common to all prostitutes about the value of the prostitutional game and its stakes, or even the value of the prostitution space's
very existence. This is demonstrated by the extremely complex and ambiguous relationship – to which we will return later, and which has already been
identified by Goffman (1963) in other stigmatized groups – between the people
exercising this activity and the condition they find themselves in, which often
leads them to adopt presentations of the self that tend towards a distancing
of the most devalued representations of prostitution. Rather than presupposing the existence of an *illusio*, or a unifying tendency, specific to the world of
prostitution and irreducible to those that govern other social worlds, it may be
more relevant to consider that a multitude of diffuse and constantly evolving
practical logics operate within this space.

From this viewpoint, seeing prostitution as a social space allows us to highlight a tension within the field theory constructed by Bourdieu, a tension
between its ambition to interpret agents' practices and representations and the
positions they adopt through the interplay of habitus and field (Bourdieu and
Wacquant 1992), and the exacting definition it gives of this concept – requiring, in particular, a prior analysis of the historical conditions under which each

field was constituted and autonomized – which specifically means that not all social spaces can be considered as fields in strict terms. But if not all social groups or configurations of interdependence necessarily constitute true fields, how and with what instruments can we envisage the practices that nevertheless arise in them? This difficulty is compounded in the analysis of social worlds which, like prostitution, are spaces of relegation with low levels of autonomy. We can thus see that most of the fields to which Bourdieu devoted himself, and whose analyses he used to construct his theory, have in common the fact that they are relatively institutionalized, socially dominant worlds, operating in what he himself called the "field of power": the fields of literature, science, business management etc. Consequently, he tended to neglect the specific features of the most dominated or weakly constituted social worlds, whose analysis thus requires distinct conceptual instruments.

This absence of central, structuring stakes in the world of prostitution also prevents us from seeing it as a *market*. Though prostitution certainly constitutes a specific form of trade, and the accumulation of economic profits constitutes the most powerful motivating force for members of the prostitution space, it is not the only one. Seeing prostitutes only as special cases of homo economicus would be reductive, and would get in the way of understanding what the struggles between competing segments owe to identitarian motives that seek either to deny or to manage the negative symbolic capital constituted by the various stigmas attached to the exercise of this activity.

As a spatial metaphor, the prostitution space also has the advantage of accounting for the specifically geographic dimension of the "sex trade" (Redoutey 2005). The structure of its positions is reflected practically in urban geography – a cartography in which prostitutes have practical expertise, and on which they rely for their evaluations and hierarchical rankings. Consequently, classification struggles in the prostitution space often take the form of *positioning struggles*. Disputes over the right to occupy a certain location (or, conversely, affirmations of this right: "I created my own place"), accusations of usurpation ("He shouldn't be here, it's always been women who have worked here, we don't want any transvestites") or strategies to devalue competing locations ("In X street, they steal from clients", "They're all drug addicts over there, they're dirty") are central to disputes between prostitutes, while any emergence of new competition results immediately in attempts to expel them from the space, as this young transvestite testifies: "Working in the street is a real problem. Because what with the girls with their pimps, the transvestites who have their own bit of territory, if you try and take a piece sometimes you negotiate, sometimes you stand up for yourself and it just becomes … a total mess. (…) I chose a place, and I thought: they'll come and hassle me, I know they will. Sure enough, the first night: 'What are you doing there, you can't be there, clear off, go further away.'" Further towards areas where social relationships are more unstable, away from the influence of the regulating actions of the "protectors", these conflicts often turn all the more bitter.

2   Internal Hierarchical Principles

Before describing the different positions that make up the prostitution space, we need to present the main properties associated with them, which prostitutes themselves use for their practical purposes of classification. These properties, which earn their bearer either legitimacy or indignity, are often mobilized in disputes between competing prostitutes; they constitute resources for justification used in tests[5] for managing rivalries (always temporarily) by defining the relative "worth" – i.e., for example, prestige, authority and the right to work – of each protagonist. These tests are forms by which the structure of the prostitution space is updated and consolidated.

Among these properties, experience, evaluated on the basis of age[6] or time spent working in prostitution (the longer the time, the greater the legitimacy), is one of the most important. Experience can also refer to specific biographical details (time in prison, past dependence on a "big pimp" etc.), which confer a specific form of authority: the "elders" who "remember the time of the pimps", when "men made the decisions", never miss an opportunity to remind their juniors of the respect due to them. The authority and legitimacy conferred by experience are closely linked to knowledge about and respect for the "rules of the trade",[7] together with belonging, now or in the past, to a "network" of pimps (i.e. a group of agents specifically responsible for ensuring these "rules" are respected). Failure to respect the rules (or rather an accusation of this failure)

---

5   We use this notion with a meaning close to the one given to it by Boltanski and Thévenot (2006), with the proviso that the tests we refer to here are not subject to the same constraints of publicity and generality as the ones described by these two authors.

6   However, age is an ambiguous evaluation criterion: while it is a positive sign of experience and commands the respect due to "veterans", it becomes a negative stigma when prostitution continues to an advanced age. It can no longer be justified with a long-term goal; it becomes a matter of survival alone. It is then viewed negatively as indicating a failure to prepare for a change of livelihood.

7   Among the informal corpus of "rules of the trade", the most frequently mentioned are the prohibitions on kissing the client, "going upstairs" with multiple clients or taking sexual pleasure from clients, the limit on the time spent with each client and the obligation to use condoms.

is punished by a charge of illegitimacy to work as a prostitute, or even attempts at expulsion from the prostitution space. In conversations between prostitutes, indignant accusations against illegitimate competitors stigmatized by their transgressive practices are frequently heard: "the one from X street, I saw her in the car kissing her client. 'Nice work!' I said to her"; "she got in with the guy in the red Volvo, the one who always wants to do it without a condom, obviously she does it without".

The type of sexual practices offered to clients is a second classification crite-rion. The most legitimate practices are the ones seen as conforming the most to the "natural" order of heterosexuality ("lovemaking", i.e. vaginal penetra-tion); in other words, conforming to the schemas of the sexual division of the social world and the division of sex work, organized according to the ordered opposing pairs active/passive, on top/underneath, dominant/dominated and masculine/feminine (Bourdieu 2001: 17–22). In this context, the "naturalness" of their practices is a resource available to women who consider themselves to have greater legitimacy in the street since their services are distinct from the practices of their transgender competitors, which are considered "deviant". Conversely, the practices that transgress most clearly against this "natural" order are more illegitimate or stigmatizing. For example, sodomy is prohib-ited (which does not mean never practiced) among women. It is more com-monly recognized, though sometimes presented as a minority pursuit, among transgender and boy prostitutes, who emphasize conversely that it is often cli-ents who ask to be sodomized. Easily the most common practice among both female and male prostitutes working in their clients' cars, but less frequent among indoor prostitutes (de Vincenzi et al. 1992), fellatio is often treated with disdain by the latter in that the price is lower than the price for penetration. The status of "specialties" such as sadomasochistic practices is ambiguous. They are valued in that higher prices can be charged than for ordinary sex, there is usually no physical contact with the client's body and there is a rela-tionship of domination over the client (which may include physical violence). However, their "dirty" (bloody or scatological), violent and deviant nature – again, diverging from the naturalized dominance relationships between men and women – lead to specialists in this area being seen with a mixture of aver-sion and respect: "In prostitution, (...) I was marginal because my clients were unusual – they were masochists. (...) [Prostitutes] think that's not normal. It's not right. Men hit, they don't get hit" (former prostitute).

The location and conditions of work are a positive marker of dominance in the prostitution space when they allow relative comfort and access to hygiene and security. People with an apartment where they can receive clients are the most favored in this respect, benefiting from satisfactory conditions of comfort, though their isolation in an enclosed space exposes them to specific forms of insecurity: as the appointment is generally made by telephone, they have no means of "testing" and potentially rejecting a client who could be dangerous (see Chapter 2). The same applies to prostitutes who receive clients in hotel rooms (often after placing a small ad on a dating site), which is why they often resort to having men on standby, paid to step in if there is a "problem", who thus find themselves in the position of a pimp. As massage parlor employees generally work as part of a team, they can count on their colleagues in the event of aggression and also benefit from a basic level of comfort (water, heating, furniture etc.).

On the other hand, prostitutes with no premises, who work in their clients' cars, in alleys between buildings, in public toilets or in wooded areas, have to face the most unfavorable conditions, given that they have no sanitation at their disposal and are particularly vulnerable to attack. Working from a car or, more frequently, a van parked beside a road or in a car park represents an intermediate position on this scale. This long-standing practice grew significantly more widespread when the offence of soliciting was reintroduced in 2003. As the law targeted the visible presence of prostitutes in urban areas, buying a van where they could discreetly wait for clients was a response that, again, provided a basic level of comfort. Depending on their age and condition, vans constitute a private space (inaccessible to the police) that can house a mattress and store water and hygiene products, where a prostitute can wait between clients, sheltered from the weather. While a concentration of this type of vehicle in a single space presents both advantages (the activity can immediately be identified by clients, encouraging custom) and disadvantages (complaints from nearby residents about disruption and harm to the reputation of the area), prostitutes parking on isolated roads are more exposed to violence.

In a space where attacks occur very frequently and arguments quickly turn to aggression, having the means of carrying out physical violence constitutes a particularly persuasive mechanism for consolidating position and reducing competition. This resource takes two distinct forms, depending on whether someone has the means to defend themselves or impose respect, or delegates the potential violence to others – "protectors" specializing in the (sometimes forced) provision of security. The capacity to carry out violence contributes to a person's reputation, positively marking their ability to resist aggression or attempts at extortion and to impose their will over their client's. Asserting physical strength is thus one of the self-presentation strategies adopted by prostitutes. Conversely, the absence of personal means of defense negatively marks out the weakest, the ill and those whose consumption of psychotropic drugs alters their perceptions (Coppel et al. 1990).

"Beauty" also contributes to reputation and to the respect given to each prostitute. This aspect is particularly important among transgender prostitutes, whose feminine "plausibility" and the success of their transformation are evaluated not only against aesthetic criteria, but also their supposed power of seducing clients. The criteria on which these mutual evaluations are based are, of course, far from stable and uniform. Condemning clients' poor taste when a competitor is more successful – "it's the hags who get the most work" – is a recurring theme in conversations between prostitutes dismayed by the shortage of business. This aspect is more significant than it might appear in that it can have serious consequences for the health of transgender prostitutes. The intensification of competition can lead to an escalation in feminization, leading to overconsumption of hormones or the use of cosmetic surgery (facial transformation or breast implants), with side-effects that can be dramatic (stroke or psychological identity disorders) in the absence of medical support. The use of hormones or silicone (Silva Duarte 2018) appears when prostitution moves from being an occasional source of income to a regular activity, involving full commitment to the status of a prostitute. Feminization is a process that affects an individual's identity as well as their physical appearance, and involves a number of steps (wearing women's clothes only in the street, then permanently, always using a female first name, taking hormones, potential anatomical sex change surgery), which not all individuals are equally willing to take. As men wanting to be penetrated constitute a significant proportion of their clients, many transgender prostitutes combine a feminine appearance with an assertion of sexual virility;[8] this results in Viagra-type products being traded and sometimes consumed in large quantities. Though largely driven by economic factors (transgender prostitutes can charge more than male prostitutes in men's clothes, and have more clients) and by competition based on appearance, feminization can nevertheless culminate in an assertion of the status of a trans woman, which is then rationalized as the inexorable conclusion of a path predestined since birth, in a logic close to the one described by Prieur (1998): "I have always felt that I was a woman" is thus a common expression among trans prostitutes who mostly began their career as a "boy".

Economic capital in the prostitution space is closely linked to the symbolic capital it helps to generate. The takings are compared at the end of each day or night of work, and contribute to how internal classifications are determined. However, the people who "work the best" and are most envied are not

---

8   Claims of the ability to perform sexually time after time or of exceptional penis size are common arguments for personal value in disputes between peers.

necessarily the ones with the most clients; they are more likely to be the ones who charge the most or manage to extort the most money from clients through bargaining. The frequent practice of extravagant expenditure, designed to be seen by the others, is all the more effective if it has no practical value, as in the case of this transvestite who took his dog out for dinner ("I bought him a steak tartare – it was very classy") in a restaurant frequented by many of his colleagues. Commercial success also provides a favorable position in the form of "savings", which can insulate against the risks of everyday life (such as inability to work in the event of illness, as many prostitutes lack social security cover), or contribute to a plan to retrain in the medium or long term. Emphasizing that they are working as prostitutes out of choice in order to make money for a specific goal (such as buying a shop or, among transgender prostitutes, having an operation) distances them from the more degrading connotations of the activity, which is no longer seen as imposed by the lack of an alternative but rather as a temporary means of achieving a goal in life in a rational, controlled way.

The accumulation of symbolic capital, notably in the form of prestige or "good reputation", is all the more crucial in that it takes place in a social world that is heavily stigmatized. It leads certain prostitutes to try to mark themselves out from the most demeaning representations of sexual promiscuity involved in their activity by laying claim to conservative values in terms of political opinions, morals or lifestyle (especially with regard to the education of children, who are generally placed in private schools), at least verbally if not in reality.[9] We can also see that symbolic capital in the prostitution space is *incorporated* capital in the sense that it is the form in which a set of essentially physical properties (health, beauty, strength, age) are seen and recognized. It is precisely because it is carried directly within individuals – and thus subject to significant variation, especially as its value depends on the perceptions and recognition of others – rather than having any external material reality that is self-evidently imposed on everyone, that it also constitutes an indicator of the low level of objectivation and the lability of the social relationships that take place in this social world.

Last but not least, "ethnic" origin has constituted a major classification criterion since the significant internationalization of prostitution in France

---

9 This chimes with the criticisms made by Sykes and Matza (1957) of subculture theories postulating a clear division, or even an inversion, between the values specific to the deviant group and those that prevail in the "normal" social world: far from being radically different, deviants generally share the same moral concepts, legitimizing their own transgressions using "neutralization techniques".

since the late 1990s. This is certainly not new – the arrival of the "Brazilians" in the 1970s, soon followed by other Latin Americans, had already had a profound impact on transgender prostitution (Silva Duarte 2018), and prostitutes included women from French-speaking Africa and Eastern Europe from the 1990s onwards. The current large numbers of female and male prostitutes from countries as diverse as Nigeria, Peru, China, Romania and the Dominican Republic has led to a close association between migration and prostitution in the popular imagination, and particularly in the minds of politicians (see Chapter 4). The world of prostitution itself is no different, and culturalist stereotypes, prejudices about skin color (Pourette 2005) and other racializing beliefs are among the most common classification criteria, attributing particular propensities to theft, failure to respect "strolls" (a stroll is an area where someone works on the street), failure to use condoms, dependence on pimps or even sorcery to specific ethnic origins. At the same time, the bonds of solidarity based on shared language or nationality constitute resources against adversity and competition.

3   A Differentiated Space

The distribution of these properties constitutes the structure of the prostitution space, and we shall now present the main positions within this space. It should be remembered first of all that this structure is constantly shifting and subject to challenge, either due to the evolving internal balance of power (such as a struggle between pimps for control of the same group of prostitutes, for example), or to the intervention of external elements (primarily the police). We must also take into account that it does not consist of stable categories, but rather of a series of positions through which an individual may pass during their career (from indoor prostitution to street prostitution, or from rent boy to transvestite, which are both common cases).

When this analysis framework was first developed in the early 1990s (Welzer-Lang, Barbosa and Mathieu 1994), the dominant positions were those occupied by women working in traditional prostitution areas in city centers (such as the Rue Saint-Denis in Paris), where they had often been based for several years, owning the room where they worked. These prostitutes, describing themselves as "traditional", were favored in several ways – they had a clientele of loyal "regulars", they provided the most legitimate services at relatively high prices under satisfactory sanitary conditions and they were rarely affected by drug addiction or HIV. Relatively socially integrated, and fully accepting – or even proclaiming – their status as prostitutes, they had a detailed knowledge of the health and social support available to them. Working for long years, they had the experience that brings authority and legitimacy in the eyes of their younger colleagues; they formed a relatively cohesive group offering mutual recognition and met in social venues such as the bars in the streets where prostitution was concentrated. The drop in recruitment (due partly to the decline or fall of the criminal networks they were often associated with) and the gentrification of the neighborhoods where they were sometimes central figures marked the end of this form of prostitution, which no longer exists in French cities except in a few residual cases.

In reality, ageing has always marked the decline of the "traditionals". When they had not been able to prepare for a life after prostitution, they found themselves having to join the relatively dominated segments, indicative of decline in their eyes, of prostitution from vans parked beside country roads (this was sometimes also a punishment inflicted by a pimp on an unruly woman) or ring roads, or in specific areas of prostitute neighborhoods. The most frequent practice (fellatio), together with the insecurity and unsafe hygiene conditions, were then and are still indicators of the devaluation that characterizes this type of prostitution.

The two segments presented above consist mostly of women, and these prostitutes work mainly during the day. Nocturnal street prostitution (or prostitution in parks and wooded areas) has a more equal gender balance, and practitioners are often younger than their colleagues working indoors or from vehicles. It corresponds to a relatively dominated position and involves the more vulnerable segments of the prostitution space. On the male side, this type of prostitution takes two distinct forms: young boys in male clothing serving homosexual clients (known as "hustlers", "rent boys" or "call boys"), and transvestites or transgender prostitutes, born male but working with a feminine appearance for clients who identify as heterosexual. Working in the street – the former often close to gay pick-up spots – their working conditions are the most precarious and hazardous of all. Taking advantage of the blurred boundaries between prostitution and gay pick-ups, hustlers rarely define themselves as prostitutes, especially as their prostitution is often occasional, responding for example to an immediate need for money imposed by a nomadic situation (Mai 2011; 2012).

In both the female and male forms of this type of prostitution, the most frequent practice is fellatio. The service is usually provided in the client's car, in an alley between buildings, in public toilets, or, more rarely and only if the client is prepared to pay more, at a hotel. Prostitutes soliciting by roads that pass through parks or woods sometimes construct temporary shelters or stretch out tarpaulins for privacy from walkers. Small-time operatives working for networks of pimps or marginal figures paid small amounts by the prostitutes themselves, lookouts and other providers of ancillary services (supplying sandwiches or condoms, car journeys etc.) generally gravitate at a distance and provide a basic level of security. However, the poor working conditions, permanent insecurity and possible presence of drug addiction make these segments among the most fragile and precarious in the prostitute population. The spaces where this type of prostitution is carried out are frequently separated along national lines. Sometimes associated with the same migration circuits and/ or networks of pimps, sharing similar experiences (of migration, dependence, debt etc.) and cultural references, and speaking the same language, prostitutes tend to gather in groups of acquaintanceship and solidarity, providing a basic level of mutual support in the event of difficulties, though this does not prevent conflicts or exploitation (Amaouche 2010; Lévy and Lieber 2009; de Montvalon 2018).

On the fringes of these populations are the prostitutes commonly referred to as "occasional", who are usually young drug addicts engaging in prostitution to earn enough money to buy drugs, of which the most common are heroin, morphine derivatives and crack (Ingold 1993; 1994). Their living conditions are the most unpredictable: often with no fixed abode, in very poor health, they try to survive in the short term through prostitution at low rates, and are more tempted than their colleagues to accept the unprotected practices that many clients ask for. Often presenting themselves without the sartorial clues indicating prostitution, largely due to their extreme poverty, they seem to blend into the background of the urban landscape, only announcing themselves to the attention of clients by remaining stationary on the pavement. They do not work in neighborhoods usually associated with prostitution, but often beside major roads, where working conditions are much more insecure and dangerous. They are particularly exposed to aggression from clients, dealers and other prostitutes, who accuse them of undercutting their prices. Not generally identifying as prostitutes but rather as drug addicts, and with few contacts (other than conflicts) with "veterans" able to pass on their experience, they are most often ignorant of – and probably uninterested in – the "rules" of an activity they do not see as their trade or a central element of their personal identity, but just as the only means they have of quickly obtaining enough money to buy the product on which they depend.

On the margins of street prostitution, other forms of the "sex trade" are practiced more discreetly due to the secrecy inherent in the illegal way they are organized, mostly under the umbrella of hotel-based pimping. Female prostitution takes place in certain bars whose customers consist almost exclusively of isolated immigrants, or in workers' hostels located near construction sites

(Moujoud 2005). Sometimes dependent on a pimp and often foreigners with no legal status, these prostitutes generally have to work in the back room of the bar or a room in the hostel, seeing large numbers of clients who queue for a trick, which explains this practice being called *abattage* (a word that comes from abattoir that means slaughterhouse). "Tours" of prostitutes from city to city are a more favorable variation on this principle. An internet ad (generally on a dating site) informs potential clients that they can make an appointment with a prostitute who will be staying for a few days in a particular hotel or apartment. Often organized by pimps who take care of booking rooms, posting ads and providing security for the prostitutes, this form of prostitution is hemmed in by police vigilance. While the police are sometimes thrown off the scent by the speed with which the prostitutes travel, they can shut down websites and hotels if it can be proved that they are aware of the activities they are hosting.

Massage parlors constitute another form of indoor prostitution, though police vigilance has made them more fragile. Under the official guise of a relaxation facility, hostesses (often undocumented Chinese immigrants) provide services whose distinction from prostitution is blurred. The employees of these parlors (and their clients) reject their categorization as prostitutes on the basis that their services are limited to "erotic massages" ending in masturbation, and that they refuse to be penetrated, which they see as the marker of "real prostitutes". However, these self-categorizations carry little weight when the police launch proceedings for hotel-based pimping, considering that their activity clearly constitutes prostitution (and when the "masseuses" are oriented towards social services specifically designed for prostitutes after the parlors are shut down). This provides a practical demonstration of how official or "external" definitions of the boundaries of the prostitution space take precedence over "indigenous" attempts to define or delimit them. This observation also applies to "hostess bars" and "champagne bars", where the employees are likely to offer paying customers more than just company. Paying for sexual services from a hostess encountered in a bar is prohibited in France, and these establishments are monitored to enforce the laws against hotel-based pimping. On the other hand, it is allowed in countries such as the Czech Republic (Darley 2007), Spain (Solana Ruiz and López Riopedre 2012) and Switzerland (Chimienti 2009), where establishments provide separate rooms where hostesses can take their clients.

This presentation of the prostitution space tends to overlook how its structure has evolved over time; it provides a synchronic view in which different generations of prostitutes and historically heterogeneous forms of prostitution are gathered together. For example, as we have already said, female prostitution in urban areas, some of which have specialized in this activity for centuries, has seen an irresistible decline over the last thirty years, freeing up spaces that are often central and can be exploited for business purposes and property speculation. Transgender prostitutes saw considerable, unprecedented growth in their activities in the early 1990s, but their "exoticism" then stagnated in favor of migrants from different continents arriving in France from the end of that decade. These latecomers opened up new prostitution districts, due partly to hostility from longer-established competitors and partly to police harassment or urban transformation. The evolution of drug addiction (dominated by heroin in the 1990s, followed by synthetic drugs such as crack) has modified the interactions between the sale of sexual services and dependency or altered states of consciousness. Finally, it is clear that new communication technologies have disrupted encounters between clients and prostitutes: the mobile phone (in the paradigmatic form of a butterfly bearing a first name and a phone number stuck to a traffic sign) and, above all, the internet have encouraged the development of a form of prostitution that has no need to display itself in public in order to thrive (Pajnik et al. 2016).

These communication facilities have especially benefited what is commonly referred to as "escorting". Rubio's study of homosexual escorting (2013) highlights the relatively favored profile of young men, some of whom are students well integrated into society, for whom prostitution has nothing to do with economic necessity, and who distinguish themselves carefully from its most debased forms. Meeting their clients through online ads, they take great care in how they present themselves and select their clients meticulously on the basis of social matching, favouring clients whose social or cultural standing is close to their own and rejecting anyone whose messages suggest a more modest background.[10] However, this selection does not altogether shelter escorts, male or female, from aggression or from relationships based on power more generally. Female escorts also have to learn to impose their will in order to control a relationship that could (most commonly) slide into violence or (more exceptionally) take an emotional or even romantic turn (Bigot 2009; Bernstein 2007). The so-called "Carlton" affair, involving former government minister Dominique Strauss-Kahn, provided a glimpse of this type of prostitution, confirming its existence in certain economic and political circles while also highlighting the haziness of its distinction from the swinger lifestyle. The same affair also showed that neither the wealth of their clients nor the

---

10   See also Lavergne (2021) on how male escorts present their identities and sexual qualities online.

euphemistic approach to the commercial nature of their services spared the escorts involved from the stigma of prostitution or the risk of aggression.

4   The Lack of Cohesion in a Destiny Group

We have not yet discussed the relationship that people working in prostitution have with this condition and identity, and how they see the "consistency" and form of existence of this "group" they never truly chose to join. If we use inverted commas to talk about prostitutes as a group, it is because this idea is far from self-evident for them. We have already mentioned the continual antagonisms, tensions and competition running through the different segments of the prostitution space and pitting them against each other. In addition, certain aspects specific to this world result in the very lowest levels of cohesion. One of the most striking examples is the competition between networks of pimps, as this prostitute describes: "When I was working on x street, I was working with girls who ... I'd been told not to talk to. I don't know why, because for me these girls ... But they, it was the same on their side, we didn't speak. And it was better not to".

The weight of these aggravated antagonisms and competition generates a widespread atmosphere of suspicion, a latent war between everyone and everyone else, which can result in exclusion from the prostitution space (in its material sense) or physical aggression, a set of practices that could be described as *collective disaggregation behaviors*. The imperatives of protecting the autonomy of the prostitution world and preserving it from external eyes, though frequently invoked, can nevertheless be transgressed for the purposes of internal management. We thus see forms of instrumentalization of the police, who can be called on secretly to resolve disputes specific to the prostitution space or obtain the right to remain in the country. The departments dedicated to suppressing pimping (sometimes still referred to in the streets by their former French name of the *brigade des mœurs* or "vice squad"), as their senior officers have admitted, have an interest in maintaining this division and competition, which enables them to prosecute the cases of pimping reported to them. It is not unusual for prostitutes under the control of a protector or drug dealer to inform on a competitor with the aim of bringing their activities to an end. As a result, any solidarity expressed in the prostitution space often tends to be minimal, limited to examples such as providing assistance in the event of an attack.

In the same way, we can see that prostitutes (and especially those in the dominant positions in the space) are constantly concerned about the reality and the limits of the collective they form, which leads them continually to recall and invoke the legitimate means of exercising prostitution that provide the basis of the "good form" (Boltanski 1987) they wish to preserve. Conversations between prostitutes are filled with references – we have seen a few examples above – to what is done and what is not done, breaches of the rules and the resulting penalties, the lack of "professional ethics" attributed, as in many other spheres of activity, to the younger generations etc. Prostitutes form a population whose collective existence is uncertain and fragile, which leads them to constantly invoke the "rules" governing their activity, which itself demonstrates the changing nature and difficulty of enforcing these rules and codes of conduct, together with the low level of objectivation of the social relationships within the space. The basic level of internal cohesion and autonomy in relation to the rest of the social world that are essential for the space to survive and maintain the relative positions of which it consists can only be guaranteed and safeguarded by continuous efforts at preservation and consolidation. These constantly need to be renewed due to their high level of fragility and instability.

The weight of the internalized stigma and shame adds its own strength to this endemic lack of cohesion. When we listen to prostitutes discussing their situation among themselves or in interviews, they seem to be driven by two opposing forces, on one hand to try to distinguish themselves from the most unfavorable representations of their condition ("I've never been a smackhead", "When I'm on the corner, I don't talk to the other girls, they have a bad attitude") and on the other to recognize the failure of these attempts, which leads them to adopt an unfavorable, resigned view of themselves ("In the end we're just whores", "We'll always be outcasts") and to devalue themselves. Prostitutes' relationships with their identity and their condition appear above all to be characterized by *ambivalence* (Goffman 1963: 137–139): either people boast of their identity with aggressive bravado, emphasizing the respectability of their status ("It's a job like any other"), or conversely, clinging to their degradation, they proclaim their exclusion and the disgrace of their condition – the same people often adopting both of these registers in turn depending on the circumstances and who they are talking to. Frequently having no other option than to incorporate the social world's negative prejudices and most disdainful representations of them, they find themselves appropriating the most insulting terms describing them for use in strategies of individual distinction through devaluing others. Calling each other "whore" or, for men, "poof" or "cocksucker", corresponds to these ambivalent distancing strategies, but with a resigned recognition of the weight of the stigma. Divisions and attempts to distinguish between "veterans" and "occasional" prostitutes, women and transvestites, transvestites and rent boys, abstainers and drug addicts, French and foreigners etc. combine to make the prostitution space look more like a landscape of perpetually antagonistic individuals than a truly unified "group".

This heteronomy of identity in which prostitutes are forced to recognize themselves is doubtless strengthened still further by the specific logic of their activity which, requiring them to attract the male eye and arouse male desire, constantly leads them to see themselves through their clients' eyes, or through what they imagine their clients' eyes to be. Their commercial success depends on their response to the socially constituted expectations of seduction – as well as a symbolic capital, physical appearance is also a condition for economic earnings. Prostitutes' constant concern for their physical appearance, and the competition that emerges between them about their power of seduction – "You have to admit, I have quite a style in the street" – or, among transgender prostitutes, about their feminine plausibility, leads to a form of alienation of their self-perception and their relationship with their body, which becomes a *body-for-others*. The words of this transvestite, who used hormones to achieve apparently female breasts while working as a prostitute and suffered the side-effects on his own sexuality, and who underwent breast removal surgery when he decided to leave the streets, are an example of this submission to the gaze and the erotic expectations of others: "It's a progression, you start as a woman and clients always want a little more, they always get a bit more demanding, and then I thought why not? Why not take hormones? (…) Your testicles shrink, you don't produce any sperm at all any more". To use the vocabulary of Merleau-Ponty (2013), we could suggest that prostitution leads to a *degradation of the body-subject* – the anchor point or point of insertion into the world through which the world is perceived – which results in the prostitute's individual body no longer being perceived as the foundation of their subjectivity but as a relatively exterior object, understood through categories of perception external to them.

This questioning of the mode of existence of the collective formed by prostitutes aligns with the concerns of a whole current of research – symbolized by the work of Boltanski (1987) on "cadres", or the French management class – challenging substantialist views of social groups to demonstrate, conversely, their socially constructed nature, the fuzziness of their boundaries and the variability of their degrees of cohesion. This type of sociological questioning has essentially concentrated on fully legitimate professional groups, and has only rarely been applied to deviant populations, whose collective dimension is often seen as self-evident. An initial consequence of the lack of interest in this issue has been to favor excessively stabilized visions of worlds that are in fact largely informal and weakly structured, as shown by Catanzaro (1991) in his study of Mafia criminality, for example. A second consequence is the tendency to neglect the experience that the people involved have of belonging to these worlds. As a conclusion, it thus appears possible to argue that while prostitution certainly constitutes a certain form of group, it is above all, for its members, a relegation group they never chose to join in a completely deliberate way, any more than they chose their "colleagues" (and the difficulty of choosing an appropriate term to describe these companions in misfortune is itself significant). It is primarily the feeling of a community of stigma and marginalization, as well as powerlessness and inability to resist, that contribute to forming basic and always fragile forms of a sense of identity. Consequently, for the people working as prostitutes, the collective they form can be considered to constitute above all what Pollak (1988) called a *destiny group*, and doubtless more so than the homosexuals he was studying.

CHAPTER 2

Violence in the Prostitution World

Certain common representations present prostitution as the consequence of a process of coercion – economic, moral or physical – which people are unable to resist.[1] It thus appears as an extreme form of subjection, with the men and women involved seen as victims. Feminist thinking in particular has often considered prostitution as a paradigmatic form of the oppression of women and a form of violence in itself. Sociologists such as Kathleen Barry (in the USA) or Marie-Victoire Louis and Colette Guillaumin (in France) have argued that prostitution is a "crime against all women" (Barry 1986: 299), that it "is probably the worst violence that can be imposed on a woman" (Louis 1991: 6) or that it constitutes a monetized form of physical and sexual use against women and an exemplary expression of "the appropriation of the class of women" by the "class of men" (Guillaumin 1978: 13).

Though devoted to the role of violence in the world of prostitution, this chapter takes an entirely different perspective. Setting aside the question of whether prostitution *in itself* constitutes violence against the people (not only women) who practice it – which is undoubtedly more a normative issue than a sociological one – the following pages will examine the many forms of violence to which prostitutes are exposed and evaluate its consequences for their daily lives. The perspective adopted is deliberately descriptive and attentive to the concrete ways in which this violence is expressed and the practices prostitutes adopt in order to guard against it. This approach is based on prostitutes' own accounts, with varying degrees of rationalization, reporting their own experiences of aggression and describing the practical knowledge or skills they use in response.

1 A Violent World

The crime news regularly reminds us that prostitution is an activity that exposes the people involved in it to multiple forms of violence. In the mid-1990s, a survey

---

1 An initial version of this text was published under the title "Quand 'la peur devient une existence': Sur la place de violence dans le monde de la prostitution" ("When 'fear becomes an existence': the role of violence in the world of prostitution"), *L'Homme et la société*, no. 143–144, 2002: 47–63.

© LILIAN MATHIEU, 2023 | DOI:10.1163/9789004541535_004

coordinated by the European Centre for the Epidemiological Monitoring of AIDS (ECEMA) tried to measure the frequency of attacks on female and male prostitutes (Serre et al. 1996). The question "Have you suffered at least one physical attack since the beginning of the year?" was put to 355 prostitutes (137 women, 26 rent boys and 192 transvestites or transgender prostitutes) visiting six French HIV prevention associations in May 1995. It was answered in the affirmative by 119 people, 41% of the respondents (no answer was given by 18% of the sample, 65 individuals). The individuals most exposed to aggression were transgender prostitutes (over half, 52%, had been attacked between January and May 1995), followed by rent boys (35%) and women, who appeared the least exposed (28%, still a significant figure). Cross-referencing these figures with several other variables measured in the same survey also highlighted the fact that the people most exposed to such attacks were the ones who drank large amounts of alcohol and had unstable housing situations (living in hotels, with friends or with no fixed abode), incorporating insecurity among a set of other vulnerability factors (lack of social security cover, drug addiction etc.). The four main reasons reported for these attacks were theft, rape, hatred of prostitutes and homophobia. When identified, the aggressor was most often a client (58% of cases), several men acting as a group in 23% of cases, isolated non-client individuals (10%) or, in 9% of cases, a "colleague", dealer, pimp or police officer.

Although they are no longer current, these statistics cast a glaring light on the very high frequency of attacks on female and male prostitutes. Prostitution emerges as a high-risk activity, directly and constantly threatening the lives (though in many cases it would be more appropriate to say the survival) of those who practice it. The qualitative data supplement this information by clarifying the rationales behind the different forms of violence taking place in the streets. More specifically, it appears that we can distinguish between two main sets of rationales, which we will examine in turn. The first are *internal* to the prostitution space – these correspond to violence caused by motivations or interests specific to the people who inhabit the prostitution space (pimps, competing prostitutes). We can then identify rationales that are *external* to the prostitution space, involving violence perpetrated by individuals from outside the world of prostitution (clients, "gangs of youths", mentally unbalanced individuals etc.).

Of all the forms of violence relating to the rationales internal to the prostitution space, the ones that come most readily to mind are those carried out by pimps to ensure the prostitutes dependent on them remain docile. And yet violence is not the only, nor even the primary, means pimps use to ensure that one or more prostitutes remain dependent. The relationships of submission and dependence between a prostitute and a pimp[2] require the latter to engage in efforts that are continuously renewed, and thus costly in terms of time, energy, services and material goods, to maintain the relationship of domination. It is not enough for the pimp to "leave it to the system" he dominates for this domination to last. Pimps often find themselves in a situation where, "unable simply to appropriate the profits of a social machine not yet able to find within itself the power to perpetuate its existence, they are condemned to the elementary forms of domination, i.e. the direct domination of one person over another (...); they cannot appropriate the work, services, assets, tributes or respect of others without 'earning' them personally, 'attaching' them to themselves – in short, creating a personal link from person to person" (Bourdieu 1976: 126). Pimps appropriate the earnings and services of prostitutes, together with their submission, an essential precondition, by establishing personal links of attachment and dependence. In its "mild" form, objective exploitation can only be subjectively overlooked when it takes the form of an enchanted relationship based on attentive care and tokens of affection at the same time as demonstrations of strength. A romantic relationship is thus the primary resource at the beginning of a pimp's dealings with a (future) prostitute enabling him to "keep" her. The suggestion of prostitution (always temporary) might be combined with a promise that the earnings generated will be devoted to buying a shop for the woman to manage or own.[3] For example, one prostitute explained that she had started walking the streets because of the feelings she had for her pimp, with whom she had fallen "head over heels in love" and who had promised a "better future" after a few months of prostitution: "I think it was a kind of sublimation, and I trusted him. It's true I gave my trust blindly, I believed it, and well, a better future and all the rest, very quickly ... And then in the end ... It didn't turn out like that".

Maintaining this kind of relationship requires the pimp to pay a price, usually in the form of gifts and other signs of affection that strengthen the prostitute's attachment. This needs to be as effective as possible in that the stigmatization of the prostitute's activity and the shame she internalizes contribute

---

2   For the social recruitment of pimps, similar from a male viewpoint to that of prostitutes, see Høigård & Finstad (1992:154-158).

3   "The guy promises you the world (...) [I had] a friend (...), for her it was 'go on the game for five years, and you'll get your hairdressing salon.' In the end she died before that, because she was no more going to get a hairdressing salon five years later than five years before" (former prostitute aged 44). From this viewpoint, the pimp has to act in relation to the (future) prostitute like a "cooler" in Goffman's terms, helping her to accept the "damage (...) done to [her] self" by her accession to the degraded status of prostitute and enabling her to engage in a "process of redefining the self along defensible lines" (Goffman 1952, p. 451).

to her social and emotional isolation, and particularly her isolation from her family.[4] The interview extract below is able to describe the pimp's attentions truthfully as strategies to consolidate an exploitative relationship and ignore the conditions for their effectiveness because it comes specifically from an ex-prostitute who, suddenly forced into prostitution when she was "sold" by her husband to settle a gambling debt, was unable to give herself up to the illusion that transmutes domination suffered into domination disregarded and accepted:

> I never got presents from my pimp because I felt that if he gave me a present, or if they gave me presents, because there were several on the list, as it was me who was paying them, it was better if they just went and played cards, and at least I wouldn't see. But there are girls who turn up with beautiful rings and say: 'Have you seen this, look what he gave me.' But not me, or else I buy my own rings, but if my pimp says 'Bring me back 50 grand and I'll buy you a ring,' count me out (ex-prostitute).

When the state of dependence can no longer be overlooked while at the same time being seen in an enchanted form, other, more brutal strategies enable the pimp to maintain control over a prostitute, such as "fines" to penalize breaches of the "rules". A series of intimidation techniques such as punishments to set an example or arbitrary violence ensure the conditions for loyalty, or at least provide a considerable deterrent against any defection. Blows and injuries are part of the process of "training" the prostitute to internalize respect for a number of rules of behavior, which are primarily designed to guarantee the pimp's own financial interests. In the extracts below, two women describe how their pimp used violence to force them to accept any client without complaining.

> Once I refused a client, right at the beginning ... And one of the girls went off to tell the guy she was going out with, and the next day the guy ... The next day, when I got back, he came and hit me (prostitute)

---

4   This helps to explain how prostitutes' denials that a pimp is exploiting their earnings may be due not only to the fear he inspires but also to their genuine desire to protect a man whom they see above all as a partner. For definitions and representations of what a "procurer" means to Norwegian prostitutes – a representation aligned with the stereotypes of the brutal, exploitative pimp and very different from what French prostitutes might refer to as their "boyfriend" – see Høigård & Finstad (1992: 133-139).

Because a good professional needs maintenance. They don't kill her because she earns money, but they keep her scared. Because when you're not scared any more, you don't earn money, because you're sick of it. (...) So you get regular warnings. And that's how you get attacked with a knife on the stairs, for example. (...) They keep the fear alive. Or with punches, so it's a so-called client who comes and beats you up and you don't know why. I got stabbed in my room, it wasn't a client. The way he pulled the knife, and the way he got me, where the knife went, if it had been a client who had stabbed me the way he wanted to stab me, believe me I wouldn't be talking to you today. I've been attacked, my door has been broken down to take my money – they keep you scared, with violence. (...) They fine you for nothing. 'You got hit, you must have done something wrong, so you're getting fined.' Which means the punches, it's him [the pimp] who hands them out, and the fines, he gets them too, so in the end you're trapped (ex-prostitute).

The second interview extract shows that violence as an instrument for keeping prostitutes docile is all the more effective when it is exercised blindly and apparently with no real motivation. The arbitrariness or incomprehensibility of the punishments, their excessiveness in relation to the "offences" committed and the unpredictable alternation between periods when the pimp shows his attachment with gifts and favors and periods of violence or disdain ultimately make it impossible to anticipate how he will behave or react. Unable to define even a basic set of possibilities or probabilities to which she can adjust, the prostitute finds it more or less impossible to predict and even more so to counter the pimp's reactions and thus to carve out a space of relative autonomy and room for maneuver. She is forced to exercise continuous self-control, so fearful is she of the consequences of the slightest accidental slip. Trapped in social relationships whose rationale is entirely stripped of the security that comes from predictability and intelligibility, the young prostitute can only try to survive in the short term, permanently on her guard, which makes any plans for greater autonomy unthinkable. In contrast, the "traditionals" or "elders", thanks to their practical knowledge of behavioral norms, the acceptable limits on their transgression and a set of behaviors comparable to what Goffman calls *secondary adjustments*,[5] can allow themselves a much more relaxed approach to the rules.

---

5   For more on secondary adjustments, a set of practices enabling an individual whose existence is closely monitored and controlled to obtain unauthorized satisfactions, or to obtain authorized satisfactions by unauthorized means, using clandestine "scams" that constitute the "tricks of the trade", see Goffman (1961: 188–207).

The reference to Goffman's *Asylums* is significant. In many ways, the organization of prostitution we have just presented can be compared with the operation of total institutions. When it is controlled by organized pimps, prostitution also presupposes relatively strict isolation from the rest of the world. In a notable divergence from total institutions, the exercise of this isolation does not impose any actual physical barrier on the inmates.[6] However, prostitutes working in the street are no less confined within a limited geographical and, above all, social space, with severe restrictions or prohibitions on communication with people outside the prostitution world (except, of course, clients), and particularly members of their families. As in total institutions, prostitution can also include techniques of conditioning or mortification (rape, brutality, humiliation etc.) to ensure that prostitutes remain in a state of submission.[7] Depersonalization techniques such as the adoption of an alias or the requirement to only wear specific clothes are also designed to strip the new arrival on the street of their previous personality. The organization of continuous, mutual surveillance between prostitutes,[8] who are encouraged to compete with each other by a system of privileges ensuring they are converted to the pimp's interests, helps to destroy each individual's autonomy by exposing their slightest actions to potential punishment.

However, without minimizing the importance or seriousness of pimps' abuses, it should be noted that these kinds of behavior are generally frowned upon among pimps. They know that a relationship of submission is much more robust and sustainable if it is not seen as such, and takes the form of free consent; consequently, using violence too often is interpreted as an admission of weakness by a pimp unable to meet the conditions for enchantment in his relationship with his "earner", and is perceived as unworthy within pimping circles: "The ones who use violence, who take all the girls' money, we call them fags," asserted a prostitute affiliated with "big pimps".

In fact, the most frequent conflicts that follow the internal logics of the prostitution space and are likely to take a violent turn are the ones between

---

6   Except when practiced in a brothel, an institution that corresponds fully to Goffman's model in that prostitutes' freedom of movement is severely controlled and restricted, including their freedom to leave.

7   Several examples of these violent conditioning techniques can be found in Mossuz-Lavau & Teixeira (2005).

8   "Where you're all much closer together is in an apartment in town, partly because there's much closer surveillance from the pimp and his enforcers, even if they're just common thugs, who are even worse (…) And when you're set up in a room by an old prostitute, she's also monitoring you. (…) Not to mention that the pimps are always in cahoots with a café or pub or whatever, so they can see how many clients you have" (ex-prostitute).

prostitutes themselves. In this world of insecurity, competition takes aggravated forms and rivalries and arguments between different categories of prostitutes (between "traditional" and "occasional" prostitutes, women and transvestites, French and foreigners, drug addicts and abstainers etc.) are very common. Failing to respect another prostitute's spot, trying to win other prostitutes' clients, engaging in unfair competition by lowering prices or accepting unprotected practices are among the most usual causes of controversy[9] and can result in physical confrontations whose consequences vary in severity.

However, the survey coordinated by ECEMA indicated that the most common assaults are those corresponding to the second type identified, i.e. assaults committed by individuals from outside the prostitution world. The most feared among these potential attackers are clients, whose reactions are always unpredictable; significantly, one young transvestite explained that, in prostitution, "the hardest part is not knowing (...) who you're dealing with when you go upstairs with a client". These attacks are most commonly motivated by theft: generally, after obtaining the required sexual service, the client uses the threat of a weapon to demand not only the money already paid for the service, but all the money in the prostitute's possession. To avoid losing all their earnings, prostitutes take care to hide their money in unexpected places:

> I had one ... who terrified me at the time (...) He held the pistol to my head and ... he said 'Give me your bag.' I didn't ask questions, I gave him my bag ... I even asked his permission to put my coat back on. He said 'I don't want your coat, put it on and get lost, turn around straight away ... I don't want you to see my registration.' And then in the end (...) when he started the car, well, all his lights were off, so I couldn't see the registration. (...) I think he stole 600 francs all the same, and I'd worked well that night. All the rest was in my boots (prostitute).

In other cases, the violence committed by clients takes the form of sexual assault. Breaking the prior agreement with the prostitute about which sexual service would be exchanged for which sum of money, the client demands other practices (often degrading or brutal in nature), using threats.[10] Prostitutes

---

9   A transvestite taken to one side by his "colleagues", who saw him as a competitor as soon as he arrived in the street, says: "Apart from twice at the very beginning when I was starting to work as a woman, but I knew they [his attackers] had been sent anyway! When you're a new arrival, for sure, the clients like that, so it's bad for the ones who are already working, who are already in place".

10   As in the case of a rent boy who, taken against his will to his client's home, was subjected to fisting and, traumatized by the rape, made several suicide attempts.

working in their clients' cars are particularly likely to fall victim to this type of attack, as they can be taken to an isolated place without being able to escape the vehicle, like this young woman who found herself miles away from the street where she worked: "There was one (…) he took me towards Saint-F. He wanted a blow job with no condom, for nothing. I was really scared that time". Clients who are rejected by prostitutes for various reasons (drunkenness, general distrust, poor reputation etc.) and cannot accept the snub can also turn violent. In this case, people working in isolated locations (such as by the road-side) where they cannot count on backup from their "colleagues" are in an especially fragile position:

> I didn't have this problem when I was working indoors because if you refuse a client he won't insist, but on the road … For me, at least, it's not the same clients, and they want to get what they came for at any price. If you refuse, it often turns nasty. (…) I had a problem the day before yester-day, which went badly. (…) It ended in a fight. (…) If I'd got into the car, I wouldn't have come back (prostitute).

We must also account for assaults committed by non-clients, who attack prostitutes, acting alone or in groups, motivated by homophobia or – in the case of "gangs of youths" – to help them construct a bold, virile façade. While these attacks often take the relatively minor form (though still maintaining a general climate of insecurity in the streets) of insults hurled from the wheel of a car driving through areas where prostitutes solicit for clients, others involve physical assault and injuries:

> There's lots of verbal aggression. People shouting: 'whore, tranny, fag.' Things like that, you see, there's … never an evening without a verbal attack. (…) They're not clients. Or maybe a client on his own. But when they're in a group, maybe just for show. (…) Once there were some sol-diers. They started by throwing stones, you see. Then afterwards they came up to me and we started talking. I told them: 'Listen, I'm here to work, I'm not here for you to attack me.' So after ten minutes' talking they got the message and left (transvestite).

2   Protective Knowledge and Skills

When they talk about their work, many prostitutes underline the general atmosphere of insecurity, the continuous prospect of being attacked by a cli-ent or a mentally unbalanced individual and the permanent risk of assault, which are a constant burden that is fully integrated into their working lives. The violent undercurrent is so significant that it is almost taken for granted, seen as an integral part of being a prostitute. For example, some individuals say they are "always on the lookout", while others declare that prostitution is a world "where you have to be constantly on your guard, where (…) you learn to live with fear, so that fear becomes a mode of operation".

However, it would be inaccurate to consider prostitutes solely as potential victims. While violence is integrated into daily practice, it is also the case that they have a number of skills intended precisely to guard against any potential assault, specific techniques for protection and defense, which the "veterans" often take charge of passing on to novices.[11] From this viewpoint, the practice of prostitution requires practical security skills to be learned and mastered, and it can be seen that these contribute to the construction of the internal hierarchy in the prostitution space. Inability to master these skills, which are considered part of every prostitute's "professional expertise", is a negative marker for those exposed to aggression due to their inexperience, weakness or naivety; this hierarchical classification is implicit in the words of this transvestite and this former prostitute stigmatizing the imprudence of their young "colleagues":

> It's true that there are places (…) the people who work there aren't careful. For me, I don't know, people who've been working for three or four months, five months, if you listen to them, like F., well she's already been attacked at least two or three times. (…) B., he's already been attacked two or three times. Why, because they're not careful enough. Maybe not mature enough in their work (transvestite).

> I remember a girl who went with legionaries, and that's no good because they were always full of beer, so you couldn't get anything out of them anyway. (…) She was going to get massacred because she didn't have the knowledge. Me, an old hand, I wasn't going to get massacred by legionaries. I preferred to lose my hour and do two extra hours the next day. But well, they don't know when they're young (ex-prostitute).

Space does not allow us to develop a detailed analysis here of the various protective techniques available to prostitutes and how they are passed on.[12] We

---

11   A detailed presentation of the skills, and particularly relationship skills, required for the practice of prostitution in Brazil (which is not very different from France in this respect) can be found in Brochier (2005).

12   This question was examined by Pryen (1999).

will limit ourselves to setting out the main elements of these specific skills that enable female and male prostitutes either to evade the most dangerous situations, or to confront violence when it cannot be avoided. These include what could be described as *avoidance strategies*, i.e. practices based on a principle of selection (clients, locations or working times), designed as far as possible to prevent prostitutes finding themselves in risky situations. For example, some choose their working hours based on the probability of being confronted with dangerous individuals: "Saturdays no, Fridays it's rare, Sundays I'll work but not Saturdays, because that's when people are in couples and lots of people go out to clubs, and then they're there to mess with us, there you go, they're drunk so" (prostitute).

The largest part of this job of selection concerns clients and is based on largely informal criteria enabling the prostitute to "sense" through face-to-face interaction whether the person is likely to be favorable, to "frame" (Goffman 1974) the client as potentially dangerous or, conversely, peaceable and problem-free. *Preformed typification*,[13] often taking the form of sifted prior (unfortunate) experiences, provide a basis for classifying the individual requesting sexual services as an acceptable client or a "shady" individual to be rejected. From this viewpoint, ethnic criteria are among those most frequently called upon in developing these typification (though the proportion involving racism alone is difficult to evaluate), as the words of this transvestite indicate:

> Let's just say, I'm not racist but in my experience, Arabs, I avoid taking them in principle. I take some, I have one or two as regular clients, and there's no problem with them, but there are some, it's always the same thing, they don't mind paying but afterwards they make such a song and dance, 'Give me my money back, do this, do that,' so you fall for it once and then afterwards ... Basically, they're trouble.

Various techniques and evaluation criteria are used to "assess" the client in advance through informal *tests* (Boltanski and Thévenot 2006) as a basis for forming judgements about potential dangers. Engaging them in conversation and monitoring their attitude enable the prostitute to estimate the margin of

---

13   This concept is inspired by the *background expectancies* described by ethnomethodologists; see in particular Garfinkel (1964), Cicourel (1995); for typification processes, see Cefaï (1994).

risk and, if necessary, refuse services or flee before the individual has time to turn violent:[14]

> If the client is weird about … Because we talk to them, and if we see that he doesn't speak or … Because for me, there are times when I don't talk at all, and if I see that the client talks, I think to myself it'll be OK, but if I see that he doesn't say anything and neither do I, after a while I start to talk and if I see that he really doesn't talk, that means … he's a bit shady … (prostitute).

> You have to be suspicious (…) Before getting in the car you had a good chat with the person, and you could tell. (…) You wouldn't get in the car with just anyone. If the guy seemed a bit fishy, you didn't go (ex-transvestite).

> You learn to evaluate everything, anticipate everything. (…) If you get a bad feeling about the client, you let him get ahead, then you get back in front of him, and then behind again – it's what we call the client dance. Or else you go upstairs very quickly to see how he's going to behave, you make him talk (ex-prostitute).

On this point, we can see that despite the fierce antagonisms and strong competition that usually reign in the streets, basic forms of solidarity are expressed between prostitutes as soon as the security or life of another is at risk: "In my day there was always a time when a girl got beaten up, maybe even your worst enemy (…) there are no more enemies, you run to help. (…) I helped a girl who'd been beaten up, two days later if I'd touched her post, she would have had a go at me, he was her post, not mine" (ex-prostitute). More generally, this solidarity takes the form of passing on information about clients (usually identified by the model, color or registration of their vehicle) who should be avoided, because they have previously been aggressive to a "colleague": "For example, you might hear 'I've tried that green BMW, and it didn't go well,' and the next time you see it, you'll say no. Still, someone has to try. And the older ones tell us" (ex-transvestite). This attention to peers' safety, despite all the rivalry and competition, can also be reflected in checking the time spent with a

---

14   This decoding does not apply only to clients, but also to the work setting, as explained by this former prostitute who worked for years from a room: "I learned to work with shadows, because my room was, and I'm not the only one to work like that, on the how many, third, fourth, fifth floor, I don't remember (…) There are shadows when you get up there. If the shadows had moved, it meant something".

client: if a neighbor on the street has still not reappeared well after the average time, this is a warning sign that can lead to an investigation in the places where the person usually takes their clients.

When avoidance strategies are ineffective and the risk of aggression cannot be evaded, other methods are available to try to divert the danger and cause the attacker to give up. A prostitute can claim – truly or falsely – that she already has a pimp and its being watched from a distance, and this is one of the most commonly used ways of getting rid of profiteers or would-be pimps:

> As they wouldn't leave me alone, I said, 'Well you can talk about it with my pimp when he comes by.' I didn't have one, I didn't care (ex-transvestite).

> I came to prostitution saying that I had a pimp who was in prison. (...) I had very clear reasons, well more or less everyone has very clear reasons, but still, for being a prostitute. And I needed the money for that, and not for a pimp (ex-prostitute).

Dissuasion strategies such as these, as well as impressing the potential attacker with a courageous, determined attitude, can also be designed to discourage any temptation of theft by presenting it implicitly as pointless. We have heard an experienced prostitute, for example, advising a colleague starting work on the street to casually tell each of her clients that he is the first of the night, so that he will think she only has a tiny amount of money in her possession.

Finally, if aggression can be neither anticipated nor diverted, prostitutes have to resort to protective strategies intended either to defend themselves or to flee. For flight to be an accessible solution, however, a number of conditions have to be met to avoid finding themselves in a position of weakness if things go wrong with a client they initially considered to be harmless. Prostitutes working in cars, for example, take care to leave the door slightly open in order to be able to escape if necessary. Prostitutes working indoors, meanwhile, deliberately lay out their rooms to guarantee easy access to the exit:

> There's the room layout aspect. (...) If you don't have your chair by the door in order to get out if necessary, if you put the client's chair there, sure, if he runs at you and you're by the window, either you jump out of the window, but if it's on the fifth floor you're a pancake, or else it's him who's near the window, and if you sense danger you get out. You see, there's the whole room layout aspect. (...) So we have loads of things in our rooms to defend ourselves (ex-prostitute).

For the same reasons, prostitutes generally refuse when clients ask them to take all their clothes off, even if they pay much more. Remaining as dressed as possible during the date reduces the risk of theft and, above all, provides a kind of guarantee that flight will be possible in the event of a "problem": "I take my trousers off, I just take one leg out and it happens in the car, so that means I don't get undressed. I take one leg out and say 'Get in front and do what you have to do'" (prostitute). The need to be able to respond to an assault quickly even during a date also helps to explain why prostitutes refuse certain sex positions seen as unsafe, such as "doggy-style", or demand that the client keeps his hands on the wheel during fellatio. More generally, prostitutes adopt a number of *techniques of the body* (Mauss 1973) specifically designed to guard against the dangers of attack: "So yes, you keep your high heels on and you have a way of bending your leg to be able to give him a good kick in the belly or elsewhere if he goes too far. (...) You will never see a prostitute take her heels off, she keeps them on to defend herself" (ex-prostitute).[15]

Facing the constant risk of assault, prostitutes generally carry a weapon. The concept of a weapon needs to be taken in the wide sense, as shown by the interview extract above, where high heeled shoes are considered a potential means of defense. On the road, many women work in the company of a dog trained to defend them against attack. However, the most common weapons are pepper sprays and knives. The choice of a type of knife can sometimes be unexpected, as in the case of a transvestite who armed himself with an oyster knife because its blade was very solid while not being long enough, according to him, to stab someone fatally. Though being armed provides reassurance and an extra dose of courage when walking the streets, it is not in itself an infallible guarantee of being able to confront aggressors: "You find yourself with a weapon against your belly ... Even if you've got your hand on a pepper spray in your coat pocket, there's nothing you can do! You hand over your money" (transvestite). In addition, in many towns prostitutes are confronted with the attitude of the police, who often search them and confiscate any prohibited weapons – helping to make them more vulnerable and strengthening their feeling of insecurity. At the same time, this repressive attitude tends to put prostitutes off informing them or making a complaint in the event of an assault.

---

15   From this viewpoint, it is useful to see prostitution as what Goffman (1974) calls a *modalization*, i.e. a formal imitation of a reference activity but with a significantly different meaning. At least for the individual practicing it, prostitution constitutes a modalization of sexuality in that its practice takes the form of a sexual act but is not invested with erotic meaning or motivated by the search for pleasure.

3   Resignation as Symbolic Violence

As we come to the end of this chapter, we must first of all underline that gender plays an important role in the relationships female and male prostitutes have with violence. While the statistical data presented above indicate that men (transvestites and rent boys) are more exposed to aggression than women, it remains the case that they seem to adopt a more marked defensive attitude than their female colleagues, willingly fighting back or physically confronting their attackers. To sum up in a sentence, women explain during interviews how scared they are, while men explain how they defend themselves.[16] Even when they adopt a feminine identity – in the long term or just when working in the street – male (or male at birth)[17] prostitutes have nonetheless been socialized according to the criteria that define masculinity, and they have internalized the expectation that they will stand up to aggressors, fight rather than fleeing, defend their honor by replying to insults etc.

Other factors contribute to this unequal distribution of skills in terms of security, of which one of the most important is consumption of psychotropic drugs. From this viewpoint, drug addicts – and particularly those dependent on heroin or crack – appear doubly fragile in the face of the risk of aggression: first because their dependence, requiring them to collect the money they need for their next fix in the urgency of withdrawal, forces them to be less selective in their choice of clients, and can lead them to accept offers, with all the risks involved, from "suspect" individuals whom their drug-free colleagues have probably already rejected. Secondly, their altered state of consciousness makes them less able to impose their will on the client and puts them in a position of weakness if he tries to rob them or force them to take part in other practices than the ones initially agreed upon (such as unprotected sexual intercourse).

But above all, in conclusion, we want to examine the effects on prostitutes of what could be described as the internalization of the violent environment. Because in the streets, as one former prostitute said, "fear becomes an existence", and the possibility of violence tends to be taken for granted as an

---

16   This is illustrated by the words of two transvestites, for which we found no equivalent among female prostitutes: "I'm not someone who can be pushed around"; "No, I'm not scared. I feel... not strong, but... The other day a guy got out of a car, he came towards me, and he tried to catch me. He didn't get very far, I can tell you".

17   The homology observed on this point between men (whether they work in male or female clothing) and people born male who have changed their sex or live permanently in a feminine identity is not intended to question the "sincerity" of this feminine identity; rather it is an indicator of what might be called *the inertia of a masculine habitus*, whose effects continue to be felt despite the change of gender or anatomical sex.

unavoidable element of the prostitute's condition. The repeated assaults experienced personally or reported by peers are eventually seen with resignation as an "occupational risk" against which almost nothing can be done. This normalized representation of violence – as well as distrust of law enforcement, which is a given in a social world on the fringes of delinquency – helps explain why female and male prostitutes who have been assaulted very rarely report their attackers, because they are convinced that "there's no point" and "the cops don't care".[18] Furthermore, by making mastery of self-protection techniques one of the principles by which prostitutes establish their hierarchy, the omnipresence of violence helps make prostitution a world marked by low levels of cohesion and solidarity, making it unlikely that any plan for collective action against a situation that affects the whole group could ever become a reality.[19] This being the case, prostitutes cannot see any other option than to try to adapt as well as possible to their continuous exposure to danger, without being able – or even imagining being able – to change the rules of the prostitution game, which they rely on to safeguard their existence.

This internalization of the prospect of aggression contributes directly to consolidating prostitutes' feelings of shame and resignation in the face of an unfortunate condition that is ultimately seen as irrevocable and with no hope of change. The fatalistic integration of the violent environment into daily existence, and its acceptance as something that it is taken for granted, can thus be considered the main elements of the *symbolic violence* to which prostitutes are subjected, as a "form of violence committed against a social agent with the agent's complicity" (Bourdieu 1992: 142; see also Bourdieu and Passeron 1977). Caught between the two forces of their ignorance of the arbitrariness of the domination they experience and their recognition of its legitimacy, prostitutes usually find themselves having to be resigned to a situation they see as immutable. In this context, physical violence and symbolic violence cannot be considered as radically distinct; each one reinforcing or legitimizing the other, they are part of the same diffuse process of stigmatization and domination.

---

18   Taking the effects of this attitude into account, the authors of the article cited above took care to specify that the figures collected during their survey probably constitute a minimum level of attacks, given the "systematic under-declaration due to an undervaluation of assaults that are considered 'normal' in sex work" (Serre et al. 1996: 414).

19   A conversation between four transvestites, observed at the end of 1998, illustrates this phenomenon: laughing loudly and cruelly, they were talking about one of their female colleagues (and competitors), unanimously presented as "dumb", who found herself one night, having been beaten and raped by a client, completely naked in the countryside around twenty miles from where she worked.

Violence, as Luc Boltanski rightly said, "ignores persons, and (…) opens up the possibility of treating human beings as things" (2012: 72). From this viewpoint, for the prostitutes who are its victims, it represents a form of denial of their humanity that contributes to the stigmatization specifically associated with their activity and reminds them every day of the negligible importance given to their existence in the social world. While it is necessary to counter an over-condescending or pessimistic vision of their unfortunate condition by underlining their capacity for resistance, it would be equally wrong to overestimate the "weapons of the weak" (J. C. Scott 1990; Broqua and Deschamps 2014) with which they equip themselves, so inadequate do these weapons appear for inverting the symbolic, political and social power relationships that marginalize them.

CHAPTER 3

Prostitution, a Zone of Social Vulnerability

> Of all the causes of prostitution (...) none is more active than lack
> of work and poverty, the inevitable consequences of the inadequate
> salaries earned by our dressmakers, seamstresses, menders and, in
> general, all those who occupy themselves with the needle.
>
> ALEXANDRE PARENT-DUCHÂTELET (1981 [1836])[1]

∴

Polemics about the status of prostitution, which are particularly virulent in France, compare it to the two opposing extremes of work and slavery.[2] The abolitionist movement considers it to be a modern form of slavery, and thus to be eliminated, while advocates for its recognition define it – as long as it is "freely" chosen and practiced – as a "trade in its own right", demanding that it be de-stigmatized to allow for better social integration.

The goal of this chapter is not to study these polemics in themselves,[3] but to analyze the relationship the sale of sexual services has with the world of work and the wage society in a more global sense. More specifically, the intention here is to consider prostitution in the context of what Castel (2003) calls *disaffiliation*, i.e. a process leading from full integration to social non-existence. This is an essential condition for a clearer understanding of the factors that cause certain individuals, both women and men, to enter prostitution and remain there. This essentially socioeconomic understanding of the phenomenon of prostitution in no way excludes any others. It merely seems that adopting this lens for analysis offers a new way of considering certain aspects of prostitution, and particularly those involved in the construction of gender relationships. For example, considering prostitution from the viewpoint of exclusion from the wage society underlines the fact that this activity is mostly carried

---

1   Quoted in Scott (1990: 4).
2   An initial version of this text was published under the title "La prostitution, zone de vulnérabilité sociale" ("Prostitution, a zone of social vulnerability"), *Nouvelles questions féministes*, vol. 21, no. 2, 2002: 55-75.
3   This is the central subject of the fourth chapter of this book.

out by women, i.e. not only the category assigned to prostitution by the patri-archal order, but also one of the most precarious in the labor market. Similarly, we can consider that the factors of economic insecurity that lead men (rent boys, transvestites and transgender prostitutes) to work in prostitution are not unrelated to the fact that they present a gender discordance (socially perceived and personally internalized as deviance) to varying degrees – a discordance which, tending to equate them with femininity and homosexuality, constitutes in itself a decisive factor of vulnerability in their pathway through prostitution.

1   Prostitution and Disaffiliation

The concept of disaffiliation aims to respond to shortcomings in analyses of the current social crisis that are based on the notion of exclusion. The first problem with this concept is its homogenization of disparate situations of insecurity (homeless people, young people caught in a cycle of traineeships and odd jobs, the long-term unemployed etc.). Another flaw, stemming from its presupposition of a clear distinction between socially integrated indi-viduals and "excluded" individuals, is that it leads to a static vision of social reality: "Exclusion is static. It designates a state, or rather several states, of pri-vation. But observing deficiencies does not allow one to assess the processes that have led to them" (Castel 2003: 15).

Conversely, discussing disaffiliation opens the possibility of a dynamic understanding of the logics that take certain individuals step by step from integration to disqualification or social non-existence. For Castel, the crisis France has been experiencing for the last four decades is not restricted to the "excluded" alone; it affects all employees, who have been placed by the trans-formations of capitalism in a position of social vulnerability, an "intermediate, unstable zone that goes along with the precariousness of work and the fragility of proximate supports" (*ibid.*: 13). Castel relates this growing vulnerability to what he describes as the crumbling of the wage-earning society: whereas the wage system imposed itself for decades as the primary mode of social integra-tion, we are now seeing this status and the protections that come with it called into question. The wage system, which only recently was still a guarantee of status, protection and participation in social life, has now become destabilized and insecure (notably due to part-time work and fixed-term contracts), and no longer provides an escape from an uncertain future or from vulnerability.

Castel's thinking builds on the work of Durkheim, who positions work as the essential factor in social integration in *The Division of Labour in Society* (1984). It is in this context that we can usefully examine the question of the social position of people working in prostitution and, beyond that, the status of their activity. In other terms, is the sale of sexual services a job, and if so, should the people working in this job be considered citizens in their own right, able to claim the same rights and protections as other workers? Or is such an activity inherently illegitimate, bringing with it the marginal status of an individual gravitating around the social body without really being part of it?

This latter view is the one that has been adopted since 1960[4] by the French state, which sees in prostitution a social maladjustment that social work professionals are employed to prevent or to save people from. It is important to note that their central mission is to persuade prostitutes of the need for them to *reintegrate* into society: as a deviant activity, prostitution cannot be seen as a job, because it is precisely access to a "real job" that is expected to cause them to give it up and return to full membership of society. Social work organizations thus logically invite prostitutes to reintegrate into society through apprenticeship or retraining in a professional activity; most are equipped with rehabilitation workshops where former prostitutes can (re)make contact with the wage society with fixed-term contracts involving handling tasks.

Perceived and defined in this way, prostitution clearly seems to fall into the category of marginality and to constitute a paradigmatic form of what Castel calls the "experience of social disengagement". However, a more attentive examination leads to a more nuanced reading. Prostitution has the specific characteristic that it is both a deviance and an activity on which it is possible to base a whole existence. Unlike other marginal individuals such as drug addicts and homeless people, prostitutes can live – and sometimes live well – from prostitution: the criterion by which their deviance is defined is also a source of income. In addition, the activity of prostitution is not prohibited by French law, meaning that it can constitute a stopgap in terms of work that is, if not legitimate, at least legal. This point is not without impact on the social perception of prostitution. Though we have clearly identified how and why it constitutes a social "scandal" in that it transgresses the legitimate forms of sexual relationships in our societies (extramarital sex with multiple partners for commercial reasons with no reproductive purpose), we have doubtless underestimated how far this scandalous dimension also comes from its particular relationship with work: as an activity that is financially rewarded but is parallel to the official

---

4   This was the year when France ratified the UN Convention for the Suppression of the Traffic in Persons and of the Exploitation of the Prostitution of Others, which constitutes the central reference point for French law on the subject. Recent legislative changes, described in the fourth and subsequent chapters of this book, have not called the Convention's principles into question.

economic channels, prostitution tends to escape all control, particularly from the state. Historians have shown that what concerned nineteenth-century moral entrepreneurs keen to rehabilitate the morals of prostituted women[5] was their economic independence (including independence from a husband) and the fact that they were not supervised by an employer. Prostitution thus constituted a radical transgression against the social order, because it enabled the economic survival of women outside the family setting and the guardianship of a father or husband, as well as outside a company and the authority of a supervisor or employer (Corbin 1996; Scott 1990).

Yet prostitution, though a lucrative activity enabling its practitioner to survive, is nonetheless situated outside the "normal" world of work and – this is a central point – its protections. In this sense, it falls into the zones of vulnerability located between social integration and social non-existence: prostitutes have a source of income, certainly, but it cannot be admitted publicly and does not give them the benefit of any social protection.[6] The money they earn from their activity and inject back into the economic system enables them to contribute on a basic level to the life of society and, in the best cases, maintain the façade of a "normal" existence, but this existence nevertheless remains extremely fragile. The danger of serious illness with no social security cover, or the prospect of ageing when you have never paid into a pension fund, for example, constitute swords of Damocles hanging permanently over prostitutes' heads.

If the sex trade does not constitute a "real" job in the absence of the protections associated with being a worker, but at most what Hughes (1958) called an *occupation* (i.e. an individual's means of filling their time and earning a living), can the vulnerability of its practitioners best be remedied by officially recognizing it as a "trade", conferring eligibility for social protection, as prostitutes' collectives claim (Mathieu 2001; 2003)? Several reasons lead us to answer in the negative. One of the first is that entering prostitution is never the result of a totally free decision; it always involves some form of obligation.

---

5 Numerically marginal, male prostitution did not arouse the same social anxiety at the time.

6 Access to various aspects of social protection (illness, occupational accidents, unemployment and retirement) in France is subject to working and paying contributions calculated on the basis of income. As they do not practice a recognized activity, and their income is not subject to official evaluation (though in principle it is taxable), prostitutes cannot benefit from this protection in their role as prostitutes.

2 Entry into Prostitution

Engaging for the first time in an activity as stigmatized as prostitution is never the result of a voluntary, deliberate choice; it is always the consequence of a constraint, or at best a form of adaptation to a situation marked by distress, poverty or violence. However, recognizing this constraint does not mean espousing the representations commonly promulgated by abolitionist activists, who only want to see prostitutes as heteronomous agents of forces outside their control – naive girls (or more rarely young men) trapped by pimps who force them through violence to sell their bodies, or socially maladjusted individuals who end up on the streets in spite of themselves due to childhood psychological trauma. This pessimism firstly commits an injustice by denying prostitutes any capacity for action or reaction in the face of this constraint: prostitution can also be a form of resistance, a way of facing a danger or an even worse situation (even greater poverty, for example). It also excludes any understanding of the conditions that keep people in prostitution, disregarding the (essentially economic) interest of choosing prostitution in the eyes of individuals in great distress who have an extremely limited range of options.

Here, for the purposes of clarification, we propose to divide the reasons for entry into prostitution into the two broad categories of direct constraint and social frustration, not forgetting that the two can be closely linked.

The *direct constraints* most commonly encountered are economic. Standing for the first time by the side of the street, or accepting offers of money from men in exchange for a sexual service, is one of the last ways of quickly earning a relatively large sum of money for destitute individuals for whom legitimate methods of economic acquisition (work, benefits) are currently inaccessible. This is the situation that most prostitutes faced in their early days. It is especially relevant to young people who have run away from home or experienced family breakdown, and particularly young homosexuals rejected by a homophobic family. It is also common among drug addicts, for whom the sex trade – without necessarily requiring them to identify as prostitutes – provides a means of earning the money they need to buy the product on which they depend.

The development of the welfare state during the nineteenth and twentieth centuries has meant that the situation of the young workers forced into prostitution between two periods of employment – studied by Walkowitz (1980) in England and mentioned by Parent-Duchâtelet in the epigraph to this chapter – no longer occurs as frequently as in the preceding century. Nevertheless, even now the closure of the job market and long-term unemployment can lead people into the streets, as shown by this interview extract:

> I had exhausted all the resources there are, not finding any work, and
> well, I knew someone, I knew she worked [as a prostitute], who said 'You
> can come to me, no problem.' (...) I was a fashion technician ... Well, that
> industry's completely closed, there's nothing left. (...) She was talking to
> me casually one day, saying OK, what are you going to do, you're going
> to be screwed, because I was in my last month of benefits. And she said
> what will you do?(prostitute, aged 39).

As we have said, seeing prostitution as a way of responding to an urgent need
for money when the people engaged in it are in danger or affected by disaffiliation should not be a reason to deny them any autonomy or capacity to choose.
Prostitution is not the only way out of extreme poverty – though it presents
other risks and requirements, theft is another response to destitution.[7] So we
can see that, even in the most constrained and urgent situations, turning to
prostitution can be the result of choosing from a range of alternative solutions,
a choice in which moral considerations may be an element:

> You can't be a dancer and a heroin addict – physically it's very hard and
> financially it's not enough. So I decided to go into prostitution, because
> it was clear to me that I would never steal an old lady's handbag or rob
> a tobacconist, or a bank, because that's not at all how I see the world.
> I wanted to earn my money honestly, because I believe I do earn my
> money honestly, even as a prostitute (transvestite, aged 32).

Another type of direct constraint can be applied by a pimp, or multiple pimps.
But once again, we need to account for the diversity of situations covered by
what is first and foremost a legal category. The traditional figure of the pimp,
even if it is often far removed from the stereotypes found in literature and film,
nonetheless exists. Several years of investigation within the world of prostitution have led to encounters with several women who entered prostitution
following pressure from a pimp – pressure that generally combined tokens of
affection with demonstrations of strength. A romantic relationship is often the
primary resource at the beginning of a pimp's dealings with a (future) prostitute enabling him to lead her into prostitution. When the state of dependence

---

7   Clearly, gender plays a decisive role in the adoption of one option or the other, theft or
    prostitution (and the same aspect applies in the alternatives of pimping or prostitution). In
    addition, theft is not the only alternative to prostitution in cases of extreme financial diffi-
    culty: begging is another option, as is selling plasma in certain countries such as the United
    States (Anderson & Snow 1994).

can no longer be overlooked while at the same time being seen in an enchanted form, other, more brutal methods enable the pimp to maintain control over a prostitute.

However, it needs to be restated that – outside the "international networks", to which we will return – this "traditional" form of pimping, associated with a specific social background and essentially exploiting women, declined sharply at the end of the twentieth century. This was due both to police repression and to organized crime transferring its activities into more lucrative sectors (mostly drug trafficking). The "big pimp" controlling several women has given way to the scrounging hustler boyfriend, a petty criminal who lives on the earnings of a prostitute partner, and to the dealer encouraging his drug addict customers to use prostitution to earn money to pay for their drugs. In this context, we can note that the partners of drug addict prostitutes are often not so much pimps in the usual meaning of the word as "companions in misery", sharing the same experience of disaffiliation and dependence; consequently, their partnership is as much about mutual support in a period of difficulty and moral distress as it is about exploitation.[8] Finally, to avoid any manichaeism, it should be pointed out that a large proportion of criminal proceedings for pimping target prostitutes guilty of exploiting or extorting money from their peers, and that in certain areas of the underclass, families (and particularly mothers) can be found who prostitute their daughters – whose earnings make a significant contribution to the family finances.

The second broad rationale for entering prostitution is *social frustration*. This sees the sex trade as one of the few means of achieving or maintaining a lifestyle to which the person's current situation, and particularly modest social origins or low levels of professional ability, do not allow access. Because the social recruitment of prostitutes is highly relevant – as emphasized by Høigård and Finstad, "it is women from the working class or the lumpenproletariat who are recruited into prostitution" (1992: 15). Of the few data available for France, Ingold's figures from the 1990s confirmed this observation, demonstrating their validity for both sexes: his study of 241 subjects (women and men), conducted in various prostitution areas of Paris, indicated that a large proportion (41%) were "from modest or very modest backgrounds, sometimes marginal" (1993: 54). The same study indicated that "with regard to professional training, if it has taken place (52%), it was most often elementary (apprenticeship,

---

8   For more on this situation, see the Norwegian study by Høigård & Finstad (1992: 133-72). It should be restated that while gender plays a decisive role in whether a person adopts the position of prostitute or pimp, the male partner may also come to engage in prostitution in the most insecure and urgent situations.

secondary school) and terminated early, only rarely resulting in a qualification" (*ibid.*).[9]

Individuals with this kind of sociological profile are particularly exposed to economic constraints, in response to which prostitution can appear as a (last) resort. However, we must be wary of oversimplification: for drug addicts and people in situations of extreme disaffiliation, prostitution can constitute a means of survival in the short term, but this is not the case for all prostitutes. Above all, these economic constraints are evaluated against certain socially constructed and subjectively perceived expectations. In other terms, prostitution is also an expedient for people whose immediate physical survival is not threatened, but who feel that their current source of revenue (through work, social security benefits etc.) does not allow them (or no longer allows them) to achieve or maintain their desired lifestyle. In some cases, when routes for legitimate upward social mobility (primarily through education) are reduced or non-existent, we see that prostitution can be perceived as one of the few methods available for achieving a future that is not accessible in any other way. This former transvestite expressed precisely this when he legitimized his prostitution based on the need "to be able to keep up" financially with the wealthy patrons of venues for gay socializing:

> I worked as a transvestite and a prostitute to be able to live the life, all night long, go to restaurants, clubs, things like that. You have to spend because in that setting (...) lots of people have a lot of money. (...) So you have to keep up. (...) The motivation is money, you see. Money does a lot. Because you can't keep up, if you don't have money you can't keep up with the lifestyle in that setting (ex-transvestite, aged 44).

From this angle of analysis, we can see that the practices of extravagant spending common among prostitutes are less the symptoms of a pathological relationship with money, as certain psychologically-oriented interpretations propose, than attempts to prove their tangible financial and social success to themselves, while also signaling, among people from modest backgrounds who have always lived with financial uncertainty, that they have no need to save money. These lavish consumption behaviors are attempts to emphasize, in their own eyes and the eyes of others, that the prostitution game is well worth playing despite the stigma and insecurity. However, this relative success,

---

9   This recruitment from the working class and underclass is both a geographical and a historical constant; for several examples relating to Europe, see Rossiaud (1996), Flandrin (1981), Corbin (1996), Walkowitz (1980), Karady (1994) and Feschet (1974).

initially sociologically improbable and obtained through methods that cannot be admitted outside the limited circle of their peers, cannot be recognized outside the prostitution space. Acquired by illegitimate means even in the eyes of prostitutes themselves, this success is condemned always to be experienced as ambiguous, fragile or incomplete.

Prostitution among migrants (from sub-Saharan Africa, the Middle East, South America or Asia) can be interpreted in a similar way, in that it reveals a close interweaving of direct constraints and feelings of social frustration. Foreigners who enter prostitution in France all come from countries with very high levels of economic inequality, with no effective social welfare systems, where professional prospects are extremely limited – especially for women. The Chinese women studied by Lévy and Lieber (2009), for example, came to France with the hope of overcoming the difficulties caused by the economic restructuring of their country. Discovering the scarcity and insecurity of the jobs accessible to them in France (especially as they were illegal migrants), they had no choice but to use their sexuality as a migratory resource, either through prostitution or through marriage with a Frenchman – with the former sometimes leading to the latter.

When this kind of prostitution is carried out independently, it constitutes a way of earning a far greater income than would be accessible in their country of origin, whether the goal is simply to accumulate money to invest in a legitimate activity (usually a shop), to support the family back home or to ensure survival in France in the case of migrants without papers unable to access the legal job market. Migrant prostitution organized and controlled by pimps follows a similar logic. Not only does pimping – like all criminal activities (Mauger 2006) – constitute a quick way of earning money and leaving unsatisfactory living conditions behind for working-class men with no future in the legal economy in their country, but prostitution fulfils a similar role for the women who are subject to them. Contrary to the stereotype of the naive young woman deceived by false promises of work as a hostess or au pair girl,[10] many migrant prostitutes know exactly what is waiting for them abroad and hope to earn substantial rewards (though they often underestimate the exploitation and violence ahead, as indicated by the interviews conducted by Mossuz-Lavau and Teixeira 2005).

Based on the foregoing, prostitution makes sense when seen in relation to the legal employment market, or more specifically its closure to the portions

---

10   The fact that cases of young women decoyed in this way are not as widespread as the public imagination suggests does not change the underlying facts: whether prostitution is anticipated or not, the goal is always a better future in a new country.

of the population – especially women – who are most economically and culturally dominated. Single mothers with no qualifications who are offered only traineeships and part-time work, homeless young people ineligible for welfare until they are 25, migrants trying to build a future in France that they cannot access in their country of origin ... all these groups are close to the New York drug dealers studied by Bourgois (1995) who, disapproving of a trade they only entered by default, ultimately dream of one day accessing a "legal job". Since entry into the underground economy of prostitution is always coerced in some way, it is clear that the distinction between "free" and "forced" prostitution defended by prostitutes' organizations is irrelevant (Doezema 1998).

3   Heightened Vulnerability

Some prostitutes can earn relatively large amounts from their activity and either finance a comfortable lifestyle in the short term or save money for a future transition to the legitimate economy. These people are in the minority within the prostitution space – most live in conditions ranging from great insecurity to extreme destitution. In other words, while prostitution is a response to a situation or a risk of disaffiliation for the people who practice it, it is usually an ineffective, sterile response, principally because the dangers and stigma inherent in the activity help to reinforce their vulnerability as soon as they arrive in the street.

There are many factors of vulnerability specific to the activity of prostitution, and they directly threaten individuals' physical integrity. They include the significant risks of contracting a sexually transmitted disease (HIV and hepatitis in particular): though various epidemiological studies conducted since the emergence of AIDS have shown that infection levels remain relatively low on the streets of France and that prostitutes quickly and overwhelmingly adopted the use of condoms (Mathieu 2000), "lapses" in prevention are always possible. These are seen most often among the most vulnerable prostitutes, who can be induced by the urgency of their situation to accept offers for unprotected sex, which many clients want, even at higher rates. Drug addicts are particularly exposed in this way – apart from the risks of infection incurred by sharing syringes, straws or pipes, their dependence requires them to earn the money they need to buy their fix for fear of withdrawal, which means they have to be less selective than others in choosing their clients. Similarly, their altered state of consciousness makes them less able to impose their will on the client and puts them in a position of weakness if he tries to force them to take part in other practices than the ones they initially agreed – and especially sexual practices without a condom.

Omnipresent in the streets, insecurity is another significant factor in making prostitutes' survival a risky business. As we have already emphasized, the attackers are usually clients motivated by theft or sexual aggression, together with those who are rejected by prostitutes for various reasons (drunkenness, poor reputation etc.) and cannot accept the snub. Assaults are also often committed by individuals who, sometimes just "for fun", start throwing stones or cans of beer at prostitutes. Again, as we have already seen, prostitutes who work in dark, isolated locations where they cannot count on support from their colleagues are all the more exposed to attack.

The attitude of police officers also makes prostitutes' living conditions more uncertain. Harassment with summonses – for soliciting between 2003 and 2016, or against clients since then – or with raids to check residence permits is a tactic for deterring prostitutes from continuing to work in a particular district (sometimes following complaints from residents or with the aim of gentrification). It is generally designed to remove them to a more isolated area where their presence will be less visible – but where they will also be much more exposed to attack, have to work under unsanitary conditions and be more difficult for social work organizations to reach. Pressure, blackmail and intimidation are also used to compel certain prostitutes to act as informers or incriminate their pimp, sometimes by threatening migrants working for pimping networks with deportation. Finally, it is not unusual for prostitutes to report that they have been insulted, beaten up, extorted or raped by police officers; several trials have shown that such accusations are not always unfounded.

As well as assaults committed by individuals from outside the prostitution space, others occur due to motivations from within, including the fierce rivalry between prostitutes. Precisely because they live in such insecure conditions, they find themselves having to compete for scarce means of subsistence. This aggravated competition may result, for example, in attempts to evict new arrivals in a nearby spot with threats or violence, based on the fear that they may take over clients attracted by their novelty. The violence within the prostitution space contributes greatly to its lack of cohesion, preventing prostitutes from coming together to defend their common interests: since the challenge of short-term survival requires immediate responses, individualist strategies always appear more plausible and accessible than collective action to transform the unfortunate condition suffered by the whole group, with results that would be less immediate and always uncertain.

The illegitimacy of the sex trade adds its own force to the fragility of the people who live from it, and contributes to consolidating or heightening their disaffiliation, depending on their always individual circumstances. Housing is one of the key indicators of this. Many people who could afford to pay rent on an apartment are excluded from this possibility because estate agents require pay slips as evidence of ability to pay, which they obviously do not have. Consequently, many have to live in hotels or squats or negotiate an agreement with a landlord who will not hesitate to evict them without notice on a whim, and who can use the threat of being accused of hotel-based pimping to impose very high rents for housing that is sometimes unsanitary. The lives of many prostitutes are affected by the lack of a place where they can put down emotional and material roots, the inability to invite and form bonds with other people, and the psychological consequences of a nomadic lifestyle, which all contribute to their isolation.

Lack of social security cover is also common: the survey led by Anne Serre et al. (1996) showed that only 39% of the prostitutes in the sample had social security cover, and the difference between sexes was significant: 54% of women had cover (69% of those with children), compared with 46% of rent boys and 27% of transvestites. Access to social security is available to prostitutes, but proves patchy in practice. Apart from the fact that the most disaffiliated among them are unaware of the eligibility conditions, or have internalized the illegitimacy of their status to such an extent that they do not allow themselves any contact with institutions of this kind, the practical difficulties are many. The introduction of universal health cover in 2000 did enable many prostitutes, alongside other groups on the margins of the employment market, to access health insurance independently of their source of income. But it also brought with it a paradox – as in principle it is reserved for people with no resources, the system requires prostitutes in a more favorable economic position to lie about their actual incomes. It also remains inaccessible to illegal immigrants, and more recent assessments have confirmed that prostitutes' health remains extremely precarious (Haute autorité de santé 2016).

These factors of vulnerability affecting all prostitutes are combined with others affecting certain specific categories. We have already spoken enough about the many dangers facing drug addicts, and there is no need to cover them again. But for many foreigners, their vulnerability is multiplied by the secrecy imposed by their illegal status. The fear of police checks resulting in deportation from the country causes a level of anxiety that is only intensified by the knowledge that for most of them a forced return to their country of origin could have dramatic consequences: North African transvestites, for example, know that if they return home with a physical appearance that does not correspond to their official sex, their chances of short-term survival are slim. Deported women forced to return to families that have been informed of their work as prostitutes are exposed to similar dangers. Secrecy maintains their distance from French society and obliges them to fall back on the group, which can be a source of protection and solidarity but where relationships of dominance and exploitation can hold sway. Transgender Latin Americans arriving in France, for example, are dependent on peers who have already arrived, who immediately provide accommodation, somewhere to work and practical advice. This moral and material support naturally comes with strings attached, mostly but not solely financial, which contributes to the ambiguity of the relationships between prostitutes and their supporters or sponsors. In these terms, nothing – except the gendered presupposition that women are more vulnerable than men – separates female and transgender migrant prostitution (de Montvalon 2018).

The difficulties inherent in giving up masculinity (and its associated privileges and advantages) can also lead to sometimes dramatic situations. Transgender people rendered more fragile by their questioning of their true identity fall prey to cosmetic surgeons or hormone sellers prepared to charge exorbitant prices for operations or products that can have extremely dangerous side effects. The difficulty of living to the full with a problematic identity or an unusual appearance leads many of them to isolate themselves and socialise solely with their colleagues in the street. Many only go out when night falls or avoid busy public spaces rather than facing the eyes of others. Some mothers engage in a comparable level of secrecy, living in terror that their work might be discovered by a social worker who could have their children taken away from them. More generally, the anxiety that their prostitution might be revealed against their will is a burden for everyone trying to hide their true source of income from their family, even if the family sometimes benefits from it.

Ultimately, the absence of social security cover and housing, the isolation, exposure to assault, internalized shame etc. combine and interweave to create vicious circles that are almost impossible to escape. Because once across the "threshold" into prostitution (always a painful step), it is extremely difficult to backtrack. Once again, however, we must be wary of oversimplification: a significant proportion of prostitutes, once they have paid the (very high) price of taking on a stigmatized identity, find that prostitution suits them to a certain extent, and are not willing to give up its benefits.[11] It would be wrong to dismiss out of hand, as just a reflection of a defensive psychological attitude, the statements of women and men who prefer to remain in the street rather

---

11   The analyses by Hirschman (1970) are relevant here, showing that the higher the costs of
      entry to a social game, the more loyal individuals are to it.

than seek rehabilitation through a legitimate professional activity. For many, taking account once again of the lifestyle to which their low level of qualification condemns them, the sex trade certainly represents an option that is not without interest, *in economic terms only*. For these people, the conditions for a potential way out of prostitution must be considered as a balance between symbolic costs, risks to life and financial gain. But even the individuals who are keenest to leave prostitution find it extremely difficult to do so. Once again, leaving aside any dissuasion that may be exerted by pimps, the analysis must take the employment market into account. Apart from the difficulties facing undocumented migrants, drug addicts and transgender people in accessing work, the degraded state of the market for low-skill or unskilled jobs is a major barrier to true rehabilitation, however much people want to "get out". These obstacles, which could be categorized as macroeconomic, are combined with other, more practical difficulties: during a recruitment interview, how do you justify a career gap, often several years long, without revealing your past as a prostitute? If this past is discovered, how do you face the hostility of colleagues or sexual harassment from a superior? How do you adjust your life when your income drops dramatically? These are the questions facing policies of assistance for prostitutes.

4   The Ambiguity of Social Policy

Public policy in the field of prostitution will be discussed in greater depth in the final chapters of this book. Here we will concentrate on how social action in support of prostitutes can unintentionally help to make their position more fragile by consolidating stigma and consequently maintaining social marginalization.

   In line with the abolitionist principles adopted in 1960, all regulations restricting the activity of prostitutes have been permanently abolished in France, and those involved in this work are no longer subject to any obligations specific to them (such as mandatory registration, medical checks etc.). Taking into account the adverse effects of both prohibitionism (which pushes the activity underground) and regulationism (which traps practitioners in a status of shame), French abolitionism prefers to leave prostitution in a kind of legal void – it is totally absent from the French penal code. While France implicitly recognizes the "freedom to prostitute oneself", the same does not apply to its exploitation (categorized as pimping), the disturbance inherent in its public expression (long criminalized as soliciting and now under the general category of disturbing public order) or, since 2016, the purchase of sexual services by clients (see Chapters 4, 5 and 6).

Allowing the activity of prostitution while preserving its informal status enables people with no other resources to ensure their own survival without being permanently labelled and marginalized as prostitutes. And yet this freedom for individuals to offer sexual services for money is limited by the state's particularly negative view of their activity: the legal framework adopted in 1960 was not satisfied with removing the last vestiges of regulationism; it also defined prostitution as a social scourge, alongside alcoholism, tuberculosis and, through a last-minute amendment, homosexuality. Considered, in accordance with the UN Convention, as "incompatible with the dignity and worth of the human person", prostitution is seen by French law as a private activity that anyone is free to practice as they see fit, but using this freedom attests to a distortion of free choice that calls for appropriate support, which must be provided by social work organizations.

The package of support specifically designed for prostitutes currently has two aspects, one social and the other relating to health, and both essentially provided by the voluntary sector with the backing of public funds. The health aspect came together in the early 1990s with a focus on the fight against AIDS, and took the form of associations distributing condoms and syringes, providing preventive information, advice and health monitoring and guiding prostitutes towards sources of health support. The social aspect, established earlier, is organized around the prevention of prostitution, support for prostitutes in social difficulties and help with rehabilitation.

Both sectors, though competing with each other, are based on the same assumption – no doubt inevitable, but with its own significant consequences – that prostitution is the central element of the identity of the people they are targeting. In other words, as the sex trade is at the center of their attention, both social workers and AIDS prevention teams tend to see the individuals they care for only as prostitutes. This identity is seen as predominant, even though prostitution may only be one element among many other reference points of an individual's identity. Above all, prostitution may be just one of many factors of vulnerability or marginality, interacting with other status reference points without it necessarily being possible to identify one that plays an overarching, ultimate role: besides being a prostitute, an individual might also be homeless, addicted to drugs, an illegal immigrant etc.

The most immediate consequence of this specialization of support is well known to the sociology of deviance: it results in the labelling of the people who constitute the "clientele", who are permanently identified and marked as prostitutes by the fact that they are in contact with organizations targeting exclusively this category. This labelling explains why many of them do all they can to avoid organizations that set out specifically to help them. This is clearly expressed by this prostitute interviewed by Stéphanie Pryen, who refuses help from the *Mouvement du Nid* organization, which specializes in prostitution, because she fears being "catalogued":

> Each time they [the members of the *Mouvement du Nid*] do anything, you're catalogued. Even if it's approaching the town hall, or applying for a traineeship, for anything, or the job center, or 'I know someone at the job center, I'll give them a call!' Well you'll see, the person at the job center, she knows you're like that (...) So I say, if you can, it's best to get out by yourself.
>
> PRYEN 1999: 71

Avoiding this labelling is not just about camouflage for people worried about the possible consequences of their activity being known; it can also be about protecting their self-image by keeping the stigma at bay for individuals who have not internalized the identity of a prostitute. This is primarily the case with people who have not worked as prostitutes for long, or only irregularly and informally; they may admit to being "on the game", but without ever presenting themselves as "prostitutes". Receiving support from a specialist organization, when it cannot be avoided, acts as a status degradation ceremony,[12] which ratifies and formalizes the prostitute's status in the eyes of people for whom it is still vague and uncertain. In most cases, this formalization of the prostitute's status makes a new life more complex and difficult to achieve.

Other difficulties are more specific to social work and involve the adoption of a framework for analyzing situations inspired essentially by psychology or psychoanalysis. It is not our intention to deny the importance of psychological factors in the processes by which people enter prostitution, nor that many prostitutes suffer with psychological issues to varying degrees. The goal is rather to question the relevance of psychological approaches in assisting people in difficulty. By looking into the individual's past – and specifically their childhood – for the origins and meaning of their current difficulties, these approaches tend to overlook the part played by the current socioeconomic conditions of their life, or their survival. This leads social workers into the risk of pathologizing (and thus invalidating with stigma) what is in fact an attempt,

---

12   In the words of Harold Garfinkel: "We use 'status degradation ceremony' to mean any work of communication between people by which the public identity of an actor is transformed and – relative to the local classification of social types – lowered" (1956: 24).

desperate though it may be, to overcome immediate material difficulties. By failing to pay attention to the socioeconomic conditions that have led to (and consolidated) the situation of prostitution, the approach fosters blame: the individual tends to be considered as personally responsible for the difficult situation they have, even unconsciously, placed themselves in. The often pessimistic view that social work brings to the existence of prostitutes denies them any coherence; they constitute a collection of pathological cases (rather than a population with elements in common in terms of social origins and trajectories), and their behavior, from which all rationality appears absent, is seen above all as a set of symptoms to be treated.

The primacy given to their psychological problems at the expense of their socioeconomic difficulties is doubtless part of the reason for the difficult relationships many prostitutes have with social workers. The emphasis that certain organizations place on reintegration is also judged harshly. Firstly because by promoting, sometimes insistently, the renunciation of prostitution in favor of a "real" job, educators and social workers constantly remind prostitutes of their social shame and contribute to reawakening the violence of their stigma. Secondly, because reintegration cannot fail to come up against what we referred to above as the economic interest of prostitution as an option. Given both the closure of the market for low-skill or unskilled jobs and the low level of professional qualifications of the vast majority of prostitutes, which removes all hope of finding a "normal" job with an income comparable to what they can earn in the streets, invitations to rehabilitation are often met only with indifference.

As we have seen, prostitution's formal proximity to work is not the same thing as assimilation. Even when, practiced regularly, it constitutes the main source of a person's income, it remains excluded from the protections specific to the world of work that guarantee true social integration. Then there is the specific force of the stigma, which – either generally or in an institutionalized way, including in forms intended to be benevolent – helps to keep prostitutes at a distance from the normal world of work.

Faced with this situation, "sex worker" movements argue for a dual normalization, both professional and symbolic, as if it was enough to consider prostitution as a "trade in its own right" and to give it specific protections for its marginalization to dissolve. We have good reason to be more pessimistic, suggesting that such recognition, which has no impact on the social reasons that cause people to enter prostitution, would not prevent it from remaining, like all the caring professions in which some (e.g. Pharo 2013) suggest including it, a mostly female, underqualified, strenuous and poorly paid job, which for these reasons is mostly occupied by migrants from poor countries. Assimilating the sex trade into care work with the intention of boosting its symbolic value may backfire when care work is situated within its gendered economic and social context:[13] unequal social structures clearly assign women to these disqualified tasks. Julia O'Connell Davidson is thus not unreasonable to ask how destigmatizing an activity that consists, for example, of inserting dildos into men's backsides and faking orgasms while straddling tired penises could make it significantly different from and preferable to other menial care tasks (1995: 9). If prostitution were recognized as a job in its own right, it would be unlikely to rise above the decidedly unappealing status of what Everett Hughes (1958) called *dirty work*.

---

13   For more on the entanglement between gender, migration and neoliberal globalization in care work, see Ehrenreich and Hochschild (2003) and Falquet et al. (2010).

CHAPTER 4

French Prostitution Policies

Genesis and Methods

The days when French politicians saw dealing with prostitution as beneath their dignity are over.[1,2] The last twenty years or so have seen a succession of parliamentary reports on the subject, and new legislative provisions have been introduced, criticized and sometimes transformed, giving rise to lively public debate each time. There is no doubt that the face of prostitution has also been transformed over a similar period. The role of foreign prostitutes has grown and their numbers have made the activity more visible, and more problematic, in the urban space.

However, it would be a mistake to think that this new vision of prostitution as a public problem results solely from its transformations, as if political mobilizations and public initiatives were automatically determined by the nature of the problem they are claiming to solve. On the contrary, taking our lead from the sociology of public problems emerging from the Chicago tradition (e.g. Spector and Kitsuse 1977), what we need to examine is the process by which a set of agents declares the existence of a situation they define as deplorable and requiring remediation. We must also understand how this process is influenced by the diversity of social situations of the agents involved – located in distinct social worlds, and thus pursuing heterogeneous goals, they are engaged in a competitive struggle to impose their definition of the problem of prostitution. Finally, our account needs to incorporate the fact that this struggle is not without effects on the practices and identities of the people concerned.

The process examined in this chapter has the specific characteristic that the diversity of agents and organizations that have contributed to it (moral entrepreneurs, feminists, social workers, the police, local residents, politicians,

---

1 An initial version of this text was published under the title "Genèse et logiques des politiques de prostitution en France" ("Genesis and logics of prostitution policies in France"), *Actes de la recherche en sciences sociales*, no. 198, 2013: 4–21.

2 Alain Corbin (1996) recalls that prostitution was not a matter for the law until the mid-twentieth century, but rather for municipal regulation. Under the Directory (1795-1799), the Assembly considered that such subjects were unworthy of it. The 1946 act prohibiting prostitution establishments was adopted with no parliamentary debate, and thereafter political interventions were limited to a few isolated outbursts from personalities declaring that they supported the "reopening of the brothels", with no effect other than a brief media spotlight.

intellectuals etc.) has not prevented it from managing to impose a dominant definition of both the problem and its solution: that prostitution is a form of violence against human dignity and requires above all a penal response. Though this definition is the subject of bitter debate, it is made harder for its opponents to dispute by the fact that it has achieved a broad consensus, attracting support from agents who are opposed to each other both ideologically (from feminism to Catholicism) and politically (from the far left to the conservative right). If we are to grasp the conditions that have led this consensus to emerge and succeed, we must account for this constituent heterogeneity by focusing the analysis on the diversity of social forces interwoven within it and locating the struggles to define prostitution within a space of debate whose references go beyond the French context.

1   A Disputed Monopoly

Understanding how a definition of prostitution as an attack on dignity took hold requires us first of all to locate its first advocates within the space of organizations claiming to be experts on the issue. During the 1990s, a number of disruptions in this space undermined the previously dominant position occupied by so-called abolitionist movements, which learned the lesson that they needed to remobilize by forging new alliances and new campaign themes.

The contemporary abolitionist movement positions itself as the heir to the abolitionism that emerged in England in the second half of the nineteenth century. This original movement primarily aimed to abolish the regulation of prostitution, which trapped prostitutes in a shameful status by forcing them to register with officials and submit to health checks (Corbin 1996; Walkowitz 1980). This moral crusade was itself composite, with puritan Christians hostile to any sexual depravity rubbing shoulders with feminist progressives opposed to prostitutes' servitude to the police. Abolitionism took off at the end of the nineteenth century with a campaign against the "white slave trade" (see Chapter 7) that received widespread media coverage. The campaign gave the movement an international profile and earned support from several states, which signed conventions against the trade at the beginning of the twentieth century, and then from the League of Nations and the United Nations (UN) that succeeded it (Chaumont 2009).

In 1949, the UN gave the abolitionists a form of consecration by presenting for ratification the Convention for the Suppression of the Traffic in Persons and of the Exploitation of the Prostitution of Others, which was directly inspired by their recommendations. The Convention underlines the link between people trafficking and prostitution, considering that both are "incompatible with the dignity and worth of the human person and endanger the welfare of the individual, the family and the community". Ratified by decrees in 1960, the Convention still constitutes the legal framework for prostitution in France. In line with its provisions, French law does not impose any regulations on prostitution but controls it with two-pronged penal and social policy. The police are responsible for suppressing the organization and exploitation of prostitution by others (*i.e.* pimping) and its disruptive public manifestations (soliciting, exhibitionism), while social workers are charged with preventing prostitution and offering rehabilitation and retraining for its victims.

One factor that made it easier for the abolitionists to move into this social work space is that the government decided not to establish the specialist local services provided for by the 1960 decrees, preferring to delegate the prevention and rehabilitation missions to the voluntary sector. This enabled what is now the main French abolitionist organization, the *Mouvement du Nid*, to gradually develop its activity, from providing moral support to prostitutes to offering social assistance and rehabilitation, setting up reception services and hostels. This process of specialization, taking place in conjunction with a professionalization of social work (Muel-Dreyfus 1983), led to a split in 1971: since then, the *Amicale du Nid*, consisting of social workers, has fulfilled the roles of prevention, assistance, accommodation and rehabilitation delegated by the public authorities, while the *Mouvement du Nid* organizes volunteers who go out to meet prostitutes and offer them moral support while also raising awareness through presentations in schools, poster campaigns, the publication of the quarterly magazine *Prostitution et société*, training for social workers and lobbying of politicians.

The French abolitionist movement
The *Mouvement du Nid* was initiated in 1937 and officially founded in 1946 by a priest, Jean-Marie Talvas. The association is part of the sphere of influence of *Action catholique ouvrière* (ACO – Workers' Catholic Action), and more specifically *Jeunesse ouvrière chrétienne* (JOC – Young Christian Workers). These origins root the organisation in the progressive and Third-Worldist wings of the Catholic church (to the extent that it even opened up to Maoist influences during the 1970s, see Mathieu 2001), as illustrated by its association with the *Comité Catholique contre la Faim et pour le Développement* (CCFD – Catholic Committee against Hunger and for Development). It is now structured into around thirty local committees run by several hundred active volunteers.

Another influential organisation, the *Fondation Scelles* emerged in 1997 from the *Équipes d'action contre le proxénétisme* (Teams for Action against Procuring), which were themselves founded in 1956 by a former parliamentarian from the *Mouvement Républicain Populaire* (MRP, a Christian center-right political party) and authorized to act as the plaintiff in trials of pimps. More conservative and elitist in its recruitment (its active members include magistrates, officials and senior civil servants) but less widely established than the *Mouvement du Nid*, the *Fondation Scelles* also provides information and works to influence "opinion" by publishing books and organizing conferences.

The French abolitionist movement also includes other, smaller—*Le Cri* ("The Scram"), *Aux captifs la libération* ("Liberation for Captives"), etc.—or more specialized—*Association contre la prostitution des enfants* ("Association against Child Prostitution"), ECPAT-*France* ("End Child Prostitution, Child Pornography and Trafficking in Children for Sexual Purposes-France"), etc.—organizations. Although the specialist social work bodies (including the largest, the *Amicale du Nid*, which manages around 15 institutions) uphold a more professional identity, they still involve themselves with the key events of abolitionist activism.

The claim of the abolitionist moral entrepreneurs[3] to have a monopoly on knowledge about and treatment of prostitution was disputed from the early 1990s, firstly due to the emergence of AIDS. The specter, promoted by several politicians, of a return to health checks on prostitutes and the need for appropriate preventive initiatives to support their health aroused the distrust of a movement that was constituted in opposition to a health-based definition of prostitution (the threat of venereal disease) in favor of understanding and treating it as a social maladjustment. The result was hostility from abolitionists with regard to the creation of AIDS prevention associations working among prostitutes, which were suspected of preparing for a return to the hated regulationism and aiming to facilitate an activity that should, on the contrary, disappear. The arguments were all the stormier in that the associations combating AIDS refused to focus their efforts on rehabilitation, instead promoting specific preventive skills that prostitutes could learn from their experience in

---

3 As the abolition of the regulation of prostitution had already been achieved, the term came to refer to the abolition of prostitution itself, an extension that was all the easier in that the movement had always thought of itself as homologous with the movement for the abolition of slavery (from which some of its founders emerged) and that the theme of the "white slave trade" had been conceived on the model of African slavery.

the streets. They even appropriated the demands for "sex work" to be recognized that had been developed during the 1980s by prostitutes' movements abroad, including in the USA and the Netherlands (Pheterson 1989; Weitzer 1991; Jenness 1993; Mathieu 2001; 2003). A split thus arose in the 1990s between social work and AIDS prevention. This was reflected not only in the voluntary medical and social work sector but also in the administrative field – whereas social work was supported by the *Direction de l'action sociale* (the Social Action Department), AIDS prevention was supported by the *Direction générale de la santé* (the Health Department) – and in the intellectual and activist spheres, where partisans of abolition opposed advocates of recognizing prostitution as a trade (Mathieu 2014a).

A counter-movement: the "sex workers"

The associations fighting AIDS among prostitutes provided the basis for a new movement in the early 2000s arguing for the recognition of "sex work", and the first priority of its campaign was to oppose the domestic security act (see below). The theme of "community health" adopted by these associations led them to promote the infection prevention skills that prostitutes could learn from their experience in the streets, and it was from their ranks that the first leaders of the "sex work" cause emerged (Mathieu 2000; 2001). The cause also benefited from support from other organizations combating AIDS (starting with *Act Up*), and intellectuals engaged in a critical debate with feminism (Marcela Iacub, Élisabeth Badinter). The mobilization of prostitutes (and their supporters) took several organizational forms—*France Prostitution, Les Putes* ("The Whores"), etc.—before the foundation in 2009 of the Sex Workers' Union (STRASS), which has over 400 members. Organizing regular public initiatives (such as *"pute* pride", modelled on gay pride, the Assises de la Prostitution conference and the days against violence against sex workers) and promoting "self-management" of the sex market, STRASS received institutional recognition in 2011 at a hearing of the Bousquet-Geoffroy parliamentary commission (see below), though without shaking the abolitionist convictions of the commission's members. The "sex workers'" movement has a very confrontational relationship with the abolitionists, whom it accuses of promoting stigma and insecurity for prostitutes and whose conferences it sometimes disrupts. The distinction it makes between prostitution as a result of free choice and of coercion also causes it to demand severe repression of people trafficking for sexual exploitation.

The emergence of AIDS prevention inspired by ideas that were heretical to its principles was not the only threat to abolitionism during the 1990s. As not all European countries had ratified the 1949 Convention, or were applying it, the fear arose that European construction could call France's abolitionist commitment into question. Anxiety focused on Dutch policy, which was on course to give up abolitionism (which had been officially adopted in 1911 but abandoned in practice for decades) in favor of recognition of professional status for prostitutes (introduced in 1999) and for their employers in specialist establishments (Outshoorn 2004; Altink, Van Liempt and Wijers 2017). It was also driven by the increasingly frequent appearance in statements from various international bodies (particularly during the 1991 Council of Europe Seminar on Action Against Trafficking in Women and then the World Conference on Women in Beijing in 1995) of a distinction, which the abolitionists considered a fallacy, between "forced" prostitution, which was unacceptable, and "free" prostitution, which needed to be recognized and regulated.

However, this fear did not first emerge within abolitionism, but within feminism. More specifically, it came from the pen of Marie-Victoire Louis, a sociologist and president of the *Association contre les violences faites aux femmes* (Association against Violence against Women). A keen participant at international conferences on prostitution and people trafficking, she devoted herself from the early 1990s to denouncing the maneuvers of the Dutch government and organizations of "sex workers" to legalize pimping.[4] Louis defended a definition of prostitution as patriarchal violence that contributes to the commodification of the human body to the benefit of clients, pimps and states. She thus provided a refreshed framework of arguments for an ageing abolitionist movement, whose charitable message was looking stuck in the past compared with the tone struck by the associations combating AIDS, which appeared more modern in their approach to sexuality. Furthermore, the sociologist, who became a key figure at abolitionist conferences, gave the movement an opportunity for an unprecedented coalition with feminism.

2   The Feminist Alliance

This coalition was far from a given, as the religious background of the abolitionist movement, with its overtones of moral conservatism, made it suspect

---

4   See in particular Louis (1992, 1999). Louis wrote an "Appeal to join the resistance against a Europe of procurers" in 1999, which was signed by many abolitionist and feminist organizations, as well as trade unions and left-wing parties.

in the eyes of feminists.[5] In fact, the feminist movement was not unanimous in rallying to the cause of abolishing prostitution; the support came chiefly from its most institutionalized components (with the notable exception of the Planning Familial network). A split between two opposing viewpoints thus appeared to emerge within French feminism, a space in which prostitution had rarely been a major topic of consideration and activism in the past (Mathieu 2014b). The first viewpoint, representing the majority, was held by longer-established figures and groups, whose past or present campaigns (against rape and for contraception and abortion) led them to consider sexuality as a potential source of danger for women and to denounce prostitution as sexist violence. The second viewpoint, younger and more informal, was inspired by homosexual movements (some of its members and theorists had previously been involved in the debate about recognizing same-sex couples) and queer thought, inclined to see sexuality as a space for the expression of individual freedom; it was from this group that demands for the recognition of "sex work" recruited some of its key supporters.

The revival of the abolitionists preceded their alliance with the feminists, as illustrated by the Journées européennes de la prévention de la prostitution (European Prostitution Prevention Days), organized in 1996 by the *European Federation for the Disappearance of Prostitution* and driven by the *Mouvement du Nid*, and the creation a year later of the *Fondation Scelles*. However, the alliance proved decisive, benefiting the abolitionists on several levels. Firstly, it enabled them to ride the renewed momentum of French feminism from 1995 onwards, when a large demonstration in Paris defended the right to abortion. The main organization arising from this revitalized movement, the *Collectif national pour le droit des femmes* (National Collective for Women's Rights), for example, rallied to the cause of abolitionism. The multiple activist positions of many feminists, who were also working in the trade union movement and left-wing or far-left parties, made it possible to spread the abolitionist message far wider than the traditional ideological and political base for the movement's recruitment. One of the most notable illustrations of this extension of

---

5   A clear understanding of the alliance's interests seems to have encouraged both camps to avoid areas of disagreement. This resulted in a number of unlikely pairings, as seen at the conference "Peuple de l'abîme : la prostitution aujourd'hui" ("People of the abyss: prostitution today"), organized in 2000 by the *Fondation Scelles,* where the feminist Marie-Victoire Louis took the stage, with no apparent qualms, immediately after the historian Pierre Chaunu, who had just been railing against contraception and homosexuality. Similar links between the religious right and feminism have been observed in the United States: see Weitzer (2007) and Bernstein (2010).

abolitionism's sphere of influence is the "Gender group" of the *Attac* association, which appropriated abolitionist ideas and translated them into alter-
globalist vocabulary, denouncing prostitution as the commodification of
human bodies, and its international expansion, legitimized by neoliberal ideology, as one of the most brutal expressions of globalization (Attac 2008).

Feminism also brought new awareness-raising, organizational and political
resources to abolitionism. A widely circulated medical argument that prostitution falls under the category of a pathological dissociation of the personality
made it possible to fight AIDS prevention on its own territory of health, on the
basis that abandoning the goal of rehabilitation would only trap prostitutes in
the repetition of a trauma (Trinquart 2002). The *Mouvement pour l'abolition
de la prostitution et de la pornographie* (MAPP, Movement for the Abolition of
Prostitution and Pornography) was founded in 1998. This gave abolitionism
the symbolic support of the *Coalition Against Trafficking in Women* (CATW),
an influential contributor to international institutions, since MAPP was its
French section, relaying the Coalition's theme of trafficking.[6] Its leader Malka
Marcovich was commissioned by the governmental *National Commission on
Violence Against Women* in 2002 to produce a report on prostitution, in which
she defended the argument that prostitution is intrinsically a form of sexist
violence (Marcovich 2002). Similarly widely circulated within the movement,
the report did not just present new arguments in favour of the disappearance
of prostitution. Its production, overseen by MEP Adeline Hazan, also made it
possible to forge links with the Socialist party (PS) then in government, whose
members (particularly local elected officials) were seeking solutions to the
problem of prostitution, as we will see below.

One final factor completed the revitalization of abolitionism. Starting in the
late 1990s, the French prostitution landscape underwent significant transformations with the arrival in the streets of large numbers of foreign prostitutes,
mostly from Eastern Europe, clearly very young and assumed to be under the
control of organized pimps. The influx received wide coverage in the press
and the audiovisual media, and was quickly seen through the long-standing
schema of human-trafficking (see Chapter 7). Although this schema played a
decisive role in the development of historical abolitionism, as we have seen,
it had gradually become obsolete (in 1991, the *Équipes d'action contre la traite
des femmes et des enfants* (Teams for Action Against the Trafficking of Women
and Children) became the *Équipes d'action contre le proxénétisme* (Teams for

---

6 With its focus on the French situation, space in this chapter does not permit us to examine
   the roles of NGOs in the emergence of trafficking as a theme in international arenas; see
   Darley (2006) and Ragaru (2007).

Action Against Procuring)) and recent forms of prostitute migration (such as South American transgender prostitutes and African women) had not so far been interpreted in these terms. In addition, the assimilation of trafficking with "forced prostitution" within international organizations had long been greeted with reluctance by those in France who rejected the idea of "free prostitution".

The renewal of the trafficking theme in France followed the abolitionist revival by several years, but gave it crucial new momentum. The young foreign woman under the control of a "network" (a word whose use grew exponentially) quickly came to stand in for the whole prostitute population in the movement's public statements.[7] Its effectiveness was partly due to its easy application to situations that abolitionists presented as symbolic, like the widely covered case of Ginka Trifonova, a young Bulgarian prostitute murdered in Paris in 1999.[8] It also owed much to its evocation of a stock of urban legends, illustrated by the occasional resurgences of rumors about kidnappings of young women by pimps, of which the Orléans rumor, studied at the time by Edgar Morin (1971), is the most famous example (see Chapter 7). Above all, this image of a naive young woman lured by false promises of employment and sold to international networks of organized pimps – and the resulting view of prostitutes as victims – suited the convictions of everyone working for the abolition of prostitution. While the heirs of historical abolitionism saw it as a resurgence of a past scourge, feminists found in it the confirmation that prostitution is a form of sexist violence (pimps and clients are always men, and most prostitutes are women), while alter-globalists and the far left viewed it as symbolizing the hubris of a neoliberalism prepared to reduce human beings to commodities while profiting from north-south inequality (with prostitutes drawn from poor countries to satisfy clients in the rich world)[9]. Other stakeholders, previously unconnected to the crusade to eliminate prostitution, also found an interest in appropriating and consolidating this schema.

---

7   For an examination of the process by which this idealized figure of a trafficking victim was developed, partly due to contributions from the Comité contre l'esclavage moderne (Committee Against Modern Slavery), see Jakšić (2016).

8   Her story opens the *Livre noir de la prostitution* ("Black Book of Prostitution") (Coquart and Huet 2000), published with the support of the *Fondation Scelles*.

9   For examples of this rhetoric, see Poulin (2005) and Attac (2008).

3   Combating Urban Disruption

The incursion of foreign prostitutes did not occur without incident. They undertook to appropriate existing soliciting areas by chasing out their former occupants (sometimes backed by armed men) or opened new ones, in city centers or residential areas, where they were a constant presence, day and night. Their visibility caused a degree of public unrest and their presence created further disruptions. The incessant traffic of clients' cars, the noise of altercations between rival prostitutes, their presence sometimes in a state of undress, the traces of their activity (used condoms, tissues, excrement) and even the sight of sex acts taking place beneath windows or in hallways aroused the anger of residents, who demanded a response from municipal authorities.

But again, it would be wrong to see the municipal policies on prostitution that developed from the 2000s as an automatic response to a demand for a "solution" to an "objective problem". The conditions under which the problem was formulated and the solutions developed must be seen in the context of changing urban populations and the political and economic priorities pursued by municipal leaders. The case of Lyon provides an illustration whose interest, apart from the perspective offered by a study extending over more than twenty years, lies in its analysis of a heightened expression of issues and mechanisms that could also be observed in other cities.[10]

Until several dozen young women moved into the streets of Lyon in summer 1999, prostitution, both male and female, had been a discreet activity, mostly practiced after nightfall on the banks of the Rhône and in certain suburban areas near major roads. Their arrival stood out for its visibility – they occupied several main roads in the city center during the day – and the disruption it caused to traffic and nearby residents. The council did not grasp the issue until 2001, when a new socialist mayor was elected. The first initiatives prioritized conciliation and relied on existing resources, including a telephone line managed by the local AIDS prevention association Cabiria, which was opened to residents who wanted to make complaints. This approach did not last long, however – in August 2002 the mayor, Gérard Collomb, adopted a municipal decree that banned soliciting in most of the city's historical and commercial center (north of the second arrondissement). This about-turn was not due to a failure of the conciliatory approach, but to the arrival of a context favorable to the adoption of repressive measures. As we will see later, the new interior

---

10   For the cities of Paris, Rennes, Nantes, Angers and Toulouse, see Hubbard (2004a; 2004b); Sanselme (2004); Danet and Guienne (2006).

minister, Nicolas Sarkozy, had already announced his intention to give the police legal means for repressing a series of urban disturbances, including prostitution, more effectively. The mayors of several cities (including Orléans, Strasbourg, Metz and Lyon) very quickly anticipated the introduction of this law by prohibiting soliciting in all or part of their municipal areas.

In Lyon, the immediate effect of the prohibition was to shift the prostitutes to the south of the second arrondissement, into the Perrache district, which is separated from the rest of the city by a railway station and by its location at the tip of the confluence between the Rhône and the Saône. Unlike the wealthier northern part of the same arrondissement, this is a working class area with a low population density and no significant commercial or leisure activities, neighboring a motorway, where several dozen prostitutes had worked for many years. As soliciting was defined by their visibility, the prostitutes equipped themselves with vans where they waited for their clients and provided their services. While this made their actual presence more discreet, the concentration of their vehicles (nearly 200 were counted on the main road, the Cours Charlemagne), made their activity more obvious and caused its own new problems – as the area had no public toilets, the prostitutes urinated in bottles that sometimes broke when the bin men collected them[11] Further municipal decrees penalizing the parking of "vehicles intended for sleeping or for professional activity" followed in 2006 and 2007, forcing the prostitutes once again to move away from the area's main traffic route towards more discreet streets, and then to abandon it completely. Chased out of Perrache, many of them tried to settle in another working-class district, Gerland. This choice was no better, as several new decrees gradually reduced the space allowed for their activity, obliging many of them to leave the city entirely and establish a presence beside suburban streets or country roads.

Various factors explain the adoption of this repressive policy at local level. The first is the pressure exercised by the municipal opposition, but also by the French state, since it was the prefect who, having organized a widely publicized evacuation of vans from Perrache in 2007, forced the mayor to adopt the decree banishing prostitutes from the area. Pressure from residents has a status all of its own, primarily because it appears to have been more anticipated or cited than actually expressed. A search through the municipal archives revealed only around a dozen letters, far from the 600 that the deputy mayor responsible for security claimed to have received in 2002, and mostly sent by

---

11   The city hall decided not to install public toilets for fear of being accused of organizing prostitution and thus pursued for pimping.

businesses rather than individuals. This does not detract from their eloquence, however, as they express the fear the "established" users of the neighborhoods feel with regard to "outsiders", whose intrusion is perceived as a territorial offence (Elias and Scotson 1965; Goffman 1971). The letters from businesses focus above all on damage to the image of the area – "Our visitors, whether French or foreign, [...] are astonished and shocked by this situation," writes a grouping of companies in Gerland – while those from residents concentrate more on expressing a fear of contamination, both sanitary and moral – "Our children are confronted on the way home from school. [...] Not to mention the condoms and other rubbish strewn across the ground throughout the area," complains a residents' association.

> **"We solemnly ask you to evacuate ..."**
> "(The) neighborhood has long seen a small network of prostitution, which has grown significantly since 15 August 2007 with the proliferation of prostitutes' vans, following the prefect's decree expelling these prostitutes from the Cours Charlemagne. This pimping poses many problems of soliciting by the prostitutes [...]. Students [...] declare that they have received repeated advances from prostitutes, and that they regularly find used condoms even in front of the institution's doors. As well as the problems of cohabitation between young students, some under age, and these prostitutes, this gives rise to a certain anxiety about exposure to a specific population (pimps, drug addicts/dealers etc.) associated with insecurity [...]. Campus employees can no longer wait for the bus or leave work without being harassed by this new population. Parking spaces for our employees, students and local residents are now increasingly scarce and we are presented with serious issues of hygiene. This all contributes to a negative image for the neighborhood, which until recently was socially harmonious and peaceful, and this new problem has an impact on the reputation of our businesses. With this petition, we solemnly ask you to evacuate all the vans and the prostitutes occupying the pavements in the area".
>   *Petition signed by 127 individuals and businesses, initiated by a vocational school and sent to the local town hall and the prefect's office on 3 September 2007.*

These letters (see box) also reveal repeated use of the vocabulary of networks and trafficking, testifying to the widespread view of prostitution through the schema of people trafficking. Municipal officials are no exception, adopting a paradoxical formulation in which the perception of prostitutes as victims legitimizes a predominantly repressive approach, and we will see further examples of this later. The mayor used these terms to justify the prostitutes' expulsion from Perrache: "Clearly we were dealing with human trafficking. We had to show the networks that Lyon was not going to become the European capital of modern slavery" (*Lyon Capitale*, 24 August 2007). Two years earlier, when city hall was challenged by opposition councilors about the problems of cleanliness caused by the presence of prostitutes near a school, the deputy mayor for social affairs and solidarity responded that "we cannot accept that, in our so-called civilized countries, women suffer violence and many of them are used as slaves".[12]

The last factor, but not the least, involves the ambitions of a city that wishes to claim a leading position in the competition between major European cities to attract businesses and wealthy residents. From this viewpoint, evicting prostitutes appears inseparable from a broader policy of urban population and management that emphasizes adjustment to the needs of businesses and social classes with high expectations in terms of "quality of life". This adjustment includes paying close attention to environmental priorities, developing significant cultural provision (an important issue for a city that has been on the UNESCO World Heritage list since 1998) (Arnaud 2008; Authier et al. 2010) and redefining problems of public order in terms of security. In addition to repressing soliciting, the municipal team also distinguished itself by expanding video surveillance, cracking down on fly-posting and noise pollution and destroying Roma settlements in order to respond to the moral demands of wealthy families in the advance guard of the gentrification affecting the heritage neighborhoods of central Lyon. Attention was also paid to the expectations of property investors, and it is no coincidence that the concentration of prostitutes in the south of the second arrondissement, which could be tolerated as long as the area was dominated by a low-income, ageing population, became unacceptable when the Confluence project was launched, aiming to make this post-industrial fringe into a new center for culture (including a major museum), politics (housing the new regional council offices) and business (a shopping center has opened and modernist buildings accommodate cutting-edge businesses).

As we have seen, Lyon is not unusual among major cities, both in France and abroad. Urban geographers and sociologists have documented the political priorities imposed in various European and North American cities over recent years, all of them aiming to expel prostitutes (among other undesirable

---

12 *Bulletin municipal officiel* (Lyon's official municipal journal), Lyon, 3 October 2005: 1751.

populations) from residential districts and city centers devoted primarily to leisure and consumption.¹³ Repressing the visible presence of prostitutes in the urban space is part of the "zero tolerance" ideological framework, which sees minor urban disorders as a prelude to more serious crime, and punishes them accordingly. This means that, for Philip Hubbard, as prostitutes are "depicted as part of a criminal class, reducing the visibility of sex work in the central city is an obvious way that policy-makers can send out a message that it is ripe for reinvestment" (2004a: 1698). The same author postulates elsewhere that policies of this kind are a source of injustices that cut across class and gender dominations (2004b). It is undeniable that repression of prostitutes in Lyon and elsewhere has the effect of pushing underground and exposing to aggression a specific category of women, often all the more vulnerable if they are illegal immigrants, in order to protect other women, who are more privileged and better socially integrated, against the feeling of insecurity caused by proximity to areas of prostitution.

4   A Question of Domestic Security

The urban space is not the only one to be defined as threatened by the presence of prostitutes – the national space is seen in the same way, due precisely to many of them having foreign origins. Although often implicit and ambiguous, this appears as a central aspect of the new problematization of prostitution that emerged in the early 2000s: while migrant prostitutes as a whole are seen as victims of pimping networks, they are the subject of more complaints from neighbors than their French colleagues.¹⁴ As a way of accounting for these migrations, the schema of people trafficking owes its success to its ability to combine particularly equivocal conceptions of prostitution and the actions to be taken. This is illustrated chiefly by the politicization of the prostitution issue initiated by Nicolas Sarkozy in May 2002.

Announced by the new interior minister following his participation in a police operation in the streets of the seventeenth arrondissement of Paris, the domestic security bill (*projet de Loi sur la sécurité intérieure* – LSI) took aim at a series of problems, including noisy gatherings in the common areas of residential buildings, the exploitation of begging, illegal settlement on private land, and soliciting, for which the penalty was set at six months'

---

13   In particular, see Hubbard (1999; 2004a;2004b); Bernstein (2007); Cameron (2004); Bernd, Helms (2003).
14   Interview with the director of the Lyon AIDS prevention association Cabiria, July 2009.

imprisonment and a fine of € 3,750. By defining soliciting as inciting others by any means, including dress or attitude, to engage in sexual relations in exchange for remuneration, the bill restored the offence of passive soliciting, which had been removed by the 1994 reform to the penal code, having long been criticized for the arbitrary power it gave the police. Foreigners guilty of soliciting could have their residence permit removed and be accompanied to the border, but if they reported or testified against their pimp they could be granted temporary leave to remain. The bill was sharply criticized by the left-wing opposition and the voluntary sector, though their shared hostility did not prevent them from appearing to be divided: associations combating AIDS and groups of "sex workers" gathered before the Senate on 5 November, while abolitionists and feminists demonstrated on 10 December behind a banner proclaiming that "human beings are not a commodity". The latter groups found themselves in the typical situation of moral entrepreneurs who, having managed to alert the authorities to their cause, nevertheless find that it is taken out of their hands and can only watch resentfully as the political responses to the problem they have raised run contrary to their recommendations (Spector and Kitsuse 1977: 143–153).

The parliamentary process resulted in several changes to the LSI's provisions on prostitution. The fact-finding missions led by the women's rights delegations in the Senate and the National Assembly (Rozier 2002; Zimmermann 2002) were critical of the penalization of soliciting, reproaching the bill for ignoring the prevention of prostitution and forcing it further underground, which would increase the vulnerability of its practitioners. However, they both welcomed the ambition of fighting more effectively against international pimping networks. The Senate responded by introducing the criminalization of human trafficking, which had previously been absent from the penal code. This was in fact a consequence of France's ratification, decided under the previous government, of the additional Protocol to the United Nations Convention against Translational Organized Crime aiming to prevent, suppress and punish trafficking in persons, especially women and children. This protocol, one of the so-called "Palermo protocols", was designed to organize cooperation between states to suppress human trafficking and repatriate its victims, whether they had consented to their migration and prostitution or not. Its addition to the LSI gave the final legislative text a more protective tone. Adopted on 18 March 2003, the bill also reduced by two months the prison term for soliciting, whose definition no longer referred to dress, and made prefects responsible for deciding whether to grant a temporary residence permit to a foreigner reporting someone for pimping or human trafficking.

As soon as it was first formulated, the LSI bill was criticized by politicians, journalists and intellectuals[15] for its underlying paradox. It seems contradictory to say the least to claim to be protecting pimps' victims by penalizing their activity, and the opposition parliamentarians did not hold back from attacking the interior minister for forcing prostitutes further underground by penalizing soliciting.[16] The minister nevertheless defended his approach by presenting police action as a salvation: "If the forces of order can take them [i.e. the prostitutes] back home, or hand them over to an NGO platform, we can take them out of the networks".[17] Because though he aimed to respond to local residents' demands – he spoke up for householders "who don't appreciate having to return home between ranks of poor underdressed girls, perverts and pimps" – the minister presented his bill above all as an instrument for combating human trafficking, invoking in turn the "unfortunate [...] prisoners of Bulgarian, Albanian and Ghanian networks. They weren't told they were going to be prostitutes. They were told any old story: that they would be models, without informing them that in reality they would be beaten and forced to walk the streets".[18]

Though the provisions about soliciting caused debate in the parliamentary arena, a clear consensus emerged between left and right with regard to the reality of trafficking and the need to stamp it out. The women's rights delegation in the National Assembly declared that it was "aware of the large-scale arrival in recent years of prostitutes, many from Eastern Europe, brought in by international criminal networks that are increasingly organized and violent" (Zimmerman 2002: 33), while its counterpart in the Senate invoked the "duty to rescue the young women who are victims of prostitution networks" (Rozier 2002: 27). The image that the abolitionists had created in advance, depicting young foreign women forced into prostitution, legitimized a policy focused on returning them to their countries of origin. If, as seemed obvious, the foreign prostitutes thronging the streets were there against their will, it would of course be appropriate "to take girls who do not speak our language and have just arrived in our territory back to their country of origin to free them from the grip of the pimps. It's a humanitarian duty!" [19]

---

15   For a social science viewpoint, see Danet & Guienne (2006) and Vernier (2005).

16   The report on the Senate debates on 14 November 2002 can be found at http://www.senat .fr/cra/s20021114/s20021114H29.html.

17   *Ibid.*

18   *Ibid.*

19   The interior minister during the Senate debate on 14 November 2002.

Though this was largely ignored by its critics in politics and the voluntary sector, the LSI was an integral part of the policy to combat illegal immigration developed in parallel by the same interior minister. Reviews of the law would later reveal that the criminalization of soliciting, as well as harming the economic and health situation of prostitutes, caused foreigners to be the primary targets,[20] and above all that the status of trafficking victim was usually trumped by a conviction for soliciting or crossing borders illegally (Jakšić 2016). Perceived primarily as undocumented migrants causing public disorder, foreign prostitutes were deported before they could call on the protections they should have been eligible for due to their status as trafficking victims. While court cases for trafficking were rare following the introduction of the LSI (partly because judges preferred the existing charge of pimping, which was better signposted by case law), deportations multiplied and the criminalization of soliciting emptied cities of their prostitutes.

This reveals a further key to the success of the definition of prostitution as an attack on dignity that is inseparable from trafficking. Depicting foreign prostitutes as victims of organized gangs of pimps authorized an approach to the question that was primarily repressive: as these prostitutes are the visible element of a hidden, threatening criminal world, the police appear best placed to respond to the disparate expectations of exasperated neighbors, voters hostile to immigration and advocates of the abolition of prostitution. Associating the themes of trafficking and criminality thus authorized a policy that combined strengthened border control,[21] the criminalization of deviant uses of public space and the regulation of sexual conduct. However, the paradox underlying a law designed to suppress the very same people it aimed to save from the grip of organized crime was too obvious and too sensitive to be sustainable in the long term, and the political field then devoted itself to seeking new solutions, lending a more attentive ear to abolitionist proposals.

---

20   National Citizens–justice–police Commission, *De nouvelles zones de non-droit. Des prostituées face à l'arbitraire policier* ("New zones of lawlessness: prostitutes faced with police arbitrariness"), 2005; National AIDS council, *VIH et commerce du sexe. Garantir l'accès universel à la prévention aux soins* ("HIV and the sex trade: guaranteeing universal access to preventive care"), opinion followed by recommendations, 2010; National Consultative Commission on Human Rights, *Avis sur la traite et l'exploitation des êtres humains en France* ("Opinion on people trafficking and exploitation in France"), 2010.

21   Among the abundant literature about how combating trafficking is allied with controlling migration, in France and elsewhere, see: Aradau (2004); Berman (2010); Chapkis (2003); Darley (2006); Ragaru (2007); Ticktin (2008), Jakšić (2011).

5   The Invention of a Panacea

The debate on prostitution leapt back into the public eye in spring 2011 with
the publication of the report by the prostitution fact-finding mission led by the
deputies (members of the National Assembly) Danielle Bousquet (from the left
wing Socialist Party or PS) and Guy Geoffroy (from the right-wing Union for a
Popular Movement or UMP). Four hundred pages long, it was a nuanced review
of French policy that emphasized its lack of coherence. While the repression
of pimping appeared effective, the social aspect was judged to be disastrous
due to lack of funding. The repression of soliciting had fulfilled its objective
in restoring public order, but had scarcely done anything to help save prostitutes from pimps; on the contrary, it had driven them further underground and
worsened their insecurity and vulnerability.

    Above all, the report stood out for its most innovative recommendation –
adding to the penal code an offence of buying sexual services. The initiative
took inspiration from the experience of Sweden, where soliciting the services
of a prostitute has been an offence since 1999. Prepared by a social democratic
government and introduced as an integral part of a law criminalizing violence
against women, the penalization of clients was said to have reduced the numbers of both prostitutes and their clients by half since its adoption, and dis-
suaded criminal networks from establishing people trafficking in the country
(Gould 2001; Kulick 2003; Florin 2012; Östergreen 2017). In the rapporteurs'
view, the measure would have several benefits if applied in France: pushing
back the traffickers, making clients understand their role in exploiting the vulnerability of others, consolidating the principle that the human body must not
be exploited and reducing the number of prostitutes. The recommendation
was followed several months later by a vote in the National Assembly in favor
of a resolution (presented by deputies from the PS, the UMP, the Greens, the
New Centre, the Communists and the Party of the Left) restating France's abolitionist position, and by the submission of a bill (that did not make it on to the
agenda) to criminalize the clients of prostitutes, with the same penalties as for
soliciting. What was universally hailed in political circles as an innovation was
in fact the culmination of a long effort to promote the Swedish policy, established as a "model", by the abolitionists and their feminist allies. The success
of their campaign was not a foregone conclusion, and was due both to shifts
within the cause of abolishing prostitution and to the state of political competition on security issues.

    We will see in the next chapter how the *Mouvement du Nid* decided only
gradually and after some delay to support an option to which it had initially
been hostile, while the *Fondation Scelles* pronounced itself in favor of the

Swedish experience from the start, presenting a favorable picture in its *Livre noir de la prostitution* ("Black Book of Prostitution") (Coquart and Huet 2000). But it was above all the influence of the feminists that gave the figure of the client a central role in the abolitionist position and caused the Swedish experience to be held up as a model. A definition of prostitution as sexist violence logically implies punishment for the guilty parties, and it was within feminist circles that the client was transfigured into a veritable folk devil (Cohen 1973). Not only did clients' behavior represent a relationship of dominance reducing prostitutes to the status of objects; they were also "objectively complicit with pimps and traffickers" (Attac 2008: 102).

The proposal to criminalize clients would have fallen on deaf ears if it had not aroused the interest of a political party – the PS – able to translate it into the political realm. Though the links between the abolitionists and the main parties grew closer from the late 1990s, when the political field began to take an interest in prostitution both locally and nationally, those with Socialist politicians emerged as the strongest. We have already pointed out that Malka Marcovich's report had been commissioned by the MEP Adeline Hazan. The report for the Senate women's rights delegation produced in 2000 by the Socialist senator Dinah Dericke included the main abolitionist positions, considering that "it is vital to attack prostitution itself, because failure to do so sufficiently has fed the phenomenon of trafficking" (Dericke 2001: 93). Soon afterwards, a report on modern slavery conducted by PS deputies, with the *Mouvement du Nid* and MAPP both giving evidence, also assimilated migrant prostitution with people trafficking, while associating both with child pornography and domestic slavery (Lazerges and Vidalies 2001).

This receptiveness among the Socialists to abolitionist arguments first took concrete form with the adoption by the Jospin government of the 4 March 2002 law providing for three years in prison and a fine of € 45,000 for clients of under-age prostitutes aged 15 to 18. During the parliamentary debates, the measure was presented as a way of saving these minors from the "networks that brought them to France, holding out the mirage of an Eldorado to trap them into a life of domestic or sexual slavery once they arrived".[22] A few months later, when the PS were once more in opposition, they submitted a bill to criminalize the clients of all prostitutes, minor or not, marking themselves out from the repressive option recommended by the UMP while still maintaining the management of prostitution within the framework of the criminal law.

---

22 National Assembly, 11 December 2001 session; http://www.assemblee-nationale.fr/11/cra /2001-2002/2001121115.asp#P229_60404.

The fact that the bill was promoted by Christophe Caresche, a MP specializing in security issues, indicated that the aim was not to advocate a social view of prostitution in opposition to its definition in terms of security, but to draw a distinction within this definition, on which a consensus had already been reached between left and right. At the same time, Caresche was also deputy mayor in charge of security and safety at Paris city hall, which was dealing, like other cities, with the disruption caused by the presence of prostitutes in residential areas, suggesting that the intention of saving them from sexist violence could be combined with the goal of making their activity more discreet.[23]

When it was introduced by the LSI, the penalization of prostitutes doubtless had the advantage of responding more directly to the demands of local residents for an end to the disturbances inherent in their trade than the penalization of clients would have done. Around a decade later, after the suppression of soliciting had mostly removed prostitution from urban landscapes and abolitionists and feminists had actively pursued their promotion of the Swedish model, this second option became easier to envisage. The almost unanimously favorable political reception for the main recommendation in the Bousquet-Geoffroy report can be explained by the humanist gloss it gave to prostitution policy while at the same time preserving the priorities of suppressing illegal immigration and cleaning up the morality of urban spaces that had already been central to the LSI. Treating foreign prostitutes as trafficking victims, a position consolidated in the report, reinforced the legitimacy of returning people who were still seen as illegal migrants to their countries of origin. Whether this return took the form of deportation appeared secondary to the consideration that, as they were assumed to have migrated due to coercion or to deception, any desire they might express to remain in France as a prostitute could only be seen as skewed and thus not to be taken into account. As the new offence, like soliciting, consisted of a publicly observable interaction between an offer and a request for sexual services, its use as a means of transferring prostitutes' activities to more discreet areas remained guaranteed.

The next chapter will look in more detail at the process behind the development of the law, finally adopted on 13 April 2016, which made the purchase of sexual services an offence punishable with a € 1,500 fine. In conclusion to this chapter, we want to emphasize the extent to which the transition of criminalizing the client rather than the prostitute appeared to be a panacea due to

---

23   Invited to Paris city hall by a colleague of Christophe Caresche shortly before he submitted his bill, the author of this book was consulted above all on ways of resolving the problems inherent in the presence of prostitutes on the boulevards of Paris. A further bill to criminalize clients was submitted by Caresche and Danielle Bousquet in July 2006.

its capacity to respond to multiple social and political expectations. It maintained the public management of prostitution within the framework of the criminal law while bringing it more into line than the LSI did with the image of the prostitute as victim, which the abolitionists and feminists had managed to make dominant. It also testified to strong political concern about the presence of undesirable individuals in both local public spaces and the national territory, with the figure of the migrant prostitute becoming a paradigmatic figure. This is not at all specific to France, and international comparisons indicate that despite often significant divergences, the policies conducted in different European countries often come together in terms of their priorities and their effects. Following on from Jane Scoular's work (2010)[24], we can see that policies as opposed to each other as those of Sweden and the Netherlands are legitimized by similar goals – countering people trafficking, of which foreign prostitutes are necessarily assumed to be victims – and have both contributed to emptying the streets of the most visible prostitutes to the benefit of more discreet forms of the sex trade.[25]

In reality, the definition of prostitution as sexist violence inseparable from trafficking, which abolitionists and feminists have managed to impose in France, does not owe its success to any superior capacity to improve the situations of people living (or surviving) from the sale of "sexual services". Neither is it due to its relevance to the sociological reality of the world of prostitution, which empirical studies have shown is far removed from the image of trafficking (Lazaridis 2001; Oso Casas 2006; Andrijasevic 2005; Jakšić 2016; Levy and Lieber 2009; Simoni 2010; de Montvalon 2018). It has more to do with the influence of an individualist interpretation, relating prostitution to the behavior of individual people (pimps, clients) responsible for their actions, which the state has a duty to punish, rather than the interplay of structural factors such as the feminization of poverty and migration. This definition thus becomes easier to appropriate and instrumentalize for a political world now converted to a security-based approach to economic and security issues.

---

24   See also Hubbard, Matthews, Scoular (2008) and Okland Jahnsen, Wagenaar (2018).
25   Consequently, the conventional distinction between the three legislative approaches to dealing with prostitution – regulationism, abolitionism and prohibitionism – has lost all relevance with the widespread adoption of policies aiming to use coercive instruments to guard against the threat of illegal immigration causing urban immorality and disturbances, despite the differences between these policies in terms of ideological justification and legal underpinning.

CHAPTER 5

Ordinary Devils

Constructing the Public Problem of Prostitutes' Clients

> Just as *'road accidents'*, formerly seen as an inevitability, have now become *'road violence'*, prostitution is being transformed into 'prostitution violence.' Just as bad drivers now have to answer for their behavior, the prostitutor client, who feeds an immense market of women, is now being confronted with his responsibilities.
>
> LEGARDINIER (2011)

∴

Coming from an activist for the abolition of prostitution, the naive quotation used as the epigraph for this chapter inevitably raises a smile from analysts of prostitution policy: the comparison between road violence and use of prostitutes cannot fail to recall the work of Joseph Gusfield on the construction of the problem of drink driving.[1] In a work that has become a classic, the American sociologist showed how blaming drunk drivers for road accidents proceeded by excluding alternative ways of formulating the problem, such as questioning vehicle quality, road maintenance or the lack of public transport (Gusfield 1981: 187). More specifically, he studied the forms of rhetoric which are calculated to induce belief (*ibid.*: 28) that the priority in reducing the number of road accidents should be to punish "bad drivers".

Taking its inspiration from Gusfield's approach, this chapter aims to study the way in which the client came to be "singled out as *the* cause" (*ibid.*: 187) of the prostitution "problem" and how the "belief was induced" that the roots of prostitution could be eradicated by attacking him. More specifically, it intends to reconstitute the process that changed perceptions of the use of prostitutes' services from something trivial and private to something both *problematic*

---

1 An initial version of this text was published under the title "Des monstres ordinaires: La construction du problème public des clients de la prostitution" ("Ordinary devils: constructing the public problem of prostitutes' clients"), *Champ pénal/Penal field*, vol. XII, 2015; https://journals.openedition.org/champpenal/9093.

and *public*. Again building on Gusfield's work, we will focus on the expression of the public problem rather than the social problem in order to underline several characteristics of the process.[2] This process begins by developing an argument and communicating it to the audience that needs to be alerted to its importance and converted to support a given interpretation. It also involves lobbying the public authorities, which in this case was effective enough that the authorities in question appropriated the problem and undertook to provide a political response. In April 2016, the problem of prostitutes' clients received a form of consecration in the adoption of the law penalizing the purchase of sexual services.

1   A Delayed Problematization

We have known since *Outsiders* that a specific feature of moral entrepreneurs is that they highlight public problems and demand an end to a situation that shocks them profoundly (Becker 1963). The crusaders for the abolition of prostitution have been no exception, and they are now among the most fervent advocates of criminalization for men who frequent prostitutes. In fact, the project to eliminate the supply of prostitutes by suppressing demand has been the core of abolitionist campaigns in recent years. But this was not always the case, and reconstituting the process by which French abolitionism came to focus on the question of prostitutes' clients is interesting for several reasons. First, in order to historicize the problematization: far from being self-evident or the result of any logical mechanism, the figure of the client eventually came to be placed at the center of the "prostitution drama" through a complex, evolving effort of diagnosis, interpretation and indignation. Secondly, in order to account for the complexity of a process that was anything but linear or peaceful, resulting from the struggle for a definition that saw different groups or fractions confronting each other with diverging views of what clients are and how they should be treated. This is a significant issue because, as Claude Gilbert and Emmanuel Henry emphasize, "defining a problem (or, more accurately, choosing a definition) means appropriating it" (Gilbert and Henry 2012: 43) – i.e., specifically, imposing oneself as the foremost specialist and the partner of choice for the public authorities. The story of how the problem of prostitutes'

---

2   The two concepts involve similar approaches, paying attention to the processes of social construction that give them access to a form of existence; Gusfield distinguishes between them by pointing out that not all social problems *become subjects of conflict or controversy in the arenas of public action*, a property that is specific to public problems (Gusfield 1981: 9).

clients emerged is thus the story of the reorganizations of the space in which the combat to eliminate prostitution has taken place.

1.1   *The Client, a Puppet*

Historical abolitionism – by which we mean the movement that emerged within English Protestant circles in the second half of the nineteenth century and campaigned for the abolition of all regulation of prostitution – paid little attention to clients. Admittedly, as soon as the movement began, the denunciation of prostitution involved stigmatizing male sexual privileges and demanding a single morality for both sexes. The charismatic leader of the nascent abolitionist movement, Josephine Butler, refuted the idea of prostitution as a necessary outlet, for example, identifying within it a "doctrine" that "women are merely pieces of flesh destined to satisfy the vilest masculine desires and (...) men are slaves of their basest appetites to the furthest degree" (reproduced in Regard 2013: 248). But above all, the movement targeted the arbitrary powers granted to the police and the medical profession: as Alain Corbin points out, "the fundamental aim [of the abolitionist project] was not the abolition of prostitution but the freeing of the prostitutes from registration, the destruction of the whole system that tended to create a marginal milieu outside common law" (Corbin 1996: 225).

Entirely devoted to fighting the key institutions of regulationism represented by brothels, French abolitionism in the first half of the twentieth century also paid only secondary attention to clients. This appeared to be inspired by the economic reasoning that supply creates demand, and the movement's writings continually denounced the ease of access to prostitution guaranteed by its regulation. For example, in the 1930s, the *Union française pour le relèvement de la moralité publique* (French Union for Improving Public Morality) declared that "the licensed brothel is a public school of depravity. Through the opportunities it offers, it provokes the need it claims only to satisfy" (Union française pour le relèvement de la moralité publique 1936a: 3). This perspective reflects a distorted conception of male sexuality, in which, instead of following instinctive urges, it is shaped and directed by specific commercial availability. The pernicious effects of these "laboratories of vice" were thought to be particularly powerful on young men, encouraged and habituated at an early age into a depravity they would have difficulty shaking off in later life, which would represent a "counter-education that tramples on all the efforts made by the family" (Gemähling 1933: 54). The priority was thus to attack the structures that created demand for prostitution, but not directly those who incarnated

it. This avoidance was also due to careful respect for individual liberty, which
had been one of the founding principles of abolitionism since its earliest origins. The Union temporaire contre la prostitution réglementée et la traite des
êtres humains (Temporary Union Against Regulated Prostitution and Human
Trafficking), for example, refused to attack prostitution per se, because that
would have been impossible "without interfering in people's private lives;
without falling into arbitrariness" (Union française pour le relèvement de la
moralité publique 1936b: 20).

Emerging from social Catholicism and destined to become France's main
abolitionist association, the *Mouvement du Nid* was no exception to this view
once the prohibition of brothels was achieved with the 13 April 1946 law: "They
want to convince parents that reopening will protect their sons against solic-
itation in the street. A thin argument, and easy to overturn. How many young
men, who would never have dared to go with a girl from the street from fear
(of diseases, chiefly), will allow themselves to be tempted by a 'house' offering
'guarantees' (...). In addition, as men who were in barracks before 46 know
(...), the simple presence of a licensed brothel is a provocation to debauchery. Far from relieving the obsession, it can sustain and develop it" (*Moissons
nouvelles*, 1955, no. 14–15: 34–35). This theory of the plasticity of male desires,
seeing them as partly determined by the state of sexual supply, was accompanied during the same period by the adoption of a predominantly psychopatho-
logical framework for interpreting prostitution. While female prostitutes were
depicted as "mentally defective", marked by a series of emotional and moral
deficiencies, as has been demonstrated elsewhere (Mathieu 2016), clients
were also viewed as easily psychologically influenced or even defective themselves.[3] The *Mouvement du Nid*'s quarterly magazine *Moissons nouvelles* ("New
Harvests") highlighted their immaturity: "A man of 40 who uses prostitutes
demonstrates a state of sexual evolution corresponding to the age of about
17 or 18" (1954, no. 27: 56). Clients were thus seen as "sexually and emotionally
underdeveloped, and, furthermore, often neurotic or unbalanced", requiring
"appropriate psychiatric and psychoanalytical treatment" (1964, no. 51: 116).

---

3 In the view of the other major player in French abolitionism in the immediate post-war
period, the *Cartel d'action morale et sociale* (Cartel for Moral and Social Action), the general
cultural context was more to blame for shaping demand for prostitution. The *Cartel* continually denounced the climate of eroticism and violence complacently sustained by literature
and cinema. It called for the public authorities and prosecutors to "combat corrupting cinema, pornographic literature and posters, the exaggerated proliferation of dance halls and
disreputable bars, nightclubs and beauty contests. (...) Finally we ask everyone, students and
young workers, soldiers and heads of families, to stop considering women as beasts of burden or instruments of pleasure" (*Rénovation* 1950, no. 11: no page numbers).

This simultaneously psychologically-oriented and pessimistic tone left a lasting mark on the abolitionist view of clients. In 1973, a *Mouvement du Nid* psychiatrist, Dr Safar, described the client as "emotionally disengaged" (Safar 1973: 25), fand even in 1996 a journalist in the movement, Claudine Legardinier, was still able to depict him as "driven by discomfort and difficulty in communicating, but wrong in seeking a response to his problems in sexual consumption, which is just a con in which the client and the prostitute are swindled while the pimp collects the winnings" (Legardinier 1996: 11). While the same author discusses the opposition between the options of suppressing clients and empowering them through education, she refrains from choosing a side.

1.2   *A Feminist Problematization*

As we have seen, abolitionism paid only secondary attention to the client for years, seeing him as a sort of puppet whose desires are manipulated by pimps, bound to the prostitute by a shared existential malaise.[4] So it was not from this movement that the initial problematization of the client's role in perpetuating the phenomenon of prostitution emerged, starting in the 1990s, but from the space of the women's movement (Bereni 2012), which at the time was in a phase of remobilization and organizational rearrangement: the main body coordinating French feminist groups and organizations, the *Collectif national pour le droit des femmes* (CNDF, the National Collective for Women's Rights), was founded in January 1996, following the November 1995 demonstration defending the right to abortion and contraception.

The French women's movement had not so far shown much interest in prostitution, apart from short-term support for prostitutes fighting police repression in 1975 (Mathieu 2001; 2014b). While the principal French feminist intellectuals – including Simone de Beauvoir and Colette Guillaumin – had devoted a few pages to the subject, they referred above all to the prostitute's situation as an extreme example of the condition facing all women, rather than an analysis of the specific issue of prostitution. Sexual themes were long monopolized by predominantly psychoanalytical analyses inspired by "differentialism", and the main struggles in feminism – particularly for fertility control and against rape – led sexuality to be considered through the lens of the risks to which it

---

4   Note however the brochure "Au marché du sexe, client qui est-tu?" ("In the sex market, who is the client?"), which compiled the proceedings of the third autumn university organized by the movement *Le Cri* in 1993. But this contribution, emerging from a dominated association in the abolitionist space, remained isolated.

exposes women. The French women's movement also stayed away for years from the "sex wars" in the United States in the 1980s, which pitted resolute opponents of pornography and prostitution, defined as sexist violence, against promoters of an emancipation of women through the diversification of their sexual repertoire (Vance 1984; *Signs* 1984; Berger and Searles and Cottle 1990).

Two moral entrepreneurs would play a decisive role in French feminism's appropriation of prostitution as a theme. The first was the journalist Florence Montreynaud, who published an illustrated book on prostitution in 1993, in which she questioned the client's view of the activity (Montreynaud 1993). The book, welcomed by the *Mouvement du Nid*, led to its author not only examining clients more closely, but also moving closer to an abolitionist position. Starting in the late 1990s, Montreynaud wrote a regular column in the *Mouvement du Nid*'s quarterly magazine *Prostitution et société* (now *P&S*) entitled "Payer pour ça" ("Paying for it"), in which she engaged in a sarcastic denunciation of the specifically masculine practice of buying sexual services. Her access to the media and the humorous tone of her columns enabled her to express broad criticism of any monetary trade in the intimacy of the human body (Montreynaud 1999).

We have already met the second moral entrepreneur: the sociologist Marie-Victoire Louis. Formerly specializing in the sociology of work, she began to take an interest in prostitution at the beginning of the 1990s, initially as an observer of the internal debates within the arenas of European institutions. These institutions were shaken by the opposition between the two approaches to prostitution respectively considered and then adopted by Sweden and the Netherlands. The former considers prostitution as sexual violence whose perpetrators – clients – must be punished, while the second undertakes to normalize the "sex trade" by recognizing it as a trade in its own right. Louis was not content with denouncing the Dutch approach as a threat to the "principle, nevertheless universal, that the human body is inalienable" (Louis 1999: 14). Within feminism and beyond, she took up a position as a whistleblower, warning of what she saw as the Dutch initiative to convert other countries to the recognition of "sex work". This was the motivation, for example, for her attacks on the community health associations, which called for the recognition of this "work" from the starting point of preventing HIV among prostitutes.

The stances of Montreynaud and Louis were broadcast widely within the space of the women's movement, and particularly within the CNDF, which adopted the expression "prostitution system" (*système prostitutionnel*) coined by Louis (2004).[5] Montreynaud was invited to the 2002 CNDF Forum, where

---

5   According to the sociologist, this concept refers to "a system of commercial domination of
    genitalia, bodies and thus human beings which, through the force, coercion and violence

she defended the idea that "if there were no clients, there would be no prostitution" (Montreynaud 2002: 195). The same workshop also involved two other moral entrepreneurs, who were both very involved in the increasingly close relationship between abolitionism and feminism. The first was Malka Marcovich, representing the *Mouvement pour l'abolition de la prostitution et de la pornographie* (MAPP, Movement for the Abolition of Prostitution and Pornography), the French wing of the *Coalition Against Trafficking in Women* (CATW), founded by the American academic Kathleen Barry. Marcovich's report for the National Committee on Violence Against Women entitled *Le système de la prostitution : une violence à l'encontre des femmes* ("The prostitution system: violence against women"), which we have already mentioned, was also circulated widely within feminist groups. It describes the "commercial sexual act" as the "keystone of the persistence of inequalities between men and women" (Marcovich 2002: no page numbers). The second entrepreneur at the CNDF Forum was the *Mouvement du Nid* journalist Claudine Legardinier, whose positions – like those of her association – were evolving significantly at the time. The article on prostitution that she wrote for the *Dictionnaire critique du féminisme* (Critical Dictionary of Feminism) ended with a now-favorable presentation of the Swedish policy of criminalizing clients, to which we must now turn (Legardinier 2000).

1.3   The Swedish Model

The problematization of the contribution made by clients to the phenomenon of prostitution would not have taken the direction it did if the policy adopted in Sweden in 1999 had not been widely promoted at the same time. Sweden was the first country to make the purchase of sexual services an offence, punishable with a fifty-day fine (with the amount calculated based on income) and six months in prison. This penal policy was part of a set of provisions aiming to combat sexist violence adopted by the social democratic government of the time, and feminist parliamentarians were its primary driving force. It is based on the idea that "Gender equality will remain unattainable so long as men buy, sell and exploit women and children by prostituting them".[6] More globally, it

---

legitimised by the law, creates the conditions for contact between 'clients' to whom pimps – natural and legal persons – guarantee in exchange for remuneration the possibility of commercial access to the genitalia of other people, female in the vast majority of cases, adult women, teenagers and young girls" (Louis 2004).

6   Report by the Swedish Ministry of Industry, Employment and Communication from 2003, cited in Hubbard, Matthews, Scoular (2008: 143).

considers prostitution as sexist violence whose primary perpetrators, clients, must thus be punished (Florin 2012; Östergreen 2017).

French feminists were the first to take an interest in the Swedish policy. The new definition of prostitution as sexist violence immediately resonated within a movement which, as we have seen, was historically constituted within the struggle against violence against women. But the "Swedish model" was legitimized above all by active promotional work carried out from the early 2000s by the Swedish government itself, whose feminist representatives – or femocrats, to use the expression popularized by Banaszak (2010) – joined a variety of forums for discussion and debate and presented the benefits of criminalizing clients. In France, they could be found at the 2002 CNDF forum and, the following year, at the European Women's Assembly, organized in parallel with the European Social Forum, and the "*Politiques urbaines face à la prostitution*" conference ("Urban policies faced with prostitution"), chaired by Legardinier and Marcovich, and they also organized a seminar on the issue at the Swedish embassy. The systematic nature of this promotion, which was also supported and amplified by the *European Women's Lobby*, is clear from the repetition of the same "elements of language" in all presentations of the Swedish innovation: a halving of the number of street prostitutes, increased popular support for a measure initially treated with suspicion, phone taps of gang members revealing their lack of interest in a country where prostitution would no longer be profitable, and even the name of the legislative package in which the criminalization of clients was included – "peace for women" – comparing prostitution with a practice of warfare.

Montreynaud, Marcovich, Louis and Legardinier all became ardent promoters of the Swedish model within the space of the women's movement in France and even beyond. The connections between certain fractions of the women's movement and the far left encouraged its promotion within the alter-globalization movement, and particularly *Attac*. In 2008, this association's "Gender" committee published a short book on the links between globalization and prostitution, which ended with the claim that "criminalizing clients/prostitutors is a key element of the policy that needs to be implemented urgently (…) to end the oldest system of exploitation in the world" (Attac 2008: 103–104).

While feminists quickly rallied to support the criminalization of clients, the proposal met most resistance within abolitionism. Hostility to any coercive measures had long been assumed within the *Mouvement du Nid*, which had always made education and empowerment the key concepts in an approach emphasizing awareness-raising above all. "The disappearance of the client does not raise the stakes of repression," said no. 91 of *P&S* in 1990, and the same position held sway in 2002: "Criminalizing clients is wrongly seen as the panacea that will avoid the need to address the question in all its complexity. Moreover, criminalizing clients means opting for a prohibitionist measure. The *Mouvement du Nid* has always been opposed to measures targeting soliciting that worsen prostitutes' exclusion and condemn them to greater exploitation, including by the state. Logically, it rejects them equally for clients" (*P&S* 2002, no. 139: 27). But in 2007, the *Mouvement du Nid*'s national committee came out in favor of "the establishment of a legal norm prohibiting the purchase of a sexual act". The split between the competing goals of education and repression within the association is clear from this justification, paradoxical to say the least, of a "sanction that should (...) not be used as a punitive measure but, on the contrary, as a lever for prevention and empowerment" (*P&S* 2007, no. 156: 28–29). Two years later, the educational dimension had faded, and the *Mouvement du Nid* firmly called for a prohibition on the purchase of any sexual service by clients, who were characterized chiefly as aggressors (*P&S* 2009, no. 166: 25).

The main French abolitionist group thus changed its course completely within the space of a few years. There are several possible explanations. The first is an influx of younger members in an association whose founders' generation, socialized within social Catholicism, was fading and being replaced by new activists with different political reference points and a greater receptiveness to feminist positions. A second is the restructuring of the abolitionist space at the time, following the creation in 1993 of a new organization, the *Fondation Scelles,* whose audience and influence expanded from 2000 onwards. The direct heir to the *Équipes d'action contre le proxénétisme* (Teams for Action against Procuring), the *Fondation Scelles* was more conservative in its sensibilities than the *Mouvement du Nid* and, more importantly, more enthusiastic about penal options.[7] It was logical that it would support the criminalization of clients from the start, making the *Mouvement du Nid* look more timid. We thus cannot exclude the possibility that the *Mouvement du Nid* rallied to an option it had rejected only a short time before due, at least partly, to a "radical flank effect" – the risk for proponents of moderate positions that they will be marginalized by others who spearhead the struggle with their more radical positions (Haines 2013).

As we can see, not only is the problematization of prostitutes' clients a recent phenomenon within French abolitionism; it was also mostly achieved against the movement's will, under the effect of a mobilization, unprecedented at least

---

7   The *Équipes d'action* were authorized to act as the plaintiff in trials of pimps, and developed expertise in the legal aspects of prostitution. The *Fondation Scelles* is chaired by a magistrate, Yves Charpenel.

in scale, of French feminism on the issue. The U-turn by the *Mouvement du Nid* in favor of an option it had long rejected shows that this problematization is the result of a struggle for a definition, in which the position defended by feminism won out over the position traditionally held by abolitionism. Furthermore, a Catholic association such as the *Mouvement du Nid* was only able to overcome the women's movement's natural distrust and make itself an acceptable partner by incorporating many of the schemas and much of the vocabulary of feminism.

2   The Construction of Devilishness

An intellectualist bias that is widespread within the sociology of social movements, and particularly within the framing theory inherited from Erving Goffman, assigns decisive importance to the "robustness" and "resonance" of militant narratives in the success of activist movements. From this viewpoint, the most coherent and refined activist arguments are the most "effective". However, criticism of this confidence in an "omnipotence of ideas" (Mathieu, 2002) should not lead us to disregard an analysis of the arguments put forward by social movement organizations. Firstly because developing them is an activist technique in its own right, and secondly because they express – though usually implicitly or unconsciously – some of the social ideas behind the engagement of those producing them. Preparing arguments, choosing vocabulary, arranging examples – these are all processes that do not happen by chance; they draw on a stock of cultural references whose content is socially determined. It would thus be useful, following Gusfield's example once again, to look at the rhetorical forms that have shaped the problematization of the client issue.

2.1   *A Devil ...*

The rhetorical processes of problematization include two dimensions (Gusfield 2009: 9 *et seq.*). One is cognitive, and involves establishing irrefutable facts to be brought to the attention of an audience. The other is moral, and makes a normative judgement about these facts by presenting them as shameful, repulsive and reprehensible. Abolitionists and feminists, now working together, engaged in discourse production which, though it was relatively abundant, was nonetheless homogeneous: the same overall portrait of clients – describing them as ordinary devils – emerged from the many fractions and currents within the campaign for their criminalization.

Before analyzing these messages, we should pay attention to the media by which they are conveyed. First of all, we can see that abolitionists' lack of interest in clients was succeeded from the early 2000s by an intense focus on their contribution to the phenomenon of prostitution. *Prostitution et société* repeatedly devoted features to them: "Clients de la prostitution : le grand secret" ("Prostitution clients: the big secret") (2001, no. 134); "Faut-il pénaliser les clients de la prostitution ?" ("Should prostitution clients be penalized?") (2002, no. 139); "On ne naît pas client, on le devient" ("One is not born, but rather becomes, a client") (2004, no. 146); "L'image du client en France" ("The image of the client in France") (2004, no. 147); "Clients de la prostitution : nouveaux regards, nouvelles politiques" ("Prostitution clients: new perspectives, new policies") (2006, no. 152); "Prostitueurs : état des lieux" ("Prostitutors: the state of play") (2008, no. 163). The *Mouvement du Nid* launched a survey of clients at the same time, conducted by Legardinier in collaboration with the sociologist Saïd Bouamama, which was promoted and commented on in its quarterly magazine (Bouamama and Legardinier, 2006). We can then observe that this discourse production emerges from a stable, restricted group of recurring names. Though claiming to provide new knowledge on the subject and to represent scientific work, it also remains limited to activist publications. Books, journals and websites produced by social movement organizations or with a clear activist dimension constitute the main channels for transmitting this knowledge, whose sources and conditions of production are rarely made clear and which usually ignores the scientific knowledge available.[8]

The dual cognitive and moral dimensions are expressed first of all in the recurring observation that clients are little known: publicizing new knowledge is equivalent to unmasking those who are protected by anonymity and silence. For example, the back cover of Bouamama and Legardinier's book announces that the authors are "breaking the silence that has always reigned over the practices of clients to question their responsibility for the rise in human trafficking, sex tourism and violence against women, but also for the maintenance of inequality between the sexes". Similarly, Christine's article in the *Alternative libertaire* magazine feature on the subject opens with the

---

8   For example, we found no citations of the benchmark scientific paper on the subject by Bajos et al. (1997), produced on the basis of a secondary analysis of responses from 20,000 French people to a detailed questionnaire about their sexuality. Neither were there any citations of data about payment for sex acts taken from later surveys of the same kind (Bajos and Bozon 2008; 2012). On the other hand, there were many mentions (though few explicit citations, no doubt for lack of translations) of the work conducted in Sweden during the 1980s by Sven-Axel Mansson, the inspiration for the promoters of Sweden's law.

observation that clients have long been "'the great unknown' in the prostitution system" (Christine 2010: 11), while *P&S* announces in its no. 163 (2008: 20) that the client has remained "faceless and nameless for centuries".

The point is not only to provide new knowledge, but to cause people to see reality in a new way, having been unable to grasp its full "truth" with their previous level of knowledge. This implies the adoption of a new vocabulary. Bouamama and Legardinier state in the preface to their book that they will only use "the word 'client' in these pages for lack of a better alternative, without burdening ourselves with the inverted commas it requires. This inappropriate term constitutes a euphemism and an insidious normalization of pimping and the trade in bodies. It is no coincidence that the French language has nothing else to offer us" (Bouamama and Legardinier 2006: 7). Montreynaud makes the same observation, challenging the word "client" as insufficiently stigmatizing in her eyes, unlike the symmetrical *"pute"* (whore). Noting that, in French, *"prostituée* [prostitute] is a past participle that supposes an action", she proposes the term "prostituant" "to refer to the person who prostitutes, by whom the act of prostitution is committed". The same author also suggests the term *putanier*, which "comes from the same root [as *"pute"*], from a Latin word that means 'to stink', because the whole thing is disgusting" (Montreynaud 2002: 196). But it is the term *prostitutor* that has gradually taken hold within the movement's rhetoric to simultaneously refer to and stigmatize those who pay prostitutes and thus sustain their activity.

The normative aspect of how clients are viewed is expressed above all by their reduction to a sub-humanity or animality. Clients seem to be guided by an instinctive, compulsive sexuality and thus need to be "civilized". In no. 166 of *P&S*, for example, from 2009, we read that "the violent nature of the prostitution relationship ruins any attempts to 'civilize' the prostitutors". The same magazine does not hesitate to use the headline "Football, beer and whores … The barbarians are back" in no. 153 (2006: 2) or to use the term "predators" in 2011 (no. 172: 19), while Legardinier resorts to the word "bestiality" (Legardinier 2012: 51). Marcovich, meanwhile, chooses the evocative word "horde" – "every weekend, hordes of Finnish men come to Tallin (…) to buy alcohol and women" (Marcovich 2006: 481) – while the World March of Women uses the verb *"s'abattre"* (descend on) to stigmatize "those who, like carrion [sic – *charognes* in the original French], descend on girls or women to turn them into easy, cheap merchandise to satisfy a macho, domineering male sexuality".[9]

9   See http://www.solidaires.org/article31535.html.

This devilishness of clients is thought to be expressed through multiple aspects of their attitudes and behaviors. Racism, for example, is detected in clients' tendency to choose prostitutes based on ethnic criteria: "Racist and colonialist sexual stereotypes play a major role: Asian women are presented as attentive and submissive, Africans as animalistic and sexually powerful, Latin Americans as free and easy" (Bouamama and Legardinier 2006: 71). The same applies to "ignorance, a disregard for others and irresponsibility", considered by the *Mouvement du Nid* as "at the heart of prostitutional clientelism" (*P&S*, 2007 no. 156: 28). This ignorance is explained primarily by shortcomings in a sexual education driven mainly or even solely by pornography: "Solitude in the face of questions about sexuality pushes people towards the only answers available, which are inegalitarian and mechanical, and come from pornography" (Legardinier 2012: 50), and clients' sexuality consequently reveals "a fantasy world shaped by pornography".[10]

Finally, and more fundamentally, the use of prostitution is said to be a form of violence. It is given a kind of dual status, both practical and ontological. It is true that many clients commit violence against prostitutes, and Legardinier points out that "most of the violent acts suffered by prostitutes – verbal, physical, sexual – are committed by clients" (Legardinier 2012: 49). But, at a more basic level, they are also guilty of the violence of prostitution itself.[11] Thus *P&S* claims (2008 no. 163: 13) that "the sex trade is an incomparable violence for everyone subject to it", while the Trotskyist party the *Ligue communiste révolutionnaire* (Revolutionary Communist League) considers it to be "the most extreme form of violence, male domination" (Ligue communiste révolutionnaire 2006: 5) and the feminist organization *Osez le féminisme* ("Dare to be feminist") argues that "prostitution – independently of the conditions under which it is exercised – is a form of violence in itself, because it is first and foremost a sexual encounter that is desired by only one of the protagonists: the prostitutor client".[12]

Within abolitionist/feminist discourse, the client has a favored incarnation in the role of a football supporter. A social life presented as exclusively

---

10   "Les motivations des prostitueurs" ("The motivations of prostitutors"), *Prostitution et société*, 2009; http://www.prostitutionetsociete.fr/eclairage/acteurs/les-motivations-des-prostitueurs.

11   The counterpart to the violence committed by clients is the status of victim given to prostitutes and the emphasis in the image painted of them on post-traumatic stress and other "dissociative" phenomena affecting them.

12   "France: la violence d'un État proxénète" ("France: the violence of a procurer state") at http://www.osezlefeminisme.fr/article/france-la-violence-d-un-etat-proxenete.

ORDINARY DEVILS   99

masculine coupled with a supposedly high consumption of alcohol are seen as
factors predisposing him to the "consumption" of prostitutes. This association
was underlined in 2006 by the petition "Buying sex is not a sport", launched to
coincide with the FIFA World Cup in Germany in protest at the 40,000 foreign
prostitutes "imported" in response to demand from supporters.[13] The success
of the petition, and of the association between popular male sports and the
use of prostitution more generally, is no doubt due to the fact that it incrim-
inated football fans (i.e. the most popular sport among working class men,
whom class condescension willingly presents as more uncouth, particularly in
terms of relations between the sexes, than the better educated social classes).
The conception of the client according to abolitionists and feminists is very
much a socially identifiable – and socially generated – portrait: violent, sexist, racist, ignorant, socializing primarily with men, consuming alcohol[14] and a
football fan, the client has all the characteristics of the cultivated middle class's
representation of the most culturally and economically deprived sections of
the working classes.[15]

2.2   ... Who Is Ordinary

Far from coherent, the abolitionist and feminist discourse contains a number
of contradictions. The fact that the traits that identify clients are socially situated does not prevent them being seen in parallel as ordinary and banal, a
necessary condition for their denunciation to be generalized and legitimized
(Boltanski 2012). The client is thus an "everyman", and there are no variables
that enable him to be described more specifically. According to Christine in
Alternative libertaire, for example, "they are ordinary men of all ages, professions, social classes, nationalities and 'races'" (Christine 2010: 11). Bouamama
and Legardinier make the same assertion, underlining that "the men we have
met are ordinary men. They do not fit into a specific category that could

---

13   The text of the petition, circulated in France by MAPP, can be found at http://sisyphe.org
      /spip.php?article2226.
14   For example, Attac highlights "the influence of the male group, the connections with alco-
      hol and Saturday nights on the town, fear and ignorance of the opposite sex, the image of
      women and their sexuality" in the use of prostitution (Attac 2008: 55).
15   The feminist/abolitionist stigmatization of clients thus has a number of similarities with
      the stigmatization of alleged working-class racism, whose characteristics and logic were
      identified by Claude Grignon: "Hate, rage, aggression, violence: the words that specialists
      in anti-racism use to stigmatize 'working-class racism' (...) are no different from the words
      of ordinary racism. (...) The emotions attributed to the 'lower' classes are automatically
      devalued as 'low' (depraved, ignoble, primitive etc.) and the emotions socially devalued as
      'low' are automatically and exclusively attributed to the 'lower' classes" (Grignon 1991: 8).

be delimited with objective characteristics" (Bouamama and Legardinier 2006: 111). The *Fondation Scelles* agrees, but innovates by including female clients: "married or not, they are men or women from all social classes, all ages and all origins. It is impossible to define a typical profile of a client" (Charpenel 2012: 161). The figure of a man who is not a client, though representing the majority of the population (Bajos et al. 1997), appears to evaporate in the face of this new avatar of the banality of evil.

This insistence on the "ordinary" but also indefinable nature of the male client fulfils several objectives. The first is to raise public awareness and convince them of the importance of the cause of criminalization. The use of prostitutes is no longer a problem restricted to a fraction of the population, and thus easy to curb, but as an evil that is all the more dangerous for being diffuse, widespread and anonymous. For Bouamama and Legardinier, "the idea that there is a minority of perverts (or sick people, damaged by life) is thus incorrect" (Bouamama and Legardinier 2006: 111). A second goal, which follows from the first, is to make clients responsible for their actions by cutting off access to any justification on the basis of a fundamental need – which Montreynaud (2002: 198) sums up with a terse "no one has ever seen a ball explode". Legardinier in turn refutes clients' "self-justifications", based on solitude or "irrepressible sexual needs" for example, countering that a desire for dominance is the sole principle behind the purchase of a prostitute's services (Legardinier 2012: 49). It is thus easy to understand why the abolitionists have so vigorously opposed any form of sexual assistance to people with disabilities: recognizing that some people might not have any alternative to a commercial, professionalized form of sexuality could only compromise this dimension of their argument (Brasseur 2017).

Legardinier emphasizes what she sees as the primary characteristic of these "ordinary men", "their attachment to all the stereotypes about sexual identities, and to a traditional patriarchal order in general" (2012: 49). Clients are depicted as attached to the traditional, unequal order in the relationship between the sexes, which legitimizes and justifies their practice in their eyes. This is the cause of their hostility to feminism and, more globally, any demand for women's emancipation: clients "present themselves as victims: of their 'needs' and of women, who are too demanding, too complicated, too selfish, too provocative, too free, too powerful" (Attac 2008: 55). Although it contradicts the thesis of a "bestial", "barbarous" sexuality, this explanation for the use of prostitutes as the result of patriarchal male socialization roots it in a historically situated context. Consequently, while this conduct is "a profoundly cultural practice" (Bouamama and Legardinier 2006: 67), it is not inevitable – it can be modified by a change in the social conditions that cause it. This is precisely the goal targeted by criminalization. The *Mouvement du Nid* underlines that "it is clearly culture and learned perceptions of male and female roles that create and sustain the prostitution system. Real long-term change can thus only come with the establishment of a true force of political initiative" (*P&S* 2008, no. 163: 31).

What could be called the thesis of the patriarchal shaping of demand for prostitution is not just about rooting calls for its criminalization in the feminist struggle. It also makes it possible to generalize and balance the criticisms it makes by enlarging the scope of prostitution's victims. If the invocation of an "everyman" client enlarges the status of persecutor to potentially include all male individuals, the reference to the patriarchy symmetrically enables the status of victim to be applied to the whole female population. Hence the insistence of feminists and abolitionists on the "collective" and "systemic" nature of prostitution, which affects gender relations as a whole. For Attac, for example, "prostitution helps to keep all women in an inferior status" (2008: 61), while for *Alternative libertaire*, "prostitution is a monetization of the patriarchy. It thus oppresses all women" (Ferrand 2010: 15). In turn, this extension of the problematization to all women has the advantage of refuting the criticism often made by organizations of "sex workers" that the women most concerned, i.e. prostitutes, are not allowed to speak for themselves. If prostitution does not only affect those involved, but all women, any woman has as much legitimacy as a prostitute in speaking out on the subject. If it is not just a case of inter-individual negotiation between prostitute and client, it becomes a specifically political issue.

3   Joint Political Construction

The process by which the problem of prostitutes' clients was constituted has globally followed the stages defined by Malcolm Spector and John Kitsuse (1977) in what they call the "natural history of social problems". The first stage was the public definition of prostitution as an offensive, deplorable reality by abolitionist and feminist moral entrepreneurs. This was followed by its appropriation by the public authorities, in this case the interior minister, who, as we saw in the previous chapter, drew on the arguments developed by the abolitionists and feminists to come up with his own "solution" to the problem – in this case, the domestic security act (LSI), which criminalized not clients, but prostitutes guilty of soliciting. As Spector and Kitsuse emphasize, this second stage often sees the original reporters of the problem dispossessed in favor of authorities who intend to resolve it by methods that are far removed from the initial proposals. This leads to the third stage in the process, which is the remobilization of the moral entrepreneurs, dissatisfied with the political response to their complaints. In this case, the third stage was a renewed combativeness in favor of criminalizing clients, expressed primarily through the "Abolition 2012" campaign led by several dozen feminist and abolitionist associations.

Illuminating though it may be, Spector and Kitsuse's perspective is not completely satisfying. The unfortunate expression "natural history", first of all, suggests that the three stages are successive and necessary, while in fact they are more interwoven and uncertain. But the most debatable aspect in this case is the proposed division between mobilized groups and institutional authorities, because more detailed analysis highlights institutional players active in the activist space together with an institutional co-opting of figures from the movement. More globally, the present problematization does not correspond to the activist challenge/political response model proposed by the two authors, but more to an effort of mutual consolidation and legitimization between partners with shared schemas of perception.

3.1   *Cross-consolidations*

As we have already emphasized, the first mentions of the "Swedish model" within the abolitionist and feminist space were relatively cautious. In her 2002 report, Marcovich suggested that it would be "important to monitor and analyze the effects of the Swedish 'Peace for Women' law, whose results in terms of prevention and rehabilitation currently appear extremely compelling" (2002: no page numbers), but held back from including the criminalization of clients among her recommendations. Similarly, in her entry in the *Dictionnaire critique du féminisme*, Legardinier concentrates chiefly on the educational aspects of the Swedish policy – which offers clients "telephone helplines or interviews with psychologists" – and the need for "prevention and education initiatives on the fundamental causes of prostitution" (2000: 166–167). The criminalization of clients was also a subject for debate within certain left-wing parties, such as the Greens and the LCR, whose brochure on the subject sets out diverging positions.

Similar caution can be found in the first official statement on the subject, the report on prostitution produced by Dinah Dericke in 2001 for the brand new Senate delegation on women's rights and equal opportunities for men and women. This relates to what Bereni and Revillard (2007) called the "institutional acclimatization" of feminist problems, which was also the stimulus for the creation at the same time of the *Observatoire de la parité* (Gender Equality Observatory) and the post of interministerial delegate for women's rights.

These measures, encouraged by growing numbers of women in politics, contributed to the emergence of a state feminism able to politicize the issues put forward by the women's movement, including prostitution.

The delegation chaired by Dericke based its thinking on hearings dominated by figures from the abolitionist and feminist movements: Marie-Victoire Louis, the MAPP, the *Mouvement du Nid*, the *Fondation Scelles*, the *International Abolitionist Federation* and *the French coordinators of the European Women's Lobby* were invited to set out their positions, while the only voice able to express alternative options was the Lyon AIDS prevention association *Cabiria*. Naturally, the report took up the abolitionist definition of the problem of clients, highlighting the need for "the 'client' to become aware: that prostitution is a failure, not only for the prostitute, but also for him; that for him it may be a trivial, meaningless act, but for the prostitute it is a form of violence; that by using the services of a prostitute, he is very likely to be an accomplice to a pimp and, quite possibly, a human trafficker" (Dericke 2001: 58). But it refrained from recommending a specific policy targeting clients ("Should he be made responsible through education or criminalization?") (*ibid.*: 95) and limited itself to a call for further thinking.

Breaking with a long tradition of political avoidance of the subject of prostitution, the Dericke report was the first parliamentary mission specifically dedicated to the topic. It did not remain isolated for long, and reports on the subject multiplied in the following years at an ever-increasing rate: the Lazerges-Vidalies report on modern slavery in 2001, the Bouquet-Geoffroy report on prostitution in 2011, the Jouanno-Godefroy report on the health and social situation of prostitutes in 2013, the Olivier report on the fight against the prostitution system in 2013, not to mention the information reports produced when bills or legislative proposals were debated[16] and the resolution "restating France's abolitionist position on the subject of prostitution" adopted by the National Assembly in December 2011.

These institutional documents were prepared through joint construction by both activists and politicians, so close were the links between the abolitionist and feminist movements and the backers of the prostitution issue within the institutional debating chambers. First of all, several important protagonists in the process were characterized by multiple roles, rubbing shoulders in the "hybrid forums" (Callon, Lascoumes and Barthe 2009) of the specialist committees or observatories, where politicians and former politicians

---

16   Including Zimmermann (2002); Rozier (2002); Gonthier-Maurin (2014) and Meunier (2014).

mix with representatives of "civil society". Legardinier, for example, was not just a journalist at *P&S*; she was a member of the *Observatoire de la parité* (Gender Equality Observatory) from 2002 to 2005. The general secretary of the *Mouvement du Nid*, Grégoire Théry, was a member of the *Haut Conseil à l'égalité entre les hommes et les femmes* (High Council on Gender Equality) that followed it. This body was chaired at the time by Danielle Bousquet, the former socialist deputy and author, with Guy Geoffroy, of the 2011 parliamentary report on prostitution, and a former activist with the Planning Familial network who still identifies as a feminist. Meanwhile, the partisan leanings of many feminists contributed – via the CNDF in particular – to converting most left-wing and far-left organizations to the cause of criminalizing clients. It was through the left wing of the political spectrum that this policy gained its legitimacy.

It is also important to put this process of political rallying around the client criminalization option into context. Another venue for encounters between politicians and activists, the "*Politiques urbaines face à la prostitution*" conference ("Urban policies faced with prostitution") organised by Marcovich and Legardinier in Nantes in 2002, is interesting not only for its exclusively feminist and abolitionist composition on the activist side, but also because, on the political side, most of the speakers were elected officials with responsibility for security issues. As we saw in the previous chapter, prostitution climbed the municipal political agenda from the late 1990s due to the arrival of foreign prostitutes, assumed to be under the control of organized pimping gangs, very visible in public spaces and responsible for disruption that caused complaints from local residents. The definition of prostitution as sexist violence requiring a penal response, promoted by feminists and abolitionists, thus resonated with elected officials sensitive to the theme of insecurity and open to repressive solutions to urban disorder.[17]

---

17   The conference proceedings can be accessed at http://www.grandesvilles.org/sites/defa
      ult/files/publications/actes-colloques/les_politiques_urbaines_face_la_prostitution_13
      283.pdf. The police as an institution, however, speaking through several police unions,
      restated its opposition to criminalizing clients (their positions are outlined in Mossuz-
      Lavau, 2015, 265–266). Apart from the practical aspects of an offence that is difficult to
      prove, this position is perhaps a legacy of the historical reluctance, reported by Berlière
      (1992), of the police to investigate clients who may include figures needing to be protected
      from scandal. The Ambiel case (an advisor to Prime Minister Raffarin prosecuted for
      soliciting the services of an under-age prostitute) and the Strauss-Kahn case (investigated
      for hosting orgies with escorts) may signal a change in this attitude, in line with reduced
      tolerance of such behavior among an increasingly feminized political world.

The prospect of a change with the 2012 presidential election led to a remobilization of the abolitionist and feminist activist space. The critical view of the effects of the LSI made it easier to argue for an alternative option targeting not prostitutes but their clients, while offering ways of evicting prostitution from public spaces. But criminalization was promoted above all through the "Abolition 2012" campaign, initiated within the voluntary sector while drawing on institutional resources. The campaign was driven forward by a conference organized in February 2010 by the *Mouvement du Nid* and 17 partner associations, constituting a *"Front de refus du système prostitutionnel"* ("Front for Rejection of the Prostitution System").[18] The fact that the conference was held at the Palais Bourbon (the French National Assembly building) with the active participation of several parliamentarians – with Danielle Bousquet chief among them – testifies to the successful interweaving of the activist and institutional driving forces. The subsequent establishment of Bousquet's fact-finding mission on prostitution was its first concrete result.

3.2   *Political Work*

This section aims to examine in more detail the specifically political job of gaining legislative approval for the problematization put forward by abolitionists and feminists by retracing the steps that led to the final adoption of the act criminalizing the purchase of sex acts in April 2016, the first version of which was voted on by the National Assembly on 4 December 2013.

The first thing to note is that a form of criminalization of prostitutes' clients already existed since the 4 March 2002 act – adopted by a socialist government – which introduced a penalty of three years in prison and a fine of € 45,000 for clients of under-age prostitutes aged 15 to 18. The fact that this measure had been included in a legislative framework focusing on parental authority, which also addressed child abuse, prefigured the association between violence and prostitution. The following year, the LSI supplemented this provision by applying the same penalties for the use of a prostitute's services if she has a specific vulnerability due to an illness, disability, physical or

---

18   The conference proceedings were published in no. 167 of *P&S* in 2009. The partner associations were the *Association française des femmes diplômées des universités, CATW, the French section of the European Women's Lobby, Concertation des luttes contre l'exploitation sexuelle, Centre national d'information sur les Droits des femmes et des familles, the feminist collective "Ruptures", Comité permanent de liaison des associations abolitionnistes, Élu(e) s contre les violences faites aux femmes, Femmes solidaires, Fédération nationale solidarité femmes, Fondation Scelles, the World March of Women, Mouvement jeunes femmes, Le CRI, Rajfire, Regards de femmes* and SOS *sexisme*.

mental deficiency or pregnancy. The ground was laid for this criminalization of the clients of under-age or vulnerable prostitutes by the Lazerges-Vidalies report on the fight against modern slavery, submitted in 2001, which devoted several pages to prostitution. For example, the report argued that "while it is legitimate to pursue and condemn individuals who indulge in the practices of 'sex tourism' outside our borders, it is also vital to suppress the comparable actions now taking place on our own soil" and "regretted that our criminal law does not punish the client of an under-age prostitute if she is below the age of 15, the 'age of consent'" (Lazerges and Vidalies 2001: 203).

The "Swedish model" was promoted much more explicitly in the Bousquet-Geoffroy report (2011), which published significant work by a committee composed of both PS and UMP deputies. Though 200 figures with a variety of positions on the subject were interviewed, the abolitionists and feminists were cited most often. With specific regard to the client, the report proposed in its turn that he is a "central but long overlooked player in the prostitution system", that "the verdict is simple: without clients, prostitution would not exist" and, citing Bouamama, that "pornography can (...) be seen as 'a frequent step in the process of becoming a client'" (Bousquet and Geoffroy 2011: 214 and 239). Considering that "criminalizing clients means making them understand that they are participating in a form of exploitation of other people's vulnerability" (*ibid.*: 232) and drawing on observations made during a trip to Stockholm, the commission proposed to "create an offence to penalize the use of prostitution". This recommendation was only one among thirty others, relating to the protection of trafficking victims and social support for prostitutes, but it was given top billing and attracted the most comment.

The forthcoming presidential and legislative elections in spring 2012 prevented the measures recommended by the Bousquet-Geoffroy report from being adopted, but nonetheless, in December 2011, a resolution was adopted "restating France's abolitionist position". Referring to the Swedish policy, and with no fear of pleonasm, the resolution declared that "the law must clearly indicate the responsibility of everyone in perpetuating the prostitution system. (...) It must (...) give clients a sense of responsibility by indicating clearly that they too have a share of the responsibility". The text was adopted unanimously by the National Assembly, testament to the fact that the feminist/abolitionist positions had now achieved political consensus. Right-wing groups were converted under the influence of Geoffroy, a UMP member who had also campaigned against the recognition of same-sex couples.

As soon as the PS returned to power, the legislative process was restarted. A few weeks after the new minister for women's rights, Najat Vallaud-Belkacem, had taken office, she declared in a column in the *Journal du dimanche* that her "objective is to see prostitution disappear", and indicated that the parties were unanimous on the need to criminalize clients. Despite a journey to Stockholm in November 2012, the minister appeared to back-pedal in February 2013, espousing a more hesitant position in the feminist magazine *Causette*. The option of criminalizing clients was not unanimously supported in the voluntary sector or in the feminist movement, and the government cautiously commissioned parliamentarians to argue for this option. The PS deputy Maud Olivier took charge of the task. In September 2013, after the inevitable trip to Stockholm, she submitted a report that followed on directly from the Bousquet-Geoffroy report's appropriation of feminist and abolitionist rhetoric. She agreed that "the client is the one that is never spoken about. And yet, without him, 'prostitution and human trafficking for the purpose of sexual exploitation would not exist.'" Mention was again made of "the influence of violent pornography on the construction of young people's representations of sexuality, the responsibility of clients in perpetuating trafficking" and the fact "that buying a sexual act constitutes violence to others, which supposes that this act and thus its punishment should be taken seriously" (Olivier 2013: 13, 96, 106 and 113).

The fusion between activist and institutional narratives was even clearer in the report submitted by Brigitte Gonthier-Maurin in June 2014, when the Senate was examining the proposed bill. Once again, there were assurances that "the few studies available of consumers of prostitution highlight the fact that the client is of all ages and all social conditions: he is an 'everyman'" (Gonthier-Maurin 2014: 27). Once again, the "links between prostitution and pornography" (*ibid.*: 7) were invoked. Once again, it was asserted that "clients of prostitutes are men who consider the bodies of these people as commodities" (19), that "on the buyer's side, prostitution is characterized by unease and discomfort" (30) and that "no sexual compulsion legitimizes renting a human body" (25). Once again the "educational" purpose of punishing clients was invoked, consisting of "setting a simple limit and recalling an essential principle: it is not tolerable for one human to buy the sexual services of another human" (48).[19]

---

19   The continuing legislative process was marginally strengthened by the adoption on 4 August 2014 of the so-called act *"pour l'égalité réelle entre les femmes et les hommes"* ("for real equality between women and men"), the first article of which stipulates that the policy for equality between women and men includes actions aiming to reinforce the combat against the prostitution system – though without specifying the means of this combat. This act did not only institutionalize a formulation and an approach – making prostitution a "system" – that had arisen directly from the feminist and abolitionist movements. It also enshrined its understanding as an obstacle to equality between the sexes; in other words, a gender issue.

This well-worn argument seemed to have reached the end of the road when the Senate's special commission, reporting on the bill in July 2014 (Meunier 2014), concluded that there was a real risk that criminalizing clients would push prostitutes further into conditions of vulnerability and danger. The article criminalizing the purchase of sexual services was thus withdrawn from the text submitted to the Senate for examination on 30 March 2015. As the right had regained their majority in the upper chamber, the debates and the vote confirmed this withdrawal of the criminalization of clients, retaining the punishment for soliciting. This reversal was greeted with anger from the abolitionist/feminist movement – the *Mouvement du Nid* describing it as a "reactionary, dishonorable and irresponsible vote"[20] – but as the French constitution gives the last word to the National Assembly, the criminalization of clients was reintroduced when the bill was finally adopted by deputies on 6 April 2016 and enacted on 13 April.[21]

Known as the act *"renforçant la lutte contre le système prostitutionnel"* ("to strengthen the fight against the prostitution system"), it repealed the offence of soliciting and introduced new measures to suppress online pimping. Above all, it made "soliciting, accepting or obtaining relations of a sexual nature from a person engaged in prostitution, including occasionally, in exchange for remuneration, a promise of remuneration, the provision of a benefit in kind or the promise of such a benefit" an offence punishable with a fine of € 1,500, raised to € 3,750 for a subsequent offence, and potentially "the obligation to complete, at his own expense where relevant, an awareness course on the fight against the purchase of sex acts". It also provided for a body to be set up in each department, presided over by the prefect, to provide "protection for victims of prostitution, pimping or human trafficking" and to give them "the assistance they need, including arranging a place in an accommodation and social reintegration center". This body is responsible for offering a "path out of prostitution and social and professional integration" to "any person who is a victim of prostitution, pimping and human trafficking for the purpose of sexual exploitation". This path is defined based on an assessment of the person's health, professional and social needs in order to enable them to access alternatives to prostitution, and is "developed and implemented, in agreement

---

20   http://www.mouvementdunid.org/PPL-prostitution-au-Senat-un-vote.

21   The act was challenged with an application for a priority ruling on constitutionality submitted by several associations of "sex workers" and public health, arguing that it contravened the principles of the right to privacy, freedom of enterprise and the necessity and proportionality of penalties. The Constitutional Court rejected their application and upheld the law in a decision issued in January 2019.

with the person being supported, by an approved association". Each former prostitute engaged in this program is awarded € 330 per month, benefits from a discount on any tax debts and, if she is foreign, may be issued a temporary residence permit (but these resources are withdrawn if she continues to work as a prostitute). The act also provided for awareness campaigns on the commodification of human bodies for both potential clients and school pupils.

Coming relatively late, the first review of the law by a state body (Inspection générale des affaires sociales 2019) came to a critical conclusion on the initial years of its application. Noting the weakness of its political leadership, the reviewers emphasized the meagre numbers of clients penalized (1,939 questioned in 2018, half of them in Paris; underdeveloped awareness courses) and of paths out of prostitution (230 beneficiaries out of a prostitute population estimated at 30,000 or 40,000 people). The departmental agencies are not working in many departments, and as prefects are responsible for granting residence permits, they are only distributed with the most extreme parsimony. The voluntary sector – and particularly the health associations that had campaigned against the bill during its drafting – was also critical, highlighting that the criminalization of clients is just a mirror image of the criminalization of soliciting, resulting in the same increased dispersion, isolation and insecurity for prostitutes, and underlining the inadequate results in terms of access to housing, residence permits, workplace integration and healthcare. A report prepared under the auspices of Doctors of the World also indicated that "despite what the law promised, including that penalizing demand (clients) would also reduce supply, interviews with associations show that there is no reduction in the number of sex workers. *The negative effects of the law are being felt on their security, their health and their living conditions in general.* The law has had a negative impact on their autonomy at work, the risks they have to take, their stigmatization and their economic situation" (Le Bail, Giametta and Rassouw 2018: 6, emphasis in the original). But as prostitution has faded from public discussion, their criticisms have received scarcely any coverage or political attention.

The adoption of the law "to strengthen the fight against the prostitution system" is part of a broader movement of the penalization of social issues (Wacquant 1999: 2004). While France's espousal of the cause of abolitionism in 1960 led to a specialized social work sector being put in place to help prostitutes and guide them towards reintegration into society, it is now the police who are asked to make prostitution disappear by punishing its clients. This evolution also suggests that the institutionalization of feminism, in France as in the United States (Bernstein 2010), goes hand in hand with its shift from a redistributive conception of justice to a punitive one. Moving from the status of a social inadequate to that of a victim of violence, the prostitute has seen the economic and social context of her activity fade from view, to be replaced by a predominantly moral condemnation. Prostitution here is no longer the result of unequal social structures but an intrinsically violent interaction between a victim and a perpetrator, subject to individualized punitive action.

CHAPTER 6

The Procurer, the Moving Target of Prostitution Policies

Treating the figure of the pimp as a "moving target" requires a few preliminary explanations. Describing him as a *target* means first of all designating him as an objective we are seeking to achieve, in this case to neutralize his negative action.[1] The pimp is thus the subject of a disapproval that has multiple forms and consequences. He is *targeted* overall by moral condemnation, which is expressed through differing discourses that may be either ordinary or specialist, but that all have a normative tone that stigmatizes his activities. Among these orders of normative discourse, the legal register has a particular place and a particular strength in that it supports specific public policies. From the legal viewpoint, the pimp is someone who breaks the law – in France, specifically articles 225 paragraphs 5 to 12 of the penal code (see box) – and is thus a target for investigation by specialist police services and sanctions from magistrates or criminal courts.

But the target is also *moving*, because the pimp is incarnated in many ways, some of which may be surprising: the pimp, as we will try to show here, sometimes crops up in unexpected places with an unexpected appearance. Even the word "incarnation" appears restrictive – certainly, pimps are above all flesh-and-blood beings, capable and guilty of reprehensible actions. But the pimp is also an entity with an almost metaphysical status, the centerpiece of a specific normative system whose invocation accounts for a wide variety of phenomena associated with him, including, first of all, the very existence of prostitution itself. The target of the pimp is thus moving in a different sense, in the switch between his incarnated form – in which he can be found in the docks of courtrooms or the cells of prisons – and his metaphysical or moral form, in which he is more present in the discursive state, whose elusive form makes it no less concerning and influential. The pimp thus has several *modes of existence*,[2] and

---

1 An initial version of this text was published under the title "Le proxénète, cible mouvante des politiques de prostitution" ("The procurer, the moving target of prostitution policies") in *Genre, sexualité & société*, no. 20, 2018; http://journals.openedition.org/gss/5055.

2 The expression, popularized by Latour (2013), originates in Boltanski's work on the modes of existence of the "cadre" group (1987).

it is this existential plurality[3] that we shall try to address in this chapter, which is organized into two phases: moral existence first, and then penal existence.

Principal articles in the French penal code relating to human trafficking and pimping

Article 225–4–1: Human trafficking is the action of recruiting, transporting, transferring, accommodating or hosting a person in exchange for remuneration or any other benefit or a promise of remuneration or of a benefit, for the purpose of having them available or making them available to a third party, even unidentified, in order either to enable the offences of pimping, sexual aggression or assault, the exploitation of begging, or working or housing conditions contrary to their dignity to be committed against this person, or to compel this person to commit a crime or an offence.

Human trafficking is punishable with seven years in prison and a fine of € 150,000.

(...)

Article 225–5: Pimping is the action, by any person, by any means, of:

1. Helping, assisting or protecting the prostitution of another;
2. Profiting from the prostitution of another, sharing the earnings or receiving subsidies from a person habitually engaging in prostitution;
3. Recruiting, grooming or taking control of a person with a view to prostitution or to exert pressure on them to prostitute themselves or to continue to do so.

Pimping is punishable with seven years in prison and a fine of €150,000.

Article 225–6: The following actions, taken by any person and by any means, are classed as pimping and punishable with the penalties specified in art. 225–5:

1. Acting as an intermediary between two people, one of whom is engaged in prostitution and the other is exploiting or remunerating the prostitution of others;
2. Assisting a pimp in justifying fictional resources;

---

3   It should be noted that this chapter does not claim to address all the modes of existence of pimping. Its specifically cultural expressions, found in cinema, literature and popular song, for example, would in themselves require a huge amount of work that is beyond our reach. For this reason, the influence of these cultural representations on the two modes of existence examined here will not be covered in this chapter.

3. Being unable to justify resources corresponding to the lifestyle while living with a person habitually engaged in prostitution or while being in habitual relationships with one or more persons engaged in prostitution;
4. Hindering the action of prevention, control, assistance or rehabilitation undertaken by qualified organizations with regard to persons in danger of prostitution or engaged in prostitution.

(…)

Article 225–10: The following actions, taken by any person acting directly or via an intermediary, are punishable with ten years in prison and a fine of € 750,000:

1. Owning, managing, operating, directing, organizing, financing or contributing to the finance of a brothel;
2. Owning, managing, operating, directing, organizing, financing or contributing to the finance of any establishment open to the public or used by the public that habitually accepts or tolerates one or more persons engaging in prostitution within the establishment or its annexes or seeking clients there with a view to prostitution;
3. Selling or making available to one or more persons premises or locations not used by the public, in the knowledge that they are engaging in prostitution there;
4. Selling, renting or making available, in any way, to one or more persons, vehicles of any kind, in the knowledge that they are engaging in prostitution there. (…)

1   The Pimp, the "Moving" Target

The moral existence of the pimp stems from the public discourse about him from organizations or individuals laying claim to a form of general interest: activists for the abolition of prostitution first of all, followed by parliamentarians responsible for drafting a law with the same goal of abolition. The close interweaving of these two orders of discourse was crystallized in a way by the campaign to criminalize clients of prostitution, a measure that was introduced by the 2016 law "to strengthen the fight against the prostitution system" mentioned in the previous chapter.

1.1   *The Abolitionist Message*

The double meaning of the "moving target" is apt: the pimp is not only a target in motion, but also a target who is *moving*, in the sense that his mere mention stimulates an emotional response. Contrary to the usual meaning of "moving" as a synonym of poignant or affecting, we should immediately clarify that the emotions are negative in this case: the pimp is someone who arouses indignation, disgust or anger, so repugnant and abominable are his activities deemed to be. It is this emotional charge that explains why the pimp occupies a central role in the pronouncements of the movement in favor of abolishing prostitution, on which we will focus first of all. The concept of a *sensitizing device* forged by Traïni is an effective description of what is going on here, i.e. a set of narratives that the movement uses to stimulate emotional reactions that predispose the people experiencing them to engage with or support the cause it promotes (Traïni 2009). In this case, the target of denunciation is moving in that it is hoped that invoking it will drive a movement in the form of a rallying of its audience to the abolitionist cause.[4]

The evocations of pimping in the abolitionist literature reveal several dominant characteristics, including shadowy omnipotence, violence and a propensity for manipulation. Pimping is presented first of all as consubstantial with prostitution, and since one cannot exist without the other, anyone who seeks the disappearance of one must also want the abolition of the other. An intellectual who is an integral part of the abolitionist movement, Marie-Victoire Louis proposed replacing the term "prostitution" with "pimping system" ("système proxénète") to highlight the fact that it could not exist without the intervention of its organizers and beneficiaries. Binding prostitutes, pimps and clients inseparably together, she said that the system is "one of the manifestations of the patriarchal domination that organises and legitimizes the sexual availability of certain humans – women of all ages in the vast majority of cases – in order to maintain and consolidate male power".[5] While the declaration that

---

4   The material on which this section is based consists of texts produced between 1999 and 2016, i.e. between the beginning of the abolitionist remobilization (strengthened by its coalition with certain elements of feminism and alter-globalization), focusing on the campaign to criminalise the clients of prostitutes and the consequent adoption of the law "to strengthen the fight against the prostitution system". The corpus is dominated by, but not limited to, texts from the two leading abolitionist organizations, the *Mouvement du Nid* and the *Fondation Scelles*, together with the Attac gender committee on the alter-globalist and feminist side. The stability of these narratives over time and the homogeneity of their references, arguments and rhetorical forms authorize us to treat them as a whole in this section.

5   Proceedings of the conference "Peuple de l'abîme : la prostitution aujourd'hui" ("People of the abyss: prostitution today"), *Fondation Scelles*, 16 May 2000: 51.

"there is no prostitute without a pimp" is an abolitionist platitude, some activists demonstrate more nuance and a concern for accuracy, following the example of Attac, which states that "at an individual level, 80 to 95% of all forms of prostitution are controlled by a pimp" (Attac 2008: 61) but immediately clarifies that the "prostitutes who claim to be independent" (note the cautious phrasing) "only represent a small minority" (*ibid.*: 77).

Significantly titled "Le proxénétisme en 2015: une hydre à mille têtes" ("Pimping in 2015: a hydra with a thousand heads"), an article in *Prostitution et société* put forward the "omnipresence" of the phenomenon and "the diversity of its forms".[6] In the body of the article, which is just under 700 words long and lists a series of pimping cases over the past year, the expression "vast network" occurs three times, suggesting the power of the pimps. The recurring use of the word "network" in the abolitionist literature is significant in itself, as Boltanski and Chiapello remind us that the term is generally associated with "organizations of a secret character (resistance networks). The latter invariably possessed a negative connotation (trafficking networks), their members being accused of seeking illicit advantages and profits through this type of association (...), and sometimes by resorting to patently illegal methods" (Boltanski and Chiapello 2017: 104).

The reference to their book *The New Spirit of Capitalism* is no coincidence. We have seen in previous chapters how French abolitionism gained a new lease of life by forming a coalition with certain segments of the alter-globalist movement, borrowing several schemas critical of neoliberalism. An author such as Poulin and an association such as Attac have made a specialty of denouncing the contribution of neoliberalism to a globalized "commodification of bodies", giving organized crime a powerful weapon. The former asserts that the trade in prostituted women and children "recruits immense populations and creates lavish profits that are recycled into the global economy" (Poulin 2003: 761), while the latter declares that "the role of human trafficking and the sex industry in criminality is considerable", specifying that "between 76 and 100% of sex businesses are controlled, financed or supported by organized crime" (Attac 2008: 24). Along the same lines, the largest French abolitionist organization, the Mouvement du Nid, continually denounces lobbying – meaning discreet or possibly secretive, and illegitimate in any case, activities intended to influence political decision-makers – by pimps. This lobbying by "a sex industry that has become all-powerful" is said to use tested methods such as "brandishing the standard of individual liberty to better defend the interests of the

---

6 http://www.prostitutionetsociete.fr/eclairage/acteurs/article/le-proxenetisme-en-2015-une
   -hydre-a-mille-tetes.

industry. The tobacco lobby focused the debate on the freedom and pleasure of smoking, obscuring the interests of manufacturers, and in the same way the sex industry has understood that it has to display concern for prostitutes. Pimps and traffickers now commonly set up associations to defend the rights of prostitutes as the ideal cover for their lobbying".[7] The goal of this lobbying is claimed to be the recognition of "sex work", legitimizing the normalization of prostitution and authorizing its exploitation by others – in other words, the legalization of pimping.

The conspiracist image of the octopus working in the dark, omnipotent and elusive, can be seen in the title of an article from *Prostitution et société*: "Réseaux : un ennemi mobile et tentaculaire" ("Networks: a mobile, many-tentacled enemy").[8] The secret power of the organizers and exploiters of prostitution is also suggested by the expression "sex industry", used as a synonym for pimping and evoking an organized world focused on the accumulation of economic benefits. The aim when using this vocabulary is to denounce the greed of the pimps (and their lack of scruples in exploiting the bodies of prostitutes) and the systematic, rational nature of their activity: organized crime is claimed to take inspiration from the business world to maximize profits while taking on some of its respectability. An all-inclusive phrase, the "sex industry" refers not only to prostitution; it also gathers into the same ignominious category other activities with greater potential legitimacy, such as pornography, sex shops, strip clubs, swingers' clubs etc. But again, the primary goal is to encourage a significant population of activists critical of contemporary capitalism to rally to the cause of abolitionism. Arguing, as in the words of Attac, that "the members of organized crime now wear the suits of respectable business men" (Attac 2008: 165) invokes an image that combines the "sharks of finance" with gangsters laundering their dirty money. Claiming, like Poulin, that the "explosion" of the sex industries is "closely linked to factors specific to neoliberal globalization" (Poulin 2004: 22) means associating the violence of prostitution with the hubris of the neoliberal market while underlining its contemporary internationalized dimension, which is itself supported by treating migrant prostitutes as victims of human trafficking.

Violence is another factor that characterizes pimps, whether it is physical – assault, rape, abduction etc. – or psychological, involving various forms of

---

7   http://www.prostitutionetsociete.fr/eclairage/point-de-vue/lobbying-proxenete-lancons-l
    -alerte.
8   *Prostitution et société*, no. 143, 2003 : 24.

deception, threats or manipulation. We have already seen that the pimp stands out for his moral indifference: nothing is off limits, including the most extreme and despicable methods, in order to subjugate the prostitutes he exploits. Attac cites the young women who "suffer abuse, blackmail, threats to their families, removal of their passports, training in mass brothels or even sale at auction" (Attac 2008: 50). Seduction, false promises of work, drugs, kidnapping and more are among the most commonly cited methods of subjugation used by pimps, supplemented, with the development of migrant prostitution, by charm and pressure on the families left behind. The disgrace is all the greater in that pimps target individuals presented as weak and vulnerable: women who are mostly young (or even still children), naive or impoverished, and ready to be seduced by prospects of a better future. Attac emphasizes the fact that pimps' victims "allow themselves to be deceived by offers holding out the prospect of a job" and that significant numbers of them are "trapped by human trafficking networks" (Attac 2008: 49). This image paints pimp and prostitute as two radically opposite figures. The former is active, rational, rich, powerful and violent and constitutes the platonic ideal of a criminal to whom no pardon or excuse can be granted. The latter is passive, easily influenced or psychologically fragile, poor and weak and represents an ideal victim figure requiring rescue and compassion.[9]

The pimp as depicted in the abolitionist literature appears as what Cohen (1973) called a *folk devil*, a personification of evil whose supposed omnipotence is equaled only by the uncertainty of his incarnations. The pimp has the status of the effective cause of the existence of prostitution: without him – and without the client, who is also designated as a "prostitutor" – no woman would ever consider practicing the fundamentally repellent activity of selling sexual services on her own initiative. It is in this sense that his existence is metaphysical: even in the absence of a concrete incarnation – i.e. a duly identified individual whose activity is empirically observable – there must be one at work somewhere, because prostitution could not exist without him.

1.2   *The Parliamentary Debate*
This kind of narrative falls into a particular register, the register of activist propaganda,[10] which, as mentioned earlier, seeks to *sensitize* an audience by

---

9   For more on the ideal victim represented by the prostitute victim of human trafficking, see Jakšić (2016).

10   The term is used here, with no pejorative connotation, to mean any persuasive action addressed to an audience in whom a change of attitude is sought (in this case, support for the abolitionist project).

challenging its moral convictions to arouse its indignation. The use of what Goffman called *dramatic realizations* (1959: 30 et seq.) is justified from the viewpoint of the abolitionist cause by the demands of a register that has no room for nuance or caution if its goals of sensitization and conversion are to be achieved. This makes its adoption in the political sphere all the more striking. Of course politicians, too, are subject to the need to convince an audience – their voters – that their positions are the right ones, and are thus predisposed to use the register of propaganda, but political representatives are nonetheless supposed to be subject also to a certain form of realism. The concrete conditions under which the public policies they define and promote are implemented – predominantly penal policies, in this case – are ill-adapted to metaphysics and demand greater adjustment to the real world.

Yet it is the moral existence of the pimp that predominates in recent political language about prostitution. We will limit ourselves here to the parliamentary debates that preceded the adoption of the law "to strengthen the fight against the prostitution system".[11] It is important to clarify that this law did not focus centrally on pimping, as most of the deputies and senators considered that the existing repressive arrangements were satisfactory (except with regard to online prostitution, which was targeted by the first article of the law[12]). Its key measure was the criminalization of clients, which replaced the offence of passive soliciting (restored by the domestic security act of 2003), backed by the introduction of new provisions to encourage prostitutes to reintegrate into society. This makes it all the more significant that pimping was mentioned repeatedly during the debates. It is equally remarkable that the arguments used by parliamentarians favorable to the proposal drew on the stock of language developed by the abolitionist movement. The expression "prostitution system", used in the law's title, was invented by Louis;[13] it occurred regularly during the debates, such as when the secretary of state (junior minister) for women's rights, Pascale Boistard, said that "we must address not only prostitution, but the prostitution system, which brings together three players – the pimp, the prostitute and the client" (Senate 30/03/2015).

---

11   The minutes of these debates can be found on the websites of the National Assembly (AN, http://www.assemblee-nationale.fr) and the Senate (http://www.senat.fr).

12   However, the scope of this article was reduced during the parliamentary debate, as the initial ambition of attacking sites presenting offers of paid-for sexual services risked infringing freedom of expression.

13   Louis uses this expression in parallel with the previously mentioned "pimping system"; see for example "Abolir la prostitution ? Non : abolir le proxénétisme" ("Abolish prostitution? No, abolish pimping"), http://www.marievictoirelouis.net/document.php?id =744#tocto2n5.

Even in the first session in the National Assembly, on 29 November 2013, the rapporteur Maud Olivier (PS) was already invoking the omnipresence and omnipotence of pimps. The entanglement of prostitution and pimping was emphasized from the start, with an emphasis on the violence and commodification she saw as consubstantial with the commercial exploitation of sexuality: "We are talking for the most part about human beings who are sold, transported and trained to become things that can be exploited for profit". As with the abolitionists, the care taken to point out that not all prostitutes are necessarily under the control of a pimp ("90% of prostitutes" are "victims of pimping", so the vast majority) is immediately cancelled out: "And if a single prostitute claims to be free, would that be enough for the slavery of all the others to become respectable and acceptable?" the same deputy asked. This reasoning is close to that of her Socialist colleague Sylvie Tolmont, who pointed out that "though certain forms of prostitution are still more violent – I'm thinking of course of those who depend on pimping networks exploiting women's poverty and vulnerability – the others are not free either" (AN 29/11/2013).

The pernicious influence of pimps and their omnipotence can also be found, particularly in the words of Maud Olivier, who said for example that "the networks are well organized, and they pay lawyers and barristers handsomely to analyze our laws" (AN 12/06/2015). This Socialist deputy made the most use of dramaturgical actions with the aim of inflating the disgrace of pimping by assimilating it into that other form of absolute evil, Islamist terrorism: "The resources of the terrorist group Daesh include earnings generated by its networks of prostitution (…). It has been shown that the women kidnapped by Boko Haram were sold to Nigerian prostitution networks – 50% of prostitutes in Great Britain are Nigerian, and 20% in France. Hostage taking and prostitution earn Boko Haram between € 500,000 and € 2 million per month" (AN 12/06/2015).

The violence, both physical and psychological, that enables pimps to subjugate prostitutes was also emphasized by the promoters of the proposed law, including the communist Laurence Cohen ("Prostitution is an extreme form of violence (…) inflicted by both clients and pimps: violence of all forms, blackmail, humiliation, insults, blows, repeated rape …", Senate 30/03/2015), the radical Alain Tourret ("Pimping is the enemy of women, the human race and society. It mistreats and brutalizes women", AN 4/12/2013) and the socialist Marie-Françoise Clergeau ("Twenty-first-century prostitution overwhelmingly concerns women from Africa and Eastern Europe, beaten and raped preventively to subjugate them to their pimps", AN 29/11/2013). The opposing pairs man–pimp–perpetrator versus woman–prostitute–victim were constantly

repeated, only very occasionally interrupted by mentions of male and transgender prostitutes (but never female pimps).[14]

Though clearly very close to abolitionist rhetoric, the parliamentary discussions still had specific features that can be attributed to the state of the
political sphere and, more specifically, the pervasiveness within it of a coercive
view of migration issues. Reading the debates, one is struck by the repeated
references to the French *territory*, which must be protected against intrusions
from pimps, who are thus necessarily presented as foreign: "France is not a
safe haven for criminal networks" (Ségolène Neuville, PS, AN 4/12/2013); "We
can act to make our territory inhospitable to pimping networks and human
traffickers" (Charles de Courson, centrist, AN 12/06/2015); "We are convinced
that, by attacking demand, the proposed law will effectively dissuade pimping networks from entering a territory where the legislation is less favorable
to criminal profits" (Claudine Lepage, PS, AN 14/10/2015); "The nomadic circuits through which young girls are recruited abroad, the 'sex tours' organized
online and the advertisements extolling the talents of masseuses require us
to equip ourselves with the means to fight their proliferation in our territory"
(Maud Olivier, PS, AN 12/06/2015). The figure of the pimp as projected by these
parliamentarians thus takes on the outline of a foreigner, and his presence in
France appears to be a penetration from outside.[15] Such an argument implicitly supposes that the French territory and citizens are free of any pimping
activity.

As we have said, the criminalization of clients was the key measure in the
legislative reform. This was put forward as relevant in view of the intrinsic
violence of prostitution but also its capacity to undermine the profits of the
pimps. At the 30 March 2015 session, the Socialist senator Roland Courteau
claimed that punishing clients "will be a strong signal to the pimping networks, and I would gamble that, by attacking demand, we will effectively
dissuade the pimping networks from entering [our] territory". Resorting to
anaphora, Pascale Boistard went further: "It's because a client pays that pimps
prostitute women. It's because a client pays that gangs of all kinds grow richer.
It's because a client pays that human trafficking is the second most lucrative
form of criminality after the drug trade" (Senate 14/10/2015). Conversely, the

---

14   This absence of female pimps, testifying to a gendered, essentialist view of the respec-
       tive statuses of perpetrators (active) and victims (passive), is addressed in Mathieu
       (2014a: 173–174).

15   This register of penetration from outside was also found in the arguments used to pro-
       mote the Swedish law that served as a model for the law "to strengthen the fight against
       the prostitution system"; see Kulick (2003).

prospect of normalizing prostitution by recognizing "sex work" was rejected precisely because it would increase the hold of organized crime and encourage its violence, as emphasised by Ségolène Neuville on the basis of the lessons learned from foreign experience: "In the Netherlands, where prostitution is very visible in windows and beneath neon lights, a police study showed that between 50% and 90% of prostitutes working in the legal 'industry' were compelled to do so by a criminal pimping network" (AN 29/11/2013).

The proposed law did meet some resistance, both on the right (where the record of the LSI was defended) and among certain Ecologists and Socialists who favored decriminalizing prostitution. But it is interesting to note that pimping also occupied a central place in the arguments put forward by opponents of the reform. The UMP deputy Marie-Louise Fort, who also saw prostitution and pimping as foreign realities, opposed any relaxation of access to residency for migrant prostitutes, claiming that "this will be an invitation to violent, illegal immigration, because pimps will have no trouble convincing people in distress to prostitute themselves in order to gain a residence permit" (AN 29/11/2013). Her UMP colleague Philippe Goujon, meanwhile, regretted the repeal of the offence of soliciting, which had enabled the police to obtain information on pimps: "In Paris, a third of the sixty or so trials [for pimping] started with information collected during police custody for soliciting" (AN 29/11/2013). A firm opponent of criminalizing clients, the Green senator Esther Benbassa nevertheless took care to argue that "the primary objective of a law on prostitution should be to shield victims of pimps against the coercion and violence that make their life a living hell" (Senate 30/03/2015). She was backed up by her Socialist colleague Jean-Pierre Godefroy, who wondered whether "the human and financial resources that would be needed to enforce this new offence couldn't be more usefully employed to fight pimping and the international networks?" (Senate 14/10/2015).

The similarities between the arguments used by abolitionists and parliamentarians supporting the proposed law are not surprising, because as we have seen the former supplied the latter plentifully with talking points and elements of language. Their messaging uniformly presents an identikit image of the pimp: he is above all a man, of foreign nationality, acting within an organized gang, using violence or manipulation, with influence and considerable resources to protect his interests, accumulating enormous profits by exploiting the bodies of the prostituted women who are his powerless victims. We have also seen that there are nuances that separate them: the parliamentarians are more explicit about the links between prostitution and migration, whereas the abolitionists, while emphasizing the international nature of the human trafficking networks, associate it more closely with neoliberal globalization. Either way, their messaging characterizes pimping by its omnipresence and its omnipotence, in line with the logic of denunciation that requires the persecutor to be magnified in order to legitimize the cause (Boltanski 2012). The metaphysical existence of the pimp is inseparable from the combat it serves and legitimizes, the combat to abolish prostitution.

2   Pimps Labelled by the Justice System

Now we turn to the second form of the pimp's existence, his penal existence. This constitutes a specific but particularly powerful variation of the normative understanding of pimping, because it involves a specific social treatment for individuals convicted by the justice system of carrying out this activity.

2.1   *The Power of Labelling*

The status of pimp is a characteristic that disqualifies the person affected by it, and thus constitutes what the sociology of deviance calls a *stigma* (Goffman 1963). The classic approach developed by Goffman is particularly relevant when applied to pimps, individuals who run the risk of being discredited as long as they have not been identified and who consequently have to keep their deviance secret by hiding their guilty activities. "Passing", "covers" and withdrawal into a social circle of "intimates" are fundamental elements of the condition of pimps.[16] As we showed in the first chapter, stigma has a contaminating dimension – while certain prostitutes can boast of having spent time with major figures from organized crime to boost their prestige within the prostitution space, most fiercely deny being exploited by one or more individuals. In the late 1990s, a Marseille prostitute defended her independence from her partner by explaining in an interview that "Bob isn't my pimp; I earn my money on my side and he earns his money on his. He's a thief".

   The equally classic propositions of Howard Becker in *Outsiders* have also remained relevant: "Social groups create deviance by making the rules whose infraction constitutes deviance, and by applying those rules to particular

---

16   Writing in the early 1960s, Goffman regretted in a note that pimps had received little study from sociologists "since there is perhaps no male occupation about which its performers are more bashful. The daily round of the pimp must be full of passing dodges not yet recorded. Further, only with the greatest difficulty can pimps be tactfully told to their faces what their occupation is" (Goffman 1963: 99, n. 58).

people and labeling them as outsiders" (Becker 1963: 9). In sociological terms, therefore, a pimp is an individual to whom this shameful label has been successfully applied. The analysis moves from the individual's personal characteristics to the social reaction to his real or supposed actions. In this case, the reaction comes primarily from the justice system: as pimping is an offence, it is the justice system that has the most authority on the subject. Its verdicts are therefore difficult to dispute and involve heavy consequences (primarily deprivation of liberty) for those it labels as pimps.[17] Others forms of labelling, on the other hand, prove more fragile and hazardous. Though they can appear relatively harmless (but not without risk) when deployed in a limited circle in the form of rumors or gossip, they are themselves subject to criminal sanction when their public expression proves unfounded: an elected member of the Ile-de-France regional council was convicted of defamation after publicly comparing the organizers of the Assises de la Prostitution conference, including the STRASS sex work union, to pimps.[18]

The justice system has the particularity of being an *institution* that is in charge, according to Luc Boltanski, of "stating the whatness of what is" (Boltanski 2011: 75), which in this case means deciding whether the facts presented to it correspond to the type defined in criminal law as pimping, and thus require the standard sentence to be imposed. Consequently, the criminal trial constitutes what the same sociologist defines as a *test*, i.e. a standardized procedure following which the individual involved will or will not be characterized as a pimp and punished under similarly standardized terms. This process has a number of notable features. First of all, it is procedural, in the sense that it takes place within a specific temporality. The test consisting of the criminal trial is the final stage in the pathway, or the career (Latour 2009; Jakšić 2016), of what is commonly called a "case", whose first stages coordinate the action of

---

17   Bourdieu underlined this higher level of performativeness of the law: "Unlike an insult hurled by a single individual, which, as private discourse uttered on the individual's own account and committing no-one but themselves, has little symbolic effectiveness, the verdict of a judge, who settles conflicts or negotiations about things or persons, proclaiming publicly what they truly are, without appeal, belongs to the class of instruments of appointment or institutional actions and represent the quintessential form of authorized, public, official speech, pronounced in the public name before the public: as judgements of attribution publicly expressed by agents acting as authorized representatives of a community, and thus constituted as models for all acts of categorization (...), these performative statements are magical acts that succeed because they are able to make themselves universally recognised, so that no-one can refuse or ignore their viewpoint and the vision they impose" (Bourdieu 1987: 13).

18   http://www.leparisien.fr/neuilly-plaisance-93360/henriette-zoughebi-condamnee-pour -avoir-diffame-les-proxenetes-10-11-2011-1711351.php.

the justice system and the police. In France, the opening of a procedure (following a report of an offence, for example) leads to an investigation conducted by police officers (or sometimes gendarmes) reporting to magistrates. Only if this procedure is successful (if the information gathered is considered sufficiently robust and conclusive) does it have any chance of resulting in a trial and – though this is not at all guaranteed, either – a conviction, i.e. a criminal labelling as a pimp.

A second notable characteristic of the process arises from the institutional status of the police and the justice system. Boltanski emphasizes that institutions are never entirely bodiless beings; on the contrary, they have to be incarnated in individual people – police officers, gendarmes, prosecuting magistrates, judges – each one defined by specific properties (attachment to an origin and a social position, educational level, age, sex etc.) and responding to specific rationales, interests and representations. Ethnographic studies of the police and the justice system in action have long shown that the understanding and management of criminal acts are shaped by "preformed typifications" and "background expectancies" arising from practical knowledge of the social world.[19] These are largely acquired through the repetition of experiences and constitute guides for action: a police officer knows from experience where to look for proof that "happy endings" are offered at a massage parlor (i.e. in the bins where paper towels smeared with sperm are disposed of) and the president of a criminal court knows that a magical ceremony known as *juju* probably preceded the migration of a Nigerian prostitute.

Organizational routines and professional cultures shape the process by which judicially labelled, i.e. convicted, pimps are produced.[20] Mainsant (2021) showed how police officers from the *Brigade de répression du proxénétisme* (anti-pimping squad) rank and select the cases reported to them. The facts considered most worthy of interest are those emerging from police work (i.e. from clues, rather than pressure from above or following a complaint[21]) and corresponding to representations of "traditional" or "high-flying" pimping, i.e. involving men who exploit women. The definition of what are considered to be "important clients" is part of the value placed on police work, which gains prestige from attacking "real criminals". Consequently, less attention is paid to

---

19   In particular, see the classic works by Aaron V Cicourel (1995) and Harvey Sacks (1972).

20   The importance of organizational routines in the criminal characterization of the facts being investigated has been emphasized since the seminal work of Sudnow (1965).

21   As a foreign prostitute informing on her pimp has the right in principle to a residence permit, the police are quick to suspect that these reports are a misuse of procedure motivated above all by the promise of legal status.

diverging forms: the more precarious fringes of the prostitution space, prostitutes' partners who do not use force, small-time operators who organize prostitutes' work and collect the earnings for others higher up the chain, exploitation between women or exploitation of transvestites and transgender prostitutes. This strongly gendered conception of police action – dominated by male police officers investigating male pimps who exploit female victims – is also racialized: at the time when Mainsant was conducting her survey, European networks were seen as more important than those involving Africans. However, this statement to the contrary, which I collected from a police commander in 2016, demonstrates that these hierarchies are neither stable nor uniform: "I prefer taking care of African prostitution – it's less complicated. Even though God knows African prostitution is complex. But with the Roma, it's epic, it's epic. It's all about clans and what-have-you".

The success of the investigations also depends on chance and on the investigators' ability to obtain relevant information. This is illustrated by an evening I spent observing a department specializing in the suppression of pimping. I accompanied two police officers for a three-hour "stake-out" in a car parked in front of a massage parlor. The aim was to find out whether the services provided in the parlor were sexual or not, and consequently whether this was a case of hotel-based pimping. The simplest method was to ask the clients leaving the establishment which services they were offered or given (it is important to note that the observation took place before the April 2016 act was passed, and there were no legal consequences for being a prostitute's client). A first man approached by the police officers when he left the parlor was aged around fifty, and appeared from his clothing to be middle-class. He claimed to have entered the establishment because he needed to relax after a tiring day. Questioned further, he answered firmly that he had been given a massage with no sexual contact, and that nothing of the kind had been offered. The officers allowed him to leave after he had promised to visit the office at a later date for his statement to be recorded. The second client was a man of around thirty who appeared much more intimidated at being questioned by the police, who took advantage of this ascendancy to ask him to come immediately to the brigade office and provide a statement. His presence in the almost-deserted police premises (it was nearly 10 pm at the time) clearly exacerbated his anxiety, and despite having claimed in the street that he had been "massaged everywhere" but "without anything sexual", he now admitted that the masseuse had masturbated him. After his departure, the police officers were exultant – they had finally obtained conclusive evidence about the offence of hotel-based pimping. If the second client had proven as unimpressionable as the first, the investigation would have remained at a standstill.

2.2   *Judicial Certification*

The police and judicial procedure can thus be considered as a long series of tests, during which the information collected is evaluated from the viewpoint of whether it supports a charge of pimping. The criminal trial is the last of these tests, when the chosen facts are submitted for examination, this time by the president of the court, the prosecutor and the lawyers (essentially those of the defendant, or more rarely those of the plaintiff), following which the accused – if he is indeed convicted for having facilitated, organized and/or exploited the prostitution of others – is officially labelled a pimp. Observing these hearings is a rich source of information on who pimps are from a judicial standpoint.

We should clarify from the outset that the thirty or so hearings observed (mostly in Paris, but also in Lyon and Grenoble) over a period of three years as part of the Proscrim research project do not constitute a representative sample that would allow any quantitative conclusions to be drawn.[22] Nevertheless, these observations highlight significant divergences, which we will examine below, from the portrait of the pimp presented by abolitionists and parliamentarians.[23] We should also add that it is hardly surprising that the penal existence of pimps differs from their metaphysical existence – i.e. the portrait drawn of them in political and abolitionist narratives – because their respective production corresponds to fundamentally different social logics.

And yet the two are not unrelated, firstly because magistrates have, to varying degrees, absorbed the perceptions of pimps put forward by the abolitionists. This absorption can occur in an informal, diffuse way,[24] but also through attendance at specific courses at the national magistrates' school, where

---

22   These data were examined separately in Favarel-Garrigues and Mathieu (2021). The trial observations were conducted by Mathilde Darley, Gilles Favarel-Garrigues, Alban Jacquemard, Milena Jakšić, Gwenaëlle Mainsant, Muriel Mille, Nadège Ragaru and myself as part of the ANR Proscrim research project led by Mathilde Darley. Its principal results were gathered together in no. 122 (2021) of the journal *Cultures et conflits* and in the book edited par Darley (2023). The other team members have no responsibility for my analyses here.

23   For a systematic study of these divergences, conducted in the United States, see Marcus et al. (2014).

24   The importance of common-sense representations among magistrates has been identified by ethnomethodologically-inspired work in the sociology of law; for a summary, see Travers (2001). The way in which racially selective schemas, partly arising from popular culture, has influenced the policing and legal framework for pimps in the United States, for example, has been addressed by Williamson and Marcus (2017).

leaders of abolitionist associations speak as experts.[25] Secondly, the way the trial is conducted requires magistrates and lawyers to examine anything that could support the charges. This is the reason for the recurring questions to defendants about their use of violence or coercion with regard to prostitutes, the sources and amount of their earnings, any transfers of money detected to their country of origin, the extent to which tasks are shared with accomplices, how foreign prostitutes are brought to France etc. Consequently, the moral existence of the pimp is very frequently incarnated in a male, foreign, violent defendant, acting within an organized gang and profiting financially from the prostitution of others.

But observing the hearings also confirms the moving – as in unstable and multiple – character of the pimp's incarnations. These diverge relatively frequently and in various ways from the identity portrait drawn by the abolitionists, sometimes to the explicit confusion or surprise of the magistrates. This is particularly the case in economic terms, because the defendants rarely stand out for their luxurious lifestyles; in several of the cases observed, they were characterized by their precarious living conditions, which they shared with the prostitutes (living in squats or slums or sharing small, overcrowded apartments) and their earnings were sometimes very low (€ 15 to € 30 per night for monitoring a prostitution area, for example, in the case of a Roma "network"). It is also the case in organizational terms, because while defendants often specialize in particular tasks (recruitment, transfer, surveillance, collecting earnings, posting advertisements on the internet, renting apartments, managing massage parlors etc.), and while foreign links are observed (often in the form of international bank transfers), the criminal associations are often small and have little in common with the many-tentacled multinationals evoked in abolitionist reports. Again, it is the case in terms of nationality, because while most of the trials observed involved foreigners, the minority of French defendants was far from negligible.

It is also the case when no violence or coercion is identified and the hearing reveals that it was the prostitutes who asked the defendant to ensure their security while they worked. This type of situation is similar to the "resource sharing" model, based on exchanges of services between pimps and prostitutes, identified by Savoie-Gargiso and Morselli (2013). This case was encountered several times during the research, including a hearing where the defendant was a young man who took charge of posting advertisements on the internet,

---

25   This is the case for Yves Charpenel, for instance, who contributes to these courses in his dual role as a legal professional (he is the first advocate-general at the court of appeal) and president of the *Fondation Scelles*.

arranging client appointments over the phone, renting apartments for prostitutes to work in and being present during dates to ensure the prostitutes were safe, all for a fixed daily payment. In his defense, the accused argued that a prostitute he had met at a nightclub had been the first to offer to pay him in exchange for his reassuring presence during her encounters with clients, and that he had not exercised any coercion on the young women, who "would have prostituted themselves without him". In response, the prosecution emphasized the gap between the defendant's lifestyle (including his nightclub outings and taste for expensive clothes) and the distress of the young girls, some of them runaways, whose "protection" he provided. The reality of this protection was also cast into doubt when it emerged that the defendant slept during the dates; the prosecutor then stigmatized the inconsistency of the service more than its illegality.

The pimp in the courtroom also departs from his abolitionist portrait if his alleged domination wavers when faced with the cries of the prostitutes learning that their partner, accused of having exploited them, has been sentenced to several years in prison. While romantic feelings constitute a classic and widely known instrument (e.g. Kennedy et al., 2007; Van San and Bovenkerk 2013) for subjugating a prostitute to her lover–pimp, the reality of the emotional attachment – sometimes consolidated by shared experiences and properties, such as migration, language or national or ethnic origin – constitutes an obstacle to a solely cynical interpretation of the relationship between them (Katona 2017; Horning and Striken 2017). Lawyers can thus use elements tending to prove the reality of their clients' feelings (photos and amorous messages on social media, tender words recorded during surveillance etc.) to prove that this is a "real couple" and that it is only the absence of any economic alternative that led them into prostitution.

More globally, we can also note that the annual number of convictions for pimping is relatively low, and even seems to be declining, despite the existence of dedicated police departments in the biggest cities.[26] The number of convictions for human trafficking (around fifteen a year) is even lower, and owes its recent increase not to a rise in cases but to the instruction to magistrates from the French justice ministry to use this charge, introduced into the penal code in 2003, more systematically.

---

26   The cumulative figures for annual convictions for "simple" and "aggravated pimping" between 2000 and 2009 gathered in the Bousquet–Geoffroy report (2011: 133) stand at around a thousand per year. The latest figures available, from 2015, show 105 convictions for simple pimping and 368 for aggravated pimping ("Les condamnations. Année 2015" ("Convictions. Year 2015"), Ministry of Justice, secretariat-general, December 2016: 21).

But the final and most important angle from which penally certified pimps differ from their abolitionist portrait is through gender, because a significant number of defendants are women charged with having organized or exploited the prostitution of other women. In a considerable number of cases, these are prostitutes with the status of "top girl", i.e. with authority delegated by a male pimp over her colleagues, whose prostitution she organizes and whose earnings she collects, sometimes with violence. They may also be women accelerating the repayment of their debt (contracted in order to be able to migrate) by exploiting in turn a prostitute who has arrived in France more recently, leading to a kind of cascade of exploitative relationships.[27] This "gender trouble" reaches its height when the figure of the prostitute–pimp demolishes the opposition between male–active–perpetrator and female–passive–victim that is such a fundamental part of the abolitionist narrative. Considering the prostitute–pimp, or simply the female pimp, as a rare form of deviance thus confirms the ascendancy identified by Cardi and Pruvost (2012) of conceptions based on an idea of what is natural, incapable of imagining violence by women as anything other than a monstrous exception.

As we have already said, it is hardly surprising that the judicial incarnation of the pimp (what we have called his penal existence) does not necessarily correspond to the image drawn of him in the abolitionist and parliamentary narratives (his moral existence). Clearly, these two orders of existence are not entirely separate, and they obviously exert a certain degree of mutual influence.[28] Nonetheless, they do not align with the same issues or fit within the same social logics. For this reason, there would be no great sociological relevance in using the divergences observed as a basis for criticizing abolitionist positions, in this case by trying to oppose "real" pimps – those encountered at trials – against the "false" pimps invoked by the advocates of abolishing prostitution. These two figures are not separated by the relationship between reality and fiction, but rather by the fact that they relate to distinct modes of existence. The metaphysical pimp invoked by abolitionists is clearly resistant to being incarnated in the men and women in the docks of courtrooms and in

---

27   This situation can be seen, for example, in trials involving women originating from sub-Saharan Africa. It has been studied by Vanessa Simoni, who reports that "certain women break free from their situation of exploitation by choosing to become exploiters in their turn, recouping part of the earnings of their prostitutes and thus accumulating the financial resources needed to repay their debt more quickly and change the nature of their relationships of dependence" (2010: 140).

28   This mutual influence is itself made even more complex by others, such as the cultural representations we have already mentioned that also outline a "good form" (Boltanski 1987) for pimping.

prison cells. But this in no way means it is inconsistent, or has no significant social power. Quite the opposite: it was the invocation of this figure that led to the 13 April 2016 act being conceived and adopted, and its consequences – for prostitutes above all – could not have been more concrete and tangible.

CHAPTER 7

Trafficking in Human Beings, from Urban Legend to Public Policy

The white slave trade, now requalified as human trafficking, constitutes the motif for one of the most widespread and widely studied urban legends.[1] One of its classic variants depicts a young girl, drugged while changing clothes in a changing room cubicle, and then delivered to a network of traffickers who put her to work as a prostitute in a foreign country. The key to its "success" is the story's fantastical structure, highly gendered and eroticized: a female character presented as vulnerable (due to her youth but also her isolation, her nudity and the effect of a drug) falls prey to malicious figures, implicitly seen as masculine, who are plotting to use her for non-consensual sexual practices (anticipated by her nudity in the changing room cubicle).

But human trafficking is not just an urban legend. It has also long been the subject of specific public policies. For instance, France ratified the UN Convention for the Suppression of the Traffic in Persons and of the Exploitation of the Prostitution of Others in 1960, introduced a new offence of human trafficking punishable with seven years in prison a € 150,000 fine in 2003 and set up an inter-ministerial mission in 2013 to protect female victims of violence and fight human trafficking (MIPROF). Experts at NGOs and international institutions have produced figures measuring both the scale of the problem and the profits it generates for its criminal organizers (Mathieu 2014a: 134–147; Chaumont 2012).

The coexistence of an urban legend and public policy is an enigma: how is it possible for considerable resources to be deployed against facts whose reality is entirely uncertain? Chaumont (2009) confronted this question by detailing how a group of experts from the League of Nations constructed a fictional trade in the 1930s on the basis of their own institutional interests and moralist certainties, even though they had more concrete, nuanced information about the logics of prostitute migrations.[2] He described what he referred to as the

---

1 An initial version of this text was published under the title in "La traite des êtres humains, de la légende urbaine à la politique publique" ("Trafficking in human beings, from urban legend to public policy") in *Émulations*, 2018; http://www.revue-emulations.net/enligne/Mathieu -traite-des-etres-humains.

2 This dimension is also central to the work of Corbin (1996), who confirms that prostitutes did indeed circulate between brothels in multiple countries but, noting their tendency to engage

"myth" – a term also used by Corbin (1996: 276) – of the white slave trade as having the specific feature, compared with legendary tales rooted in working-class communities, of having been created within the privileged classes and spread top-down, in an abuse of moral, intellectual and political authority.

However, resolving the enigma by attributing trafficking to myth may not be entirely satisfactory, because locating it between the alternatives of truth and falsehood overlooks the essential aspect of the *plausibility* of the trafficking motif, the guarantor of its social and political effectiveness. This chapter aims to subject the unilateralism of Chaumont's thesis to a critical examination: on one hand, it is unlikely that the fictional motif promulgated by the experts at the League of Nations arose from nothing, and, on the other, it would not have achieved so much success had it not been reinforced by a fund of beliefs about the risks to the virtue of imprudent young girls. In reality, rather than being opposites, the urban legend and the public policy seem to have been mutually reinforcing, confirming and consolidating one another.

1   Top-Down or Bottom-Up Trafficking?

Seen in its legendary dimension, the trafficking motif appears as a modern transposition of the fairy tale of Little Red Riding Hood (Doezema 2010): a heroine with the characteristics of fragility (femininity, youth, naivety, possibly beauty) undertakes a journey away from her home which, by isolating her socially (in the forest or the changing room cubicle), exposes her to a danger that takes the form of a male figure (the wolf or the pimp) with superior strength who wants to harm her physical integrity (eating her or subjugating her sexually).

Fine (1992) points out that the impersonal nature of modern urban life offers favorable conditions for a transposition of this motif to the anonymous locations of shopping centers.[3] The phenomenon is probably as old as urbanization, as suggested by the rumor that arose in Paris in the mid-eighteenth

---

deliberately in these migrations, refutes the claim that they were necessarily compelled or duped by evil pimps.

3   The version he quotes has several distinctive features: the victim is isolated from her friends and family in the toilets of a shopping centre rather than a changing room cubicle, and she is abducted by two women, one pretending to be her mother; but she is still drugged and destined for white slavery. Varela reports a different version specific to Argentina in the 2010s, in which young women intended for trafficking are taken prisoner in a white Transit-type van; she adds that the first versions, dating from the 1990s, took as their victims not young women but children, whose organs were harvested for sale (Varela 2015: 137, n. 48).

century that the forces of order were kidnapping children from their parents to deliver them to aristocrats, who would try to heal themselves from terrible diseases by bathing in their blood (Farge and Revel 1991). Here we can recognize the themes of vulnerability (the victims are defined by their youth) reinforced by isolation (the children are kidnapped while outside the surveillance of their parents), making possible their subjugation to individuals as powerful (aristocrats) as they are repugnant (their diseases testify to their physical and moral degeneracy) for a horrific physical fate (bleeding to death).

The analysis framework based on Chaumont hardly applies here. The story is based on a hierarchical structure that opposes degenerate, malignant, dominant characters against vulnerable, dominated ones. It is also difficult to imagine that circulating the tale could have been of use to those in power, as the rumors in Paris led to a revolt during which an officer was lynched. The same roots at the bottom of the social scale can be seen in what constitutes the most classic expression of the trafficking motif – since it was the object of a sociological study conducted in the heat of the action – which was the rumor emerging in spring 1969 about the changing room cubicles of clothes shops in Orléans run by Jews. The team put together by Edgar Morin just after the height of the rumor succeeded in reconstituting its stages, the paths by which it spread and its main fantastical elements.[4] Above all, it identified the primary "conductive medium" for the panic as young women and girls, who could not be immune to the threatening and erotic overtones of the motif, and who were lacking in the cognitive instruments that would enable them to resist fanciful rumors – whom Morin described as "politically under-developed areas" intensively consuming "mass culture" (1971: 96).[5]

The mass media doubtless offer one of the keys by which the opposition between legends distilled respectively at the top (Chaumont) or the bottom (Morin) of the social scale can be overcome. The study by Walkowitz (1992) of what was the first systematic crystallization of the schema of the white slave trade[6] – the series of sensationalist articles published by journalist W T Stead

---

4   As well as the features already identified (young female victims, isolation in the urban space, use of drugs, forced prostitution etc.), we see here the figure of the Jew as an incarnation of malevolence according to the classic antisemitic schema combining greed and secrecy.

5   The fact that the author of this book experienced an echo of the Orléans rumor in 2014 among high school pupils (who wanted to interview me for a collective project on prostitution) at one of the most select private schools in Lyon suggests that this analysis needs to be qualified or updated.

6   It was preceded a few years before by the "white slave trade affair", a scandal that grew from the discovery that young British girls, some aged under 21, were among the residents of a Brussels brothel "protected" by the Belgian police (Chaumont and Machiels 2009).

in the *Pall Mall Gazette* in 1885 – is particularly illuminating here. Stead's text refers explicitly to a fund of mythology – the ancient legend of the Minotaur – in his introduction to the narrative of an investigation in the back streets of London in which he discovered that "there is in full operation among us a system of which the violation of virgins is one of the ordinary incidents; (...) the arrangements for procuring, certifying, violating, repairing, and disposing of these ruined victims (...) are made with a simplicity and efficiency incredible to all" (Stead 1885). Walkowitz (1992) underlines the degree to which Stead's text succeeds in combining two antithetical registers, pornography on one hand and melodrama, very popular with nineteenth-century female readers, on the other, by emphasizing themes such as "the transgression of class boundaries in the male pursuit of the female object of desire, the association of sex and violence, and the presumption of aggressive male sexuality bearing down on a passive asexual female" (97). The text is also unusual in that it challenges not only the rich aristocrats willing to purchase young girls to submit them to their debauchery but also the unworthy proletarian mothers prepared to sell their children.

The narrative resources deployed by Stead were undeniably effective. A genuine moral panic,[7] the public uproar caused by his revelations led to a mass movement amplified by puritan moral entrepreneurs that culminated in legislative reform raising the age of sexual consent for girls from thirteen to sixteen, granted the police extensive powers to control brothels and suppress street prostitution and introduced severe penalties for obscene publications and homosexuality. The trial of Stead – who, to prove the facts he was denouncing, had himself undertaken to buy a girl from her mother – was not enough to dampen the conviction that the movements and leisure activities of working-class girls had to be closely controlled for their own protection. Walkowitz (1992) also emphasizes the degree to which Stead's account downplays the economic aspect of the facts that enraged him: more than the greed of their mothers or the perversity of rich aristocrats, it was endemic unemployment and poverty that led so many young English girls into prostitution. In this case, Chaumont's thesis (2009) appears to be confirmed: claims of uncertain veracity of girls being abducted were used to support the introduction of measures that restricted individual freedoms in the interests of both economic and moral conservatism. But it is highly likely that Stead's writing achieved such resonance largely because it strengthened or ratified a fund of diffuse,

---

7   Charles Krinsky (2013) defines moral panics as episodes during which the public feels concern, anxiety, fear or anger over a perceived threat to social order. For more on this concept, see also Cohen (1973) and Goode and Ben Yehuda (1994).

hazy beliefs – we vaguely know, because we have heard it somewhere, that girls are abducted and subjected to sexual abuse, and pronouncements legitimized by the ceremonial trappings of intellectual and moral authority provide confirmation.

2 The Uses and Institutionalizations of a Legendary Motif

Stead found a significant ally in the person of Josephine Butler, the leader of the movement to abolish the regulation of prostitution. The denunciation of the white slave trade gave English abolitionism new momentum just at the point when, having succeeded in having mandatory health checks on prostitutes repealed, it ran the risk of finding itself without a cause to defend (Walkowitz 1992; Mathieu 2014a).[8] The *International Abolitionist Federation,* founded and led by Butler, joined forces with several apostles of public decency to campaign against international travel by prostitutes. These prostitute migrations, motivated by both the poverty of the young working-class women and the demand for renewal in brothel personnel, were publicized by abolitionists and appropriated by the political authorities in several countries on the basis of the slavery narrative. From the turn of the twentieth century, a process of institutionalization of the white slave trade began, primarily in the form of international agreements. In 1901, the first of these formalized an arrangement between sixteen countries to fight the traffic in under-age girls and non-consenting adult women (by fraud, abuse, abuse of authority, violence, threats or any other form of coercion). This was to be achieved primarily through exchanges of intelligence between countries, monitoring at railway stations and ports, campaigns to warn girls and repatriation of victims.[9]

Other texts followed: in 1910, an International Convention for the Suppression of the White Slave Traffic provided for the penalization of procuring girls under the age of twenty, but also women over twenty in cases of coercion or deception, for the purpose of prostitution. In 1921 and then 1933, the League of

---

8   As we have already indicated, the theme of trafficking could not fail to resonate within a movement that arose directly from the campaign to abolish the slave trade, within the same British Protestant circles. The white slave trade was in fact constructed by the abolitionists through explicit homology with the trade in Africans reduced to slavery in America.

9   As early as 1903, the theme was the subject of a political and economic science thesis that was moved by "the recruitment of unfortunate, honest girls, promised splendid positions abroad but finding themselves obliged, on reaching their destination, to give themselves up to debauchery"; later, the author wondered at "the surprising excess of naivety" of the girls who let themselves be seduced by these promises (Appleton 1903: 10, 28).

Nations took up the fight against trafficking, establishing a permanent dedicated technical committee, the one studied by Chaumont (2009), and refining methods of fighting the scourge (trafficking was gradually expanded to include children of both sexes and adult women independently of consent, providing measures designed to control women undertaking to migrate alone). After the Second World War, the UN opened for ratification the Convention for the Suppression of the Traffic in Persons and of the Exploitation of the Prostitution of Others, its preamble characterizing trafficking as inseparable from prostitution. In 1958, two years before ratifying the convention, the French state established a policing mechanism specifically designed to combat trafficking, the Central Office for the Suppression of Human Trafficking (OCRTEH), which still works today to collect information and conduct national and international investigations into trafficking.

This institutional appropriation was supported by the French abolitionist movement, which saw the fight against trafficking as a central theme. Before the Second World War, it was associated with the denunciation of brothels (accused of using trafficking to renew their staff) and reproduced the narrative structure based on the abuse of the future victims' naivety: "The means by which these thugs succeed in capturing the prey on which they have set their sights vary widely. Sometimes it will be through soliciting, sometimes the promise of an illusory position, or a promise of engagement; sometimes even a wedding actually celebrated. If deception is not enough, they have no fear of resorting to violence or narcotics to overcome the resistance of their victims" (*Union temporaire contre la prostitution réglementée et la traite des femmes* (Temporary Union Against Regulated Prostitution and Human Trafficking) 1938: 13). The motif did not vanish once brothels were outlawed in 1946 – it was a recurring theme for one of the movement's central intellectuals, Odette Philippon, for example. The writings of this author, who presented herself as a "social investigator", are full of stories of naive girls abducted or seduced and then sold and forced into prostitution. In what was presented as a book for young people (and particularly girls), Philippon warns against locations that are dangerous for "young people too prone to independence": public dances, cinemas, existentialist cellars, hitch-hiking and … changing rooms, because "behind the curtains occur (…) obscenities" (Philippon 1958: 30).

Yet the reality of the phenomenon remained difficult to pin down. Corbin points out that the legal mechanisms put in place in the early twentieth century only rarely resulted in criminal proceedings, and even more rarely in convictions, which for him "demonstrates the prevalence of fantasy in this matter" (1996: 296). A study of the annual reports from the head of department in the Rhône police confirms that this was still the case in the late 1940s.

In accordance with the very broad, vague definition of trafficking set out in an interior ministry circular dated 4 May 1939 ("the term 'trafficking of women and children' should be considered to encompass (...) all aspects of commercial prostitution"), the reports list all the offences associated with prostitution (soliciting, running an illegal brothel, pimping etc.) and even beyond (corruption of a minor, indecent exposure, indecent assault on a minor of the same sex, obscene publications etc.), but do not include any offences of trafficking in the strict sense. The lack of abductions of girls to force them into prostitution was confirmed at national level by a report from the vice squad in 1956 declaring that trafficking investigations "have generally only succeeded in establishing either that the reported 'case' does not exist or that it involves a runaway voluntarily leaving home and has no connection with any pimping case," as reported by Mainsant (2012: 105). In the same year, however, the Popular Republican Movement (MRP) deputy Francine Lefebvre declared in the abolitionist press that no fewer than 100,000 French women had been abducted for the white slave trade.[10]

The theme of trafficking faded from the discourse and concerns of the abolitionist movement from the 1960s onwards, partly due to the relative delegitimization of the image of the naive girl debased by predatory male sexuality, to which the nascent feminist movement no doubt contributed.[11] It is true that *Esclavage*, the magazine of the *Équipes d'action contre la traite des femmes et des enfants* (Teams for Action Against the Trafficking of Women and Children) was still able in 1979 to warn "our girls" against hitch-hiking, public dances, flirting with strangers, hasty marriages and the jobs of dancer, stripper or nude model, portrayed as gateways to prostitution.[12] But the same association, noting the obsolescence of the trafficking theme, decided to rebrand in the early 1990s as *Équipes d'Action Contre le Proxénétisme* (Teams for Action against Procuring).

---

10   *Moissons nouvelles* no. 18, 1956 (the *Mouvement du Nid* magazine, *Moissons nouvelles* was full of melodramatic tales of poor girls duped into prostitution through their own credulity, having often been seduced and then abandoned with a child outside marriage).

11   The resonance of Morin's book (1971), explicitly attributing legendary status to abductions of girls coerced into prostitution, may also have helped to delegitimize the theme of trafficking. As we will see later, its contemporary revival makes naivety a characteristic specific to young foreign women.

12   *Esclavage* no. 25, 1979.

3   Renewal and Consecration

In retrospect, this choice must have appeared premature and unfortunate to
the *Équipes d'action,* because the late 1990s saw a spectacular rebirth of the
subject of trafficking. This was due to the combined action of several factors.
The first was that trafficking once again became topical in international institutions, consecrated by the so-called "Palermo" protocol to the UN Convention
Against Transnational Organized Crime, opened for signatures in 2000, which
defined human trafficking as "the recruitment, transportation, transfer, har-
boring or receipt of persons, by means of the threat or use of force or other
forms of coercion, of abduction, of fraud, of deception, of the abuse of power
or of a position of vulnerability or of the giving or receiving of payments or
benefits to achieve the consent of a person having control over another person,
for the purpose of exploitation" (including "the exploitation of the prostitution of others or other forms of sexual exploitation"). The adoption of this text
certainly reflected the international community's concern with regard to the
growth of organized crime, but also the new international policy challenge of
controlling migration.

    The new overlap between female migration and prostitution was the second
element favorable to the re-emergence of trafficking. Starting in the late 1990s,
this took the form of the visible presence of young foreign women (first from
Eastern Europe, then sub-Saharan Africa and, to a lesser extent, Asia) on the
pavements of major French cities. When the schema of trafficking was revived
to account for their revival, it was completely reversed: where previously it had
referred to the migration of young French women travelling abroad, it now
covered foreign women brought to France for the purpose of prostitution. The
trafficking victim, however, remained defined by her fundamental vulnerability, reflected in both her youth and her cultural otherness.

    Abolitionist associations seized on this new reality of prostitution to engage
in a remobilization that was given additional vitality thanks to support from
significant fractions of the feminist and alter-globalist movements and the
adaptation of the trafficking motif to the needs of the media. From the early
2000s, reports multiplied in the audiovisual and printed press about "Slave
girls from the East" (*Le Monde* 1 December 2000), the "New sexual slavery"
(*Le Nouvel observateur* 22 August 2002) and the "Networks of shame" (M6 18
March 2007). These frequently used the narratives of the abolitionists, who
were able to supply well-worn arguments and former prostitutes willing to
give statements. One example among many is the feature "Revelations on the
explosion of sex trafficking" in the *Nouvel observateur* of 12–18 November 2009,
whose main article is based exclusively on abolitionist positions. It argues that

"Europe is the primary destination for trafficking for sexual purposes (...); 80% of female prostitutes in Europe are foreign. Often undocumented, wanted by the immigration police, they are the ideal laborers for pimps of all kinds, exploited at will. (...) 'We stop one network here. Ten others set up elsewhere,' notes Malka Marcovich. (...) What should be done? 'Practice a true abolitionist policy', as many associations including the Mouvement du Nid demand? For Malka Marcovich, 'the only effective measure would be to target demand by criminalizing the client.'"

Under the title "The Moldovan network", the same feature also contains the story of Irina, presented as exemplifying the pathway taken by some 10,000 young Moldovan women, of whom "a large majority believe they are setting off to work as saleswomen, waitresses or dancers" and who find themselves, like her, "imprisoned in a Turkish brothel, working intensively like a ghost". This is followed by the experience of her compatriot Lena, "a tall blonde with bobbed hair", to whom a young man "played the Prince Charming, explaining that she deserved much better than Chişinău, her monotonous life and her poverty wages. Lena was completely convinced. She ended up on the streets of Moscow". The mystery of the "extreme naivety of certain girls" – already a surprise to Appleton in his 1903 thesis cited in a footnote – could be explained by psychological factors, and the article claimed that "85% of trafficking victims have suffered abuse within their families".[13]

The recurrence of these melodramatic tales in abolitionist publications indicates that the movement had clearly understood the virtues of storytelling as a tool for communication and raising awareness of its cause (Poletta 2006; Traïni 2009).[14] Each issue of the Mouvement du Nid's magazine contains a story, written in the first person, describing the descent into hell of a young woman in a vulnerable position who believed or wanted to believe that prostitution could provide a better future.[15] When the story involves a foreigner, deception and credulity are cited as the reasons for her accepting an offer of

---

13 Psychological othering is combined with cultural othering in the case of Nigerian prostitutes, whose migration is said to be preceded by a voodoo ceremony (juju) designed to subjugate them through the fear of magical punishment if they seek to escape their exploiters.

14 This storytelling is all the more effective, now and in the past, when it addresses an offer of engagement (support for abolitionism and its demands) relating to what Boltanski (2009) conceptualized as "poltics of pity".

15 The stories are those of people cared for by the Mouvement du Nid, but narrated by the association's journalists. We should also clarify that contemporary abolitionism has a selective relationship with its heritage: while Butler remains a revered figure, Stead has been expurgated from the movement's official history.

migration that rapidly turns into a nightmare. Raïssa, for example, an Albanian woman who met a "normal man" ("at least, that's what I thought") who convinced her "that in the West, [she] could have a better life and a good job", "did not understand" when her compatriot who welcomed her to Paris asked her to go with her to the prostitution area of Porte d'Auteuil.[16]

We have seen how intense lobbying enabled the French abolitionist movement to plant prostitution on the political agenda. Encountering politicians' concern about the migration issue, the movement's use of the trafficking theme proved effective in convincing them that predominantly penal measures should take priority in order to abolish prostitution. Not only did parliamentarians appropriate abolitionist arguments when drafting the law "to strengthen the fight against the prostitution system"; they also reproduced their forms, including storytelling based on the motif of the naive young woman deceived by false promises and transferred to France by a "network" of pimps. For example, the chapter on trafficking in the report by Danielle Bousquet and Guy Geoffroy contains accounts with a now-familiar narrative structure, such as this one:

> Arriving in France at the age of seventeen via a trafficking network whose true purpose she did not know, Baina was threatened with a knife, raped and forced into prostitution. She reports that her pimps had indoctrinated her so effectively that it was impossible for her to leave prostitution and escape. She was not even allowed to talk to the associations working on the ground, because that could put 'the evil eye' on the whole community.
>
> BOUSQUET and GEOFFROY 2011: 43–44

As we can see, the conviction that organized criminals abuse the weakness of naive young women to transfer them from their countries of origin and force them into prostitution provides support for public policies mobilizing the resources of several government services (police, justice system, social affairs and women's rights). And yet much sociological research – such as Davies (2009) and Montvalon (2018) – identifies divergences between this narrative structure and the actual migratory routes of foreign prostitutes in France. Other work, highlighting the scarcity of criminal convictions for human trafficking, emphasizes the institutional mechanisms that lead from the omnipresence

---

16   Claudine Legardinier, "Raïssa : Les clients ? Je ne veux plus jamais en parler. Plus jamais y penser" ("Raïssa: Clients? I never want to talk about them again. Or think about them"); http://www.prostitutionetsociete.fr/temoignages/raissa-les-clients-je-ne-veux-plus.

of trafficking victims in the discourse to their metamorphosis into offenders guilty of crossing borders illegally (Jakšić 2016).

The fact that such an observation ultimately appears to support Chaumont's thesis (2009) – that the trafficking argument legitimizes coercive policies with regard to migrants – still does not fully account for its effectiveness. This seems to lie less in the capacity of the mass media, abolitionist activists and demagogic politicians to manipulate credulous minds[17] than in the mutual reinforcement of urban legend and public policy. The two come together to produce what we could call, in line with Berger and Luckmann (1966), the "plausibility structure" of trafficking, with public policy building on the belief in the probability of abductions or deceptions of young women for the purposes of sexual subjugation, while this belief is ratified by the authority of action taken at governmental level. The fact that the fight against trafficking is enforced via police practices aiming to restrict the international mobility of women suspected from the outset to be victims of vile human traffickers, forcing these women to be exploited by people smugglers to cross borders illegally, helps to give it a new form of existence, that of the self-fulfilling prophecy.

---

17   Certainly, there is nothing to suggest that those invoking the motif of trafficking to support their abolitionist positions do so out of pure demagoguery and do not share the widespread belief in the reality of these cases of young women deceived or abducted into prostitution abroad – or, to put it another way, that credulity is a distinctive feature only of the culturally deprived sections of the population.

Conclusion

Towards an International Comparison of Perverse Effects

Prostitution is an occupation in the informal economy that enables women, men and transgender people to earn their means of subsistence by providing sexual services in exchange for remuneration. Practiced regularly, drawing on specific knowledge and skills and delivering an income stream that covers at least a person's basic needs, it can be compared with what is normally considered a trade – while being located some distance from the "normal" job market, partly because it does not confer eligibility for social protection. This informality does not mean the absence of a legal framework, or at least an indirect one: activities associated or correlated with the sale of sexual services (public expression, exploitation, organization, facilitation, encouragement etc.) are defined by standards and potentially punished, while resources are put in place, if not to eradicate prostitution, then at least to reduce its harmful consequences for those that practice it. It is a fact that this framework for prostitution is based on assumptions about the nature of both the activity and, fundamentally, the people engaged in it. These assumptions involve a particular type of performativity, since the public policies they inspire contribute to shaping the exercise of prostitution into specific forms, which are all practical adaptations to the framework they define.

These are the general conclusions of this book, which has shown the extent to which the exercise of the sex trade, social representations and public policies are interwoven and interdependent in France: a definition of prostitution as sexist violence has successfully taken hold in recent years and legitimized the introduction of primarily coercive measures that have increased the secrecy and insecurity of prostitutes, consequently appearing to legitimize the denunciation of its intrinsic violence and calls for even greater repression. This sustains a system of representations, norms and practices within which we can distinguish between winners – sworn opponents of prostitution claiming to be on "the side of good", local and national politicians presenting themselves as uncompromising in the face of crime and immigration, residents and businesses living in a "cleaned up" environment etc. – and losers – prostitutes facing greater insecurity, small- and large-scale pimps repressed, clients driven away, but also social workers straining to make contact with prostitutes scattered and driven further underground, and police officers who feel that catching people in the act of fellatio in cars is not a central part of their job.

This is the specifically French application of the book's conclusions, but in reality the assertions that open this final chapter are much more general in scope and apply to many countries. Yet we know that political options and methods of enforcement in this area vary widely[1], and most examinations of the subject begin with the unoriginal distinction between regulationism (which subjects prostitution to administrative control and favors specialist establishments), prohibitionism (which bans it) and abolitionism (which encourages its complete abandonment). And there is no shortage of works establishing scholarly typologies, placing the United States and China among the prohibitionists, the Netherlands and Greece among the regulationists and Italy and Sweden among the abolitionists, for example.

The weakness of these typologies is inherent in the attempt at classification itself: the categories it employs are caught in struggles for definitions, and their meanings, far from being stable, evolve with the shifting balances of power between partisans of one option or another. Abolitionism, for example, does not mean the same thing in Italy and Sweden. In the former country, it refers to a policy adopted in 1958 to abolish all regulation of prostitution while providing for the repression of soliciting, pimping and the purchase of sexual services from a minor aged under sixteen (Crowhurst 2012). Sweden, meanwhile, has adopted a project to abolish prostitution itself by punishing the client, an essential component of the prostitutional transaction – which is equivalent to prohibiting prostitution, because while prostitutes can offer their services, buying them is prohibited (Florin 2012; Östergreen 2017). The problem with categorization is thus clear: Swedish abolitionism resembles prohibitionism, but is far removed from that of China, for example, which punishes prostitutes. France has officially remained abolitionist, but has changed the target of this abolition from regulation, enshrined in law in 1960, to prostitution itself since 2016.

The same uncertainty of classification applies to the category of regulationism. Historically, the "French system" was spread in the wake of the Napoleonic conquests, but most of the countries that hoped that keeping registers of prostitutes, checking their health and confining them within specialist

---

1 For a recent summary of prostitution policies in Europe and beyond, see Wagenaar and Okland Jahnsen (2018). The work edited by Scoular and Sanders (2010) played a major role in my thinking about the questions examined here, as did my participation in the COST action "Comparing European Prostitution Policies: Understanding Scales and Cultures of Governance" led by Isabel Crowhurst between 2013 and 2018.

establishments would be enough to curb the disruption inherent in their activity have gradually given up this idea. This is the case in the Netherlands, where the regulation of prostitution was abolished in 1911 (Outshoorn 2004). The legislation introduced in 2000 – which abolitionist activists persist in stigmatizing as "regulationist" – has little in common with the former "French system", since it aims to normalize the exercise of prostitution, hoping that bringing prostitutes out of the darkness into the light will enable them to benefit from a series of protections against exploitation by others and give them access to better social integration. Unlike the historical regulationism, which imprisoned "renegades", prostitutes who operate outside this "professional" framework are not *inherently* exposed to sanctions.

But we should look more closely at this "inherently": prostitutes who work away from the windows and sex clubs (where working conditions are controlled) do so in a more informal, isolated way, and are among the most vulnerable members of the national prostitution space. They are thus witnesses to the inability of any efforts at recognizing and institutionalizing prostitution to grasp the subject in its entirety, and particularly to integrate its most fragile segments. These are currently composed mostly of undocumented migrants: while they are not subject to repression as prostitutes, they are as undesirable foreigners, and thus risk deportation.

All western countries (and beyond), regardless of their prostitution policies, are confronted with the migrant flows inherent in worsening global inequalities, wars and climate disasters. Stirred up by political competition that makes migrants the scapegoats for all economic and social problems, policies of closing borders and deporting undesirable foreigners inevitably come to be applied to prostitution. As the ostracization of undocumented migrants leads to their disaffiliation, and as poverty is highly gendered, it is hardly surprising that a considerable proportion and sometimes the majority of prostitutes are migrant women. More apparently paradoxical – though in reality predictable – is the tendency for the repression of both migration and prostitution to itself generate illegality: it is because borders are more difficult to cross, and because living in secrecy is precarious, that migrants have no alternative than to allow themselves to be exploited by people smuggling networks, suppliers of forged papers or accommodation, bosses of prostitution zones etc. An anecdotal example illustrates this mechanism, which is well known to sociologists of deviance: from 2003, the prostitutes of Lyon equipped themselves with vans to escape the penalties for soliciting; those without driving licenses paid young dropouts to move their vehicles, exposing them to arrest for facilitating the prostitution of others. In other words, by attacking soliciting, the law made it necessary to resort to a new kind of pimping.

The policies adopted to restrict or even block migrant prostitution vary from one country to another, but they all contribute to limiting the international travel of women if they could be suspected at first glance of carrying out this activity (on the basis of their country of origin or their age). From this point of view, the claimed humanity of measures to combat trafficking is not far removed from the patriarchal paternalism that prevented women from travelling alone in the 1930s in the name of fighting the same traffic (Chaumont 2009). While there are clearly nuances that could be identified between the different national systems for supporting trafficking victims, the emphasis they place on returning people to their countries of origin is a highly significant dimension of this transnational reflex.[2] The fact that Dutch policy distinguishes between free (officially recognized) and coerced (unacceptable) prostitution, and defines lack of a residence permit as a criterion for coercion, demonstrates all the ambiguity of this claimed humanity (Doezema 1998). We should also point out that these specific provisions have only a minor impact on the people concerned, and that the general measures for restricting illegal immigration play a much greater role (Chapkis 2003; Agustin 2006). As Jakšić (2016) showed in her study of the French situation, the image of the trafficking victim tends to fade away over the course of their contact with institutions, to be replaced by the image of the illegal border crossing offender, which she also is – which she *chiefly* is, in fact.

But the most important features specific to France are not to do with containing migrant prostitution. As we saw in the fourth chapter, the successively adopted measures have tended to make an activity that creates a variety of disturbances increasingly invisible. Whether law enforcement targets prostitutes (soliciting) or clients (criminalizing the purchase of sexual services), the nature of the offence is the same – a transaction between supply and demand for a sexual service identifiable by the police – and the consequence is also the same: shifting this transaction towards more discreet areas, or at least out of sight of the police.[3] Frequently mentioned throughout the book, the

---

2 French associations underline the extent to which obtaining a residence permit (always limited in duration and difficult to renew) is a stumbling block to the so-called "paths out of prostitution".

3 This was implicitly confirmed on 15 December 2017 by the former socialist deputy Catherine Coutelle, an advocate of criminalizing clients, at the "Prostitution and exit paths in Nouvelle-Aquitaine" conference, designed to provide an initial review of the 13 April 2016 act and organized by the *Ippo* association, which had invited me. Responding to a Bordeaux resident who complained about the disturbance caused by a group of prostitutes in his neighborhood, she said that the police were focused on more urgent tasks than penalizing clients, which was thus presented as an instrument for keeping prostitutes' activities at arm's length.

movement of prostitutes from city centers to the outskirts or country roads, the growth of online advertisements, the multiplication of butterflies on urban street furniture … are all testament to the effectiveness, *at least on this level*,[4] of policies aiming to eliminate prostitution.

International comparisons indicate that while all major cities tend to reduce the visibility of prostitution and the disturbances it causes, the measures they adopt – and those that prostitutes invent to adapt or get round them – vary widely, but the trend is to favor confining it to enclosed locations away from exterior eyes, however much those eyes may or may not know or care what goes on inside. These enclosed locations take various forms from one country to another: massage parlors in the UK, cabarets and champagne bars in Switzerland, sex clubs in Germany and the Netherlands, *puticlubs* in Spain etc. Generally offering alcohol, sometimes dancing and possibly relaxation facilities, these establishments vary also in how explicitly or euphemistically they accommodate the sex trade, limiting themselves in some cases to allowing contact to be made between the supply and demand for sexual services (which are then provided in nearby hotels or at the prostitute's home) or providing dedicated space within the premises (like the separate rooms in Swiss cabarets). Though the relationships between the managers of these establishments and the prostitutes are extremely diverse – particularly in terms of the independence and autonomy of the latter in their working practices[5] – and present highly contrasting economic statuses[6], they often have the advantage for local

---

4   Both social workers and specialist police officers are keen to emphasize the extent to which this forced discretion makes their work more difficult and harms those they are responsible for helping. Prostitutes working online are more difficult to reach for social workers, public health associations travel hundreds of kilometers to meet a target group who are now scattered across the countryside and police officers have lost access to the information that street prostitutes used to give them when regular contact generated mutual trust. This increase in the distance between prostitutes and these categories of "rescuers" makes the former more vulnerable and frustrates the work of the latter.

5   Some establishments, such as cabarets and hostess bars, let prostitutes work as they please, counting on their presence to attract clients whose alcohol consumption is their only source of revenue. While the payment for sexual services is paid directly to the "hostess", who keeps it all, her ability to make clients drink is a precondition for acceptance of her presence. Other establishments regulate prostitutes' practices by requiring them to be present regularly, pay a percentage of their earnings or a form of rent and undergo regular health checks, or even define the services they can offer (and particularly whether condoms are used). The degrees of exploitation and violence prostitutes experience are naturally correlated to their level of vulnerability (especially in terms of whether they are present in the country legally).

6   There is a wide gulf, for example, between the brothel prostitution studied by Absi (2013) in the mining areas of Bolivia and the Czech sex clubs described by Darley (2007), whether in terms of the socioeconomic circumstances of the clients, the conditions of comfort or the prostitutes' level of freedom with regard to the owners.

authorities of restricting the sex trade to defined zones, obscuring its shocking manifestations and channeling its clients. The primary purpose is always to make prostitution discreet, not by removing it completely from the urban landscape but by limiting it to defined areas, which can either be carefully avoided or visited "not by chance". The rural location of many Spanish *puticlubs*, like the windows of Belgian and Dutch red-light districts and the restricted authorization for soliciting in certain streets in Switzerland (Chimienti 2009) and Luxembourg (Mayer 2012) are illustrations of this.

Tolerating prostitution while restricting it to dedicated areas helps to give it a basic collective foundation. The employees of the same sex club or massage parlor, neighbors in the same prostitution street and prostitutes frequenting the same bar can forge bonds of mutual recognition which, though founded on competition, are also likely to create a form of solidarity based on shared experience. Concentrating activities in one place also makes police surveillance easier and guarantees a basic level of assistance in the event of aggression. This is not the case with apartment-based prostitution, which generally leaves the prostitute alone with a client she has only spoken to on the phone, with no means of "testing" how dangerous he may be in advance. Exposure to assault is a particularly acute issue in this case, along with social isolation. Fearing that their activity could be discovered by the neighbors, prostitutes working from home take care to reduce their contact with those around them as far as possible, which obviously has both social and psychological consequences.

The practical issue raised by this type of prostitution is the question of how supply and demand come into contact. The methods for posting advertisements inviting clients to make an appointment vary widely between countries. In England, highly suggestive postcards have accumulated in phone boxes, while Argentina has seen the spread of detachable adds (*papelitos*) on city walls, leading to diverging processes of explication and euphemizing of the nature of the services they offer (Daich 2015). The internet is now the most common means of identifying prostitutes working in private spaces, which again prompts new forms of dependence (on webmasters, specialist sites, "security guards" and tour organizers) or at least organization (taking and posting alluring photographs, renting apartments, managing calls, arranging security etc.). This working method, which as we have seen is growing strongly in France, appears to be characteristic of countries where the goal of eradicating prostitution is applied with the most determination. We have also seen that it is one of the arrangements that places prostitutes in the most vulnerable situations. Consequently, the sociological concept of *perverse effects* (Boudon

2017) could constitute the most accurate summary of how the "rescuers" currently dominant (at least in France) affect the condition of the prostitutes they intend, often sincerely but somewhat inadequately, to rescue.

Afterword

A Plea for the Ethnography of Prostitution

Raymond Roussel, the author of *Impressions of Africa*, set out in *How I Wrote Certain of My Books* the literary processes he had used to write his novels, which gave them the disconcerting dimension that made them famous.[1] In this methodological afterword, I would like to engage in a somewhat similar exercise by describing how I produced several of my analyses of prostitution. More specifically, I shall try to show that these analyses would not have been possible without the use of an ethnographic approach or, to put it another way, that ethnographic observation enabled me to access meaningful situations or social scenes that revealed important aspects of the prostitution world that would have remained unknown to me if, for example, I had contented myself with conducting interviews or handing out questionnaires. The first section of this chapter sets out a research journey that took several years, focusing on the different methods of investigation I was led to use, with ethnography coming to occupy a central role. The next two sections address the way in which long-term immersion in the prostitution world enabled me to develop two of my main areas of analysis: understanding this specific world as a social space (Chapter 1 of this book) and as a zone of vulnerability (Chapter 3).

1   An Ethnography of Prostitution

As I explained in the introduction, the first investigation on prostitution in which I was involved began in 1991 as part of a DEA dissertation,[2] which was itself part of a collective research project on the "new territories of prostitution in Lyon" commissioned by the *Amicale du Nid* in Lyon and awarded public funding under the fight against AIDS (Welzer-Lang, Barbosa and Mathieu 1994). The survey scheme centered on individual interviews, with active contributions from *Amicale du Nid* social workers. It was they who suggested to

---

1 This text was published for the first time under the title "Usages et pertinences de l'ethnographie pour la sociologie de la prostitution" ("Uses and relevance of ethnography for the sociology of prostitution") in Marylène Lieber, Janine Dahinden, Ellen Hertz (eds), *Cachez ce travail que je ne saurais voir*, Lausanne, Antipodes, 2010: 33–45.
2 The DEA (diploma of advanced studies, now called a research master's) was a French qualification taken in preparation for doctoral studies.

the prostitutes they were providing with social support, female and male, that they could meet our team of sociologists in an interview setting. While this approach enabled us to conduct around twenty interviews, it nevertheless presented several limitations. The first was that we had no knowledge or control over what might motivate a female or male prostitute to accept the principle of an interview, and we could only suppose that in some cases it might be to do with their interest in not harming the support relationship they had with the social worker by refusing. The second limitation lay in the fact that the form of a sociological interview is fairly close to the psychotherapeutic interviews through which the social workers carried out part of their support work. The consequence of this, which was all the more significant in that most prostitutes have only a vague idea of what a sociologist is and that some of the interviews took place at the association's premises, was that we collected accounts formulated to support a request for help that we were unable to fulfil. The third limitation was that we only had access to the people supported by the social workers, leaving aside a whole section of the prostitute population they did not know – possibly because prostitutes did not feel they needed their services.

My colleague Odette Barbosa and I also followed these social workers in their daytime or nocturnal rounds in the prostitution areas, during which they made contact with prostitutes who did not yet know about their organization, but also "caught up with" people they had known for a long time and who no longer required so much social support. As well as giving us a detailed geographical knowledge of the local supply of prostitutes, these rounds were a chance for us to be introduced by these people known and recognized by the prostitutes, and they also resulted in a few interviews. But above all they were the prelude to an initial ethnographic approach, as we continued these rounds in the evenings without the social workers. We stopped to exchange a few words with the people we had been introduced to. A basic "How's it going this evening?" followed by a "We won't keep you long" inevitably led the prostitutes to express their immediate concerns, which were significant in themselves and frequently involved desperate shortages of clients, the assaults and insults they had suffered and the recurring requests for unprotected sex. It was during these rounds that we were finally able to talk to prostitutes who had refused any contact with the social workers, and to our pleased surprise they agreed to be interviewed by us. This favorable reception may have been partly due to the fact that we were expected: the "grapevine" had certainly passed on the information, not only that two young sociologists were doing the rounds and wanted to talk to prostitutes, but also that we were not "dangerous", or at least suspected of links to the police or morally hostile to their activities.

A little later, the part of my thesis devoted to AIDS prevention associations working with prostitutes (Mathieu 2000; 2001) led me to adopt ethnography as my main method of collecting data. More specifically, observing the activities of these associations, which at the time was my central goal, enabled me to gather very rich information about the sociability and living conditions of the prostitutes who constituted their "clients". Between 1994 and 1999, repeated periods each lasting several weeks in the premises of the Lyon association *Cabiria*, where a reception desk was open every day, and in the association's camper van during its nocturnal rounds through the prostitution areas, constituted my main "observation post".[3] This was where I was able to supplement the knowledge of the prostitution world I had gained through my DEA interviews and observations. In fact, I quickly came to realize that this initial knowledge was at best insufficient and at worst very truncated, and clearly needed to be revised in the light of what I had learned through direct observation of interactions between prostitutes within the association. Consequently, I put away my tape recorder and began keeping a log book in which I recorded my observations from day to day.

These data undoubtedly benefited from being produced through regular, long-term immersion, because this enabled me to be seen as a part of the landscape of the association, with no need for reserve or mistrust. Anyone who might have had any suspicions about me, the "new guys" and "new girls", were quickly reassured by the fact that the "veterans" knew me and accepted me. I did not hide my status as a sociologist, but this, without being clearly defined, did not cause any anxiety. At best, I was considered to be part of the association staff, a little less streetwise and competent than the others, but nonetheless able to make coffee, hand out condoms and syringes and drive the camper van.

This long immersion in the associations' premises enabled me to informally collect the female and male prostitutes' statements about themselves, including their origins and social trajectories, their activity in the streets but also their lives beyond: their family and romantic lives, their leisure activities, their tastes (in music, reading, fashion etc.), their many problems of varying severity (housing, health, administration, difficulties with the justice system) etc. It quickly became clear to me that these accounts were much richer than anything I had collected during interviews, for reasons relating to the conditions under which each type of discourse is produced. When prostitutes talk among themselves (whether or not the sociologist is involved in the conversation),

---

3   The Marseille association *Autres regards*, which operates along similar lines, also hosted me for a three-month observation in 1998. The data collected in this way enabled me to qualify what my previous observations drew from the Lyon context alone.

their words are more spontaneous and less controlled than during an interview, which gives a kind of solemnity as well as an objectivity to the conversation, since it is recorded on tape and consists of answers to explicit questions.
The interview is also somewhat reminiscent of certain types of school assessment – which is all the more delicate in that most prostitutes do not have altogether positive memories of a school career that was often cut short. Above
all, the staging of the interview (withdrawing to a room "where we won't be
disturbed", switching on the tape recorder, alternating between questions and
answers etc.) underlines a social – and primarily cultural – hierarchy that can
inhibit and almost completely silence even subjects who are among the most
forthcoming in ordinary conversation.[4]

There is no reason to suppose that what is expressed in informal interactions
is any more "authentic" than what is said during an interview.[5] Any discussion
between several people obeys a situational logic that determines much of what
is said, and the analysis has to reconstruct this. In this case, for example, it was
essential to incorporate what the statements owed to the competition underlying the relationships between prostitutes, and especially the need to save face
(Goffman 1959) in a world where maintaining a good reputation, and staying
away from the most shameful stigmas, are constant priorities. Consequently,
whether they were gathered during interviews or informal conversations, the
subjects' statements provide raw material that cannot be exploited without
reconstituting the conditions under which they were produced. However, in
the case of the prostitutes, these statements are often denser in information
than those collected in interviews. Informal discussions with people I had previously interviewed taught me much more about them and their social trajectories than the interviews themselves, during which they were reluctant to
say much.

By observing discussions between prostitutes, which took the privileged
form of gossip (Elias and Scotson 1965), I also had access not only to individual
journeys but also to the world of prostitution itself, i.e. its drivers, modes and
norms of operation, and the specific principles by which the hierarchy was
ordered, which were thus revealed on a practical level. Many of the discussions were part of the debate about what is done or not done, the bad man-
ners of this or that competitor, their bad taste, their failures and shortcomings

---

4   For more on the symbolic power relationships framing interviews with members of domi-
    nated groups, see Mauger (1994).
5   Mauger usefully warns against "the illusion that there is a 'truth', an 'essence' of the subjects'
    practices, representations and opinions that has to be observed *in situ* (...) and without their
    knowledge" (1994: 129).

etc. – in short, a whole normative world that would never have been expressed in abstract or general terms, disconnected from the immediate context, but which was delivered to me directly through these debates and polemics. I was thus able to identify the shifting nature of the social relationships within this world, their normative structure, but also the complexity and ambivalence of these relationships, based simultaneously on the solidarity and camaraderie inherent in a destiny community and on aggravated competition and everyone-for-themselves.

This favored observatory was artificial in a way: would these interactions have been conceivable without the association that hosted them but also made them possible? No doubt some of them could have taken place elsewhere, in the streets or in bars, in a more diffuse – and thus more elusive – way, but some of them, such as conversations between prostitutes working a long way away from each other, would certainly not have been possible without the association's premises providing a meeting place. Yet the artificiality of these encounters does not imply any artificiality of the logics and principles of the prostitution world expressed in them; they merely offered a favorable context for the expression of these logics and principles, which already existed.

2   The Expression of Competition

Clearly, the data collection mechanisms I was able to use were not developed in advance, and were not designed to confirm or refute hypotheses that had also been defined in advance. It is more the case that they were put in place as both opportunities and constraints arose, and were adapted or adjusted as new data were incorporated. From this viewpoint, and although I only discovered this reference late, my survey approach was close to the "grounded theory" of Glazer and Strauss (1967), i.e. a survey approach that has no prior hypothesis for the fieldwork to validate or refute, but which conversely reorients and redefines itself as access to new data opens up new avenues of thought. The theoretical dimension is not a prerequisite in this case – we are not "testing" an already-formalized theory by applying it to a new situation on the ground. It is rather the product of analyzing the data, and the result of development that takes place during or even after their collection and analysis.

The conditions under which I came to see the world of prostitution in terms of a social space provide an illustration of this approach in which theory is based on field data. Again, it was observations of interactions rather than individual interviews that played a decisive role. In early 1992, a Lyon transvestite undertook to gather a number of his colleagues together to form a professional streetwalkers' coordination group (the *Coordination des péripatéticiennes professionnelles,* CDPP), which would be officially responsible for arguing for professional recognition on behalf of prostitutes. But observations of its meetings revealed that the CDPP was also pursuing other goals, of which the first was to define criteria for distinguishing between "real professionals" and others among the local prostitution population. The former should be recognized as having the right, or at least the legitimacy, to work wherever they wanted, while the latter were disqualified on the basis that they represented unfair competition and had to leave the areas near where the former worked. The primary targets for this distinction were young transvestites who, due to their exuberance and their flashy clothes, but also to accusations of undercutting the competition and not respecting the "rules of the trade", were suspected of luring away the clients of the more "traditional" prostitutes for themselves. Naturally, the offending individuals heard about the accusations made against them and came to defend their right to work where and how they liked at a particularly stormy CDPP meeting.

For a young sociologist brought up on Bourdieu's sociology, as I was at the time, these arguments, despite their confused nature, were strangely familiar. What was at stake in these debates about professionalism was a definition of the legitimate exercise of prostitution. But more than that, what my observations of the CDPP meetings showed me was the struggle to define this legitimate exercise – i.e. an aspect of what Pierre Bourdieu called a *field* (Bourdieu 2021). The similarity did not end there: the conflict gave rise to an opposition between different categories of prostitutes, each of which, in order to demonstrate its legitimacy in working where and how it liked, cited various characteristics that it contrasted with other characteristics attributed to rival categories, which it presented as invalidating. The women, for example, claimed "not to cause trouble", i.e. to be discreet and not to make the neighbors angry, while the transvestites were stigmatized as noisy, provocative and disorderly. Some women prided themselves on having known the "good old days" when decisions "were made man to man", which for them was a way of drawing value from their experience and acquiring by proxy a little legitimacy based on the strength that pimps used to have. The transvestites, meanwhile, put forward their youth and their attraction for clients, and boasted of high earnings. What was expressed in the invocation of these valuable qualities and the stigmatization of the others was an assertion of the different *positions* occupied in the world of street prostitutes, positions defined by control of various types of *capital* (another sociological concept from Bourdieu), such as power of seduction, earnings, seniority and experience or physical strength.

Field theory thus proved relevant in understanding the logic of a world that I proposed to call the *prostitution space*, which, like fields, appeared to be structured by competitive relationships – competition for economic earnings first of all, but this is not the only dimension. Other priorities were also involved, and particularly symbolic priorities in terms of prestige or, conversely, stigma. The conflicts and arguments sketched out the opposing figures of the professional prostitute – in control of her destiny, independent of a pimp, with her presence in the street legitimized by a specific project (earning enough to "get out" by buying a shop, for example), an expert in her "trade" who respects its rules – and her foil, the "occasional" prostitute who, conversely, submits to her situation – often considered to be dependent on a pimp or on drugs, she is thought of as engaging in prostitution as a last resort without knowing or being able to respect its rules. Each speaker took care in her self-presentation to resemble the former figure as closely as possible and distance herself from the latter, such as denying drug addiction or claiming to respect the "rules of the trade".

The remainder of the research confirmed to me the importance of these logics of competition and the meaning of the symbolic or material markers put forward in arguments – though I also came to understand that these markers do not necessarily correspond to the reality of prostitutes' practices. For example, my long-term presence allowed to observe that the "rules of the trade" exist above all as a discursive device, but that no-one or almost no-one respects them. Similarly, following the same population over time enabled me to understand the shifts from one position to another, and the different aspects of changes in status. Observing the transition from the status of a "rent boy" to that of a transvestite, for instance, enabled me to understand the economic rationales (transvestites have a wider client base and offer more expensive services), but also those specific to investment in the activity: becoming a transvestite signals a longer-term commitment or installation within the prostitution space, while rent boys are often only temporarily involved in prostitution. I was also able to observe both the transformations and the continuities within the competitive struggles. Once the transvestites had made room for themselves and been accepted by the women, the two formerly rival categories came together in the mid-1990s to try to exclude a new group of competitors, African prostitutes who had settled in the center of Lyon. They in their turn then had to achieve recognition and assert their right to establish a new position in the prostitution space.

3   Prostitution and Disaffiliation

Observing the CDPP meetings showed the extent to which exceptional situations (attempts at collective organization are fairly rare in the prostitution space; see Mathieu 2001; 2003) can draw attention to certain structural characteristics of the social world being studied and offer a frame of reference for more ordinary situations – such as, in this case, positive self-presentations based on physical appearance or high earnings, often accompanied by stigmatization of the ugliness or professional shortcomings of competitors. It is still essential, however, for the importance of the characteristic revealed by its first empirical identification to be confirmed by enough additional observations. One observation in isolation, especially under exceptional circumstances, adds little to an overall sociological understanding. If it is repeated, even in transposed forms (such as ordinary conversations), this indicates conversely that it highlights an important property of the group in question. In other words, as Passeron (1991) underlined, the robustness of a sociological assertion is tested by its degree of exemplification – i.e. its attestation by empirical phenomena, whose relevance is defined by the level of reiteration and the rigor of the observation protocols. In simple terms, a single observation in this case drew attention to an unknown dimension and prompted a series of facts that had previously been neglected or obscure to be seen in a new light.

The same process was repeated with regard to a second dimension for analyzing prostitution, the dimension that approaches it through Castel's concept (2003) of *disaffiliation*. In a society where work (and the associated protections, specifically against illness, old age and unemployment) bears the most responsibility for social integration, anyone who has a distended or detached relationship with it finds themselves in a situation of lower integration and greater vulnerability – precisely the situation described by disaffiliation. As we saw in the third chapter, the concept was proposed by Castel to push back against the idea of a clear distinction between integration and social marginality presupposed by the notion, common in France since the 1990s, of exclusion. Conversely, talking about processes of disaffiliation, leading from complete integration to "social non-existence", enables us to identify different zones of social vulnerability, marked by different degrees of precariousness and uncertainty about the future, affecting much larger segments of the population (people on benefits, employees on fixed-term or part-time contracts, interns, recipients of solidarity funds etc.) than the homeless, presented as the ideal exemplars of "exclusion".

Prostitution appeared to me as a specific form of disaffiliation on an occasion when I again observed a particularly significant situation.[6] Accompanying a group of transvestites outside a metro station where a young man with all the hallmarks of the homeless "excluded" was sitting on a blanket, a cup for a begging bowl in front of him, I heard one of my companions say to another: "Did you see? It's X. He's fallen a long way," to which the fatalistic reply was: "It could happen to any of us". I deduced that the young beggar was a former prostitute who had had to leave prostitution for one reason or another and fall back on another way of raising money in the informal economy. After this, I took a different approach to the words of prostitutes who boasted of having robbed a client or stolen something from a department store, or who, less favored by luck, complained of having to sleep on cardboard in the hall of a building after failing to earn enough to pay for a night at the hotel.

What is revealed in these interactions is that there is no clear break between the sex trade and other activities in the legal and informal economies, and that it is one of a set of other income-generating activities ("legal" work, theft, drug dealing, begging etc.) carried out either in parallel or instead.[7] Prostitution falls on the continuum between the two poles of social integration and total marginality, while consisting of situations that are themselves contrasting. Some prostitutes, with the resources and autonomy necessary to manage their earnings and their lives rationally, can preserve the façade of a "normal" existence and maintain a relatively comfortable lifestyle – while at the same time their exclusion from social protection and the illegitimacy of their activity makes them vulnerable to chance events. Others, more numerous, work on a hand-to-mouth basis and face serious difficulties with housing, either being accommodated by friends, living in hotels or, in the most serious cases, sleeping in the street.

The conversations I heard between prostitutes were often infused with these specifically social anxieties. How do you pay for a hotel room when clients are scarce? Where you can you find a hotel owner who is sufficiently indulgent but does not take advantage of the customer's illegitimacy to demand sexual favors

---

6   Though he makes occasional references to prostitution in his wide-ranging examination of the wage system, Castel does not include it as a contemporary figure of disaffiliation. In fact, he has been criticized for a particular lack of attention to the gender dimension, which we know to be a crucial factor in the phenomena of poverty.

7   This explains why the same people can sometimes be supported by associations specializing in different types of clients (homeless people, undocumented migrants, drug users, people re-entering the workplace etc.), and why any analysis needs to take into account the *plurality of statuses* of people who, while working as prostitutes, may also be drug addicts, illegal immigrants, ex-prisoners, transgenders etc.

or raise prices disproportionately? How can you arrange a stable home, if by chance an opportunity arises, when you have no pay slips? And if you do manage to arrange a home, how do you hide from your neighbors an activity that requires you to go out every night, heavily made up and in suggestive clothes, or even with an appearance that does not match the gender identity you live with during the day? These nervous exchanges revealed the fragility of status that marks the prostitute's condition and legitimizes its positioning as a zone of vulnerability.

More generally, this avenue of analysis provided an approach to prostitution in its relationships with the world of work, but not just through the alternatives of "a job like any other" or "slavery" to which it tends to be reduced by activist polemics. It made it possible to consider what it has in common with, but also what separates it from, recognized activities (Pryen 1999). It also enabled an understanding of the contemporary situation of female and male prostitutes within the context of historical analyses of prostitution in past centuries, and particularly those of Corbin (1996), Walkowitz (1980) and Scott (1990). These authors have shown the extent to which it was their exclusion from the employment market in the nineteenth century that drove young working-class women into prostitution, but also to which the economic independence they achieved by selling their services, challenging the gender relations that were based on women's material dependence on men, lay at the heart of the moral condemnation and social anxiety they aroused within the middle classes. Beyond the major transformations that sexual identities and the global economy have undergone since the nineteenth century, it appears that these issues specific to gender relations and the class structure remain at the center of the reality of prostitution: the vast majority of prostitutes are still women, and to a lesser extent men, from the poorest backgrounds. In other words, ethnographic observation must not forget that it is also the interplay of social structures (gender relations, social stratification, the globalization of economic exchange etc.) that is expressed and can be observed in face-to-face interactions.

Included as an afterword, this chapter aimed chiefly to set out the conditions under which the principal data this book is based on were collected. It is also an invitation to think more deeply about methods and sources in the study of prostitution. The question is not just about sociological technique, and is not just of interest to social science professionals. As we have seen over the preceding chapters, the public debates and political movements relating to prostitution draw on a scientific legitimacy and often use sociological data in their arguments. In particular, statistics are frequently invoked that claim to reveal high levels of sexual abuse suffered by prostitutes in childhood, exploitation by pimps, various psychological disorders, the presence of minors among prostitutes etc. – with no clarification of how these figures were produced or how representative were the samples of the population studied. Faced with the avalanches of figures – each more terrifying than the last[8] – that feed into abolitionist propaganda, a simple reminder of the conditions for producing scientific knowledge appears necessary to guard against both moral panics and political instrumentalization. And while there is no question of placing quantitative and qualitative methods in opposition to each other, it is legitimate to recall that one advantage the latter have over the former is that they can better capture a significant detail: the experience that the people involved have of their social condition and the meaning they give it.

---

8   For more on the abuse of unverifiable statistics in abolitionist rhetoric, See Chaumont (2012) and Mathieu (2012).

References

Absi, Pascale. 2013. "Femmes de maison. Les avatars boliviens du réglementarisme" ["Women from the House. Bolivian avatars of regulationism"], *Actes de la recherche en sciences sociales*, no. 198: 79–92.

Agustin, Laura. 2006. "The Disappearing of a Migration Category: Migrants Who Sell Sex", *Journal of Ethnic and Migration Studies*, 32 (1): 29–47.

Altink, Sietske, Van Liempt, Ils and Wijers, Marjan. 2017. "The Netherlands". In *Assessing Prostitution Policies in Europe*, edited by Okland Jahnsen, Synnove, and Wagenaar, Hendrik. 62–76. London & New York: Routledge.

Amaouche, Malika. 2010. "Les 'traditionnelles' du Bois de Vincennes, une ethnographie du travail sexuel" ["Traditional prostitutes in the Bois de Vincennes: an ethnography of sex work"]. In *Cachez ce travail que je ne saurais voir*, edited by Lieber, Marylène, Dahinden, Janine, and Hertz Ellen. 47–60. Lausanne: Antipodes.

Anderson, Leon, Snow, David. 1994. "L'industrie du plasma" ["The plasma industry"]. *Actes de la recherche en sciences sociales* 104: 25–33.

Andrijasevic, Rutvica. 2005. "La traite des femmes d'Europe de l'Est en Italie : analyse critique des représentations" ["Trafficking in women in Eastern Europe and Italy: Critical analysis of representations"]. *Revue européenne des migrations internationales* 21 (1): 155–175.

Appleton, Paul. 1903. *La Traite des blanches* ["The trafficking in women"]. Doctoral thesis in political and economic science defended before the law faculty in Lyon. Paris: Arthur Rousseau éditeur.

Aradau, Claudia. 2004. "The Perverse Politics of Four-Letter Words: Risk and Pity in the Securitisation of Human Trafficking". *Millennium. Journal of International Studies* 33 (2): 251–277.

Arnaud, Lionel. 2008. *Réinventer la ville. Artistes, minorités ethniques et militants au service des politiques de développement urbain* ["Reinventing the city. Artists, ethnic minorities and activists at the service of urban development policies"]. Rennes: PUR.

ATTAC. 2008. *Mondialisation de la prostitution, atteinte globale à la dignité humaine* ["Globalization of prostitution, a global harm to human dignity"], Paris: Mille-et-une-nuits.

Authier, Jean-Yves, Grafmeyer, Yves, Mallon, Isabelle, and Vogel, Marie. 2010. *Sociologie de Lyon* ["Sociology of Lyon"]. Paris: La Découverte.

Bajos, Nathalie, and Bozon, Michel (eds.). 2008. *Enquête sur la sexualité en France* ["Enquiry on sexuality in France"]. Paris: La Découverte.

Bajos, Nathalie, and Bozon, Michel. 2012. "Sexualité et appartenance sociale à l'âge adulte" ["Sexuality and social belonging in adulthood"]. *Raison présente* 183: 23–44.

Bajos, Nathalie, Pryen, Stéphanie, Warszawski, Josiane, and Serre, Anne. 1997. "Sexualité vénale et gestion du risque de transmission sexuelle du sida" ["Venal sexuality and managing the risk of sexual transmission of AIDS"]. *Sciences sociales et santé* 15 (3): 31–60.

Banaszak, Lee Ann. 2010 *The Women's Movement Inside and Outside the State*. Cambridge: Cambridge University Press.

Barry, Kathleen. 1986. "La prostitution est un crime" ["Prostitution is a crime"]. *Déviance et société* 10 (3): 299–303.

Becker, Howard S. 1963. *Outsiders*. Glencoe: Free Press.

Bereni, Laure. 2012. "Penser la transversalité des mobilisations féministes : l'espace de la cause des femmes" ["Thinking the transversality of feminist mobilizations: the space of the cause of women"]. In *Les Féministes de la deuxième vague,* edited by Bard, Christine. 27–41. Rennes: PUR.

Bereni, Laure, and Revillard, Anne. 2007. "Des quotas à la parité : 'féminisme d'État' et représentation politique (1974–2007)" ["From quotas to parity: 'state feminism' and political representation (1974–2007)"]. *Genèses* 67: 5–23.

Berger, Peter, and Luckmann, Thomas. 1966. *The Social Construction of Reality*. New York: Doubleday.

Berlière, Jean-Marc. 1992. *La Police des mœurs sous la IIIe République* ["Vice squads under the 3rd Republic"]. Paris: Seuil.

Berman, Jacqueline. 2010. "Biopolitical Management, Economic Calculation and 'Trafficked Women'". *International Migration* 48 (4):84–113.

Bernstein, Elizabeth. 2007. *Temporarily Yours. Intimacy, Authenticity, and the Commerce of Sex*. Chicago: Chicago University Press.

Bernstein, Elizabeth. 2010. "Militarized Humanitarianism Meets Carceral Feminism: The Politics of Sex, Rights, and Freedom in Contemporary Antitrafficking Campaigns". *Signs* 36 (1): 45–71.

Bernd, Belina, and Helms, Gesa. 2003. "Zero Tolerance for the Industrial Past and Other Threats: Policing and Urban Entrepreneurialism in Britain and Germany". *Urban Studies* 40 (9): 1845–1867.

Bigot, Sylvie. 2009. "La prostitution sur Internet : entre marchandisation de la sexualité et contractualisation de relations affectives" ["Prostitution on the Internet: between the commodification of sexuality and the contractualization of affective relationships"]. *Genre, sexualité et société* 2, online.

Boltanski, Luc. 1987. *The Making of a Class: Cadres in French Society*. Cambridge and Paris: Cambridge university Press and Éditions de la MSH.

Boltanski, Luc. 2009. *Distant Suffering. Morality, Media, and Politics*. Cambridge: Cambridge University press.

Boltanski, Luc. 2011. *On Critique. A Sociology of Emancipation*. Cambridge: Polity Press.

Boltanski, Luc. 2012. *Love and Justice as Competences*. Cambridge: Polity Press.

Boltanski, Luc, and Chiapello, Eve. 2017. *The New Spirit of Capitalism*. London: Verso.

Boltanski, Luc, and Thévenot, Laurent. 2006. *On Justification. Economies of Worth*. Princeton: Princeton University Press.

Bouamama Saïd, and Legardinier, Claudine. 2006. *Les Clients de la prostitution. L'enquête* ["Clients of prostitution. The enquiry"]. Paris: Presses de la Renaissance.

Bourdieu, Pierre. 1976. "Les modes de domination" ["The modes of domination"]. *Actes de la recherche en sciences sociales* 2–3: 122–132.

Bourdieu, Pierre. 1984. *Questions de sociologie* ["Questions of sociology"]. Paris: Minuit.

Bourdieu, Pierre. 1987. "The Force of Law". *Hastings Law Journal* 38 (5): 805–853.

Bourdieu, Pierre, and Wacquant, Loïc J. 1992. *An Invitation to Reflexive Sociology*. Chicago: University of Chicago Press.

Bourdieu, Pierre. 1992b. *Language and Symbolic Power*. Cambridge: Harvard University Press.

Bourdieu, Pierre. 2001. *Masculine Domination*. Cambridge: Polity Press.

Bourdieu, Pierre. 2021. *Microcosmes. Théorie des champs* ["Microcosms. Theory of fields"]. Paris: Raisons d'agir.

Bourdieu, Pierre, and Passeron, Jean-Claude. 1977. *Reproduction in Education, Society and Culture*. New York: Sage.

Boudon, Raymond. 2017. *The Unintended Consequences of Social Action*. New York: Palgrave MacMillan.

Bourgois, Philippe. 1995. *In Search of Respect*. Cambridge: Cambridge University Press.

Bousquet, Danièle, and Geoffroy, Guy. 2011. *Prostitution : l'exigence de responsabilité. En finir avec le mythe du "plus vieux métier du monde"* ["Prostitution: the demand for responsibility. Putting an end to the myth of the 'oldest profession in the world'"]. Paris: Assemblée nationale, Commission des lois [French National Assembly, Laws Commission], no. 3334.

Brasseur, Pierre. 2017. *L'invention de l'assistance sexuelle. Socio-histoire d'un problème public français* ["The invention of sexual assistance. Socio-history of a French public problem"]. Doctoral thesis in sociology: Université de Lille.

Brochier, Christophe. 2005. "Le travail des prostituées à Rio de Janeiro" ["The work of prostitutes in Rio de Janeiro"]. *Revue française de sociologie* 46 (1): 75–113.

Broqua, Christophe, and Deschamps, Catherine (eds.). 2014. *L'échange économico-sexuel* ["The economic-sexual exchange"]. Paris: Editions de l'EHESS.

Brunet, Jean-Baptiste. 1990. "Évolution de la législation française sur les maladies sexuellement transmissibles" ["Evolution of the French legislation on sexually transmitted diseases"]. In *Santé publique et maladies à transmission sexuelle*, edited by Job-Spira, Nathalie, Spencer, Brenda, Moatti, Jean-Paul, and Bouvet, Élisabeth, 113–121. Paris: John Libbey Eurotext.

Bucher, Rue, and Strauss, Anselm. 1961. "Professions in Process". *American Journal of Sociology* 66 (4): 325–334.

Callon, Michel, Lascoumes, Pierre, Barthe, Yannick. 2009. *Acting in an Uncertain World: an Essay on Technical Democracy*. Cambridge: MIT Press.

Cameron, Samuel. 2004. "Space, Risk and Opportunity: The Evolution of Paid Sex Markets". *Urban Studies* 41 (9): 1643–1657.

Cardi, Coline, and Pruvost, Geneviève (eds.). 2012. *Penser la violence des femmes* ["Thinking the violence by women"]. Paris: La Découverte.

Castel, Robert. 2003. *From Manual Workers to Wage Laborers: Transformation of the Social Question*. New Brunswick, N.J.: Transaction.

Catanzaro, Raimondo. 1991. "Cosche—Cosa nostra : la structure organisationnelle de la criminalité mafieuse en Sicile" ["Cosche—Cosa nostra: the organizational structure of mafia crime in Sicily"]. *Cultures et conflits* 3: 9–23.

Cefaï, Daniel. 1994. "Type, typicalité, typification" ["Type, typicality, typification"]. In "L'enquête sur les catégories". *Raisons pratiques*, edited by Fradin, Bernard, Quéré, Louis, and Widmer, Jean, 5: 105–128.

Chapkis, Wendy. 2003. "Trafficking, Migration and the Law. Protecting Innocents, Punishing Immigrants". *Gender & Society* 17 (6): 923–937.

Charpenel, Yves (ed.). 2012. *Rapport mondial sur l'exploitation sexuelle* ["World report on sexual exploitation"]. Paris: Economica.

Chaumont, Jean-Michel. 2009. *Le Mythe de la traite des blanches. Enquête sur la fabrication d'un fléau* ["The Myth of the White Slave Trade. Investigation into the making of a scourge"]. Paris: La Découverte.

Chaumont, Jean-Michel. 2012. "Le militant, l'idéologue et le chercheur" ["The activist, the ideologist and the researcher"]. *Le Débat* 172: 120–130.

Chaumont, Jean-Michel, and Machiels, Corinne (eds.). 2009. *Du sordide au mythe. L'affaire de la traite des blanches (Bruxelles, 1880)* ["From sordid to myth. The affair of the white slave trade (Brussels, 1880)"]. Louvain-la-Neuve: Presses universitaires de Louvain.

Chimienti, Milena. 2009. *Prostitution et migration. La dynamique de l'agir faible* ["Prostitution and migration. The dynamics of the weak agency"]. Zurich: Seismo.

Christine. 2010. "Ce très ordinaire désir de domination" ["This very ordinary desire for domination"]. *Alternative libertaire* 197: 11.

Cicourel, Aaron V. 1995. *The Social Organization of Juvenile Justice*. New York: Transaction Publishers.

Crowhurst, Isabel. 2012. "Approaches to the Regulation and Governance of Prostitution in Contemporary Italy". *Sexuality Research and Social Policy* 9 (3): 223–232.

Cohen, Stanley. 1973. *Folk Devils and Moral Panics*. St Albans: Paladin.

Coppel, Anne, Braggiotti, Lydia, de Vincenzi; Isabelle, Besson, Sylvie, Ancelle, Rosemary, Brunet, Jean-Baptiste. 1990. *Recherche-action prostitution et santé publique* ["Action research on prostitution and public health"]. Paris: Centre collaborateur OMS sur le SIDA/Institut de médecine et d'épidémiologie africaine et tropicale.

Coquart, Elizabeth, and Huet Philippe. 2000. *Livre noir de la prostitution* ["The Black book of prostitution"]. Paris: Albin Michel.

Corbin, Alain. 1996. *Women for Hire: Prostitution and Sexuality in France after 1850*. Cambridge: Harvard University Press.

Cusson, Maurice. 1992. "Déviance". In *Traité de sociologie*. 389–422. Paris: PUF.

Daich, Deborah. 2015. "Publicitando el sexo: papelitos, prostitución y políticas anti-trata en la Ciudad Autónoma de Buenos Aires" ["Publicizing sex: paper slips, prostitution and anti-trafficking policies in the Autonomous City of Buenos Aires"]. In *Género y violencia en el mercado del sexo*, edited by Daich, Deborah, and Sirimarco, Mariana. 151–172. Buenos Aires: Biblos.

Danet, Jean, and Guienne Véronique (eds.). 2006. *Action publique et prostitution* ["Public action and prostitution"]. Rennes: PUR.

Darley, Mathilde. 2006. "Le statut de la victime dans la lutte contre la traite des femmes" ["The status of the victim in the fight against trafficking in women"]. *Critique internationale* 30: 103–122.

Darley, Mathilde. 2007. "La prostitution en club dans les régions frontalières de la République tchèque" ["Club prostitution in the border regions of the Czech Republic"]. *Revue française de sociologie* 48(2): 273–306.

Darley, Mathilde (ed.). 2023. *Trafficking and Sex Work: Gender, Race and Public Order*. NY: Routledge.

Davies, John. 2009. *"My Name Is Not Natasha". How Albanian Women in France Use Trafficking to Overcome Social Exclusion (1998–2001)*. Amsterdam: Amsterdam University Press.

de Montvalon, Prune. 2018. "Les prostituées et leurs passeurs à l'épreuve des frontières. Négociations autour du passage vers le statut de victime" ["Prostitutes and their smugglers challenged by borders. Negotiations around the passage to victim status"]. Doctoral thesis in socio-anthropology: Université Sorbonne Paris-Cité.

Dericke, Dinah. 2001. *Les Politiques publiques et la prostitution. Rapport d'information sur l'activité de la Délégation aux droits des femmes et à l'égalité des chances entre les hommes et les femmes pour l'année 2000* ["Public policies and prostitution. Information report on the activities of the Delegation for women's rights and equal opportunities for men and women for the year 2000"]. Sénat no. 209.

Deschamps, Catherine. 2005. "Mobilisations parisiennes des prostitué(e)s" ["Parisian prostitutes' mobilizations"]. In *La prostitution à Paris*, edited by Handman, Marie-Elisabeth, and Mossuz-Lavau, Janine. 91–119. Paris: La Martinière.

Doezema, Jo. 1998. "Forced to Choose: Beyond the Voluntary v. Forced Prostitution Dichotomy". In *Global Sex Workers*, edited by Kamala Kempadoo and Jo Doezema. 34–50. New York: Routledge.

Doezema, Jo. 2010. *Sex Slaves and Discourse Masters. The Construction of Trafficking*. London: Zed Books.

De Vincenzi, Isabelle, Braggiotti, Lydia, El-Amri, Mounir, Ancelle-Park, Rosemary, and Brunet, Jean-Baptiste. 1992. "Infection par le VIH dans une population de prostituées à Paris" ["HIV infection in a population of prostitutes in Paris"]. *Bulletin épidémiologique hebdomadaire* 47: 223–224.

Durkheim, Émile. 1984. *The Division of Labour in Society*. New York: Palgrave Macmillan.

Ehrenreich, Barbara, and Hochschild, Arlie R. (eds.). 2003. *Global Women. Nannies, Maids and Sex Workers in the New Economy*. London: Granta Books.

Elias, Norbert. 1984. *What Is Sociology?* New York: Columbia University Press.

Elias, Norbert, and Scotson, John L. 1965. *The Established and the Outsiders*. New York: Sage.

Falquet, Jules, Hirara, Héléna, Kergoat, Danièle, Labari, Brahim, Le Feuvre, Nicky, and Sow, Fatou (eds.). 2010. *Le Sexe de la mondialisation. Genre, classe, race et nouvelle division du travail* ["The Sex of Globalization. Gender, Class, Race and the New Division of Labor"]. Paris: Presses de Sciences-Po.

Feschet, Jean. 1974. *A 16 ans au trottoir* ["At 16 years old on the sidewalk"]. Paris: Editions ouvrières.

Farge, Arlette, and Jacques Revel. 1991. *The Rules of Rebellion: Child Abductions in Paris in 1750*. Cambridge: Polity Press.

Favarel-Garrigues, Gilles, and Mathieu, Lilian. 2021. "Proxénètes en procès" ["Procurers on trail"]. *Cultures & Conflits* 122: 67–93.

Ferrand, Annie. 2010. "Pour l'abolition. Arrêter le mensonge" ["For abolition. Stopping the lies"]. *Alternative libertaire* 197: 15.

Fine, Gary A. 1992. *Manufacturing Tales*. Knoxville: University of Tennessee Press.

Flandrin, Jean-Louis. 1981. *Le sexe et l'Occident. Évolution des attitudes et des comportements* ["Sex and the West. Evolution of attitudes and behaviors"]. Paris: Seuil.

Florin, Ola. 2012. "A Particular Kind of Violence: Swedish Social Policy Puzzles of a Multipurpose Criminal Law". *Sexual Research and Social Policy* 9 (3): 269–278.

Garfinkel, Harold. 1956. "Conditions of Successful Degradation Ceremonies". *American Journal of Sociology* 61: 420–424.

Garfinkel, Harold. 1964. "Studies of the Routine Grounds of Everyday Activities". *Social Problems* 11 (3): 225–250.

Gemähling, Paul. 1933. *La Réglementation administrative de la prostitution jugée d'après les faits* ["Administrative Regulation of Prostitution Judged on the Facts"]. Bordeaux: Éditions du Relèvement social and Paris: Recueil Sirey.

Gilbert, Claude, and Henry, Emmanuel. 2012. "La définition des problèmes publics : entre publicité et discrétion" ["The definition of public problems: between publicity and discretion"]. *Revue française de sociologie* 53 (1): 35–59.

Glaser, Barney G. and Strauss, Anselm L. 1967. *The discovery of grounded theory: strategies for qualitative research*. Chicago: Aldine.

Goffman, Erving. 1952. "On Cooling the Mark Out. Some Aspects of Adaptation to Failure". *Psychiatry* 15: 451–463.

Goffman, Erving. 1959. *The Presentation of Self in Everyday Life*. New York: Doubleday.

Goffman, Erving. 1961. *Asylums. Essays on the Social Situations of Mental Patients and Other Inmates*. New York: Doubleday.

Goffman, Erving. 1963. *Stigma: Notes on the Management of Spoiled Identity*. Harmondsworth: Penguin.

Goffman, Erving. 1971. *Relations in Public*. New York: Basic Books.

Goffman Erving. 1974. *Frame Analysis. An Essay on the Organization of Experience*. London: Harper and Row.

Gonthier-Maurin, Brigitte. 2014. *Rapport d'information fait au nom de la Délégation au droit des femmes et à l'égalité des chances entre les hommes et les femmes sur la proposition de loi n° 207 (2013–2014), adoptée par l'Assemblée nationale, renforçant la lutte contre le système prostitutionnel* ["Information report on behalf of the Delegation for Women's Rights and Equal Opportunities for Men and Women on the bill n° 207 (2013–2014), adopted by the National Assembly, reinforcing the fight against the prostitutional system"]. Paris: Sénat no. 590.

Goode, Erich, and Ben-Yehuda Nachman. 1994. *Moral Panics. The Social Construction of Deviance*. Oxford: Blackwell.

Gould, Arthur. 2001. "The Criminalization of Buying Sex: the Politics of Prostitution in Sweden". *Journal of Social Policy* 30 (3): 437–456.

Grignon, Claude. 1991. "Racisme et racisme de classe, bis" ["Racism and class racism, bis"]. *Critiques sociales* 2: 3–12.

Guillaumin, Colette. 1978. "Pratique du pouvoir et idée de nature : 1. L'appropriation des femmes" ["Practice of power and idea of nature: 1. The appropriation of women"]. *Questions féministes* 2: 5–50.

Gusfield, Joseph. 1963. *Symbolic Crusade. Status Politics and the American Temperance Movement*. Chicago: Chicago University Press.

Gusfield Joseph. 1981. *The Culture of Public Problems*. Chicago: University of Chicago Press.

Haines, Herbert H. 2013. "Radical Flank Effect". In *The Wiley-Blackwell Encyclopedia of Social and Political Movements* edited by Snow, David A., Della Porta, Donatella, Klandermans, Bert, and McAdam, Doug. Malden and Oxford: Blackwell.

Haute autorité de santé. 2016. *État de santé des personnes en situation de prostitution et des travailleurs du sexe et identification des facteurs de vulnérabilité sanitaire* ["Health status of people in prostitution and sex workers and identification of health vulnerability factors"]. Paris: Ministère de la Santé.

Hirschman, Albert O. 1970. *Exit, Voice and Loyalty*. Cambridge: Harvard University Press.

Høigård, Cecilie, and Finstad, Liv. 1992. *Backstreets. Prostitution, Money and Love*. Cambridge: Polity Press.

Horning, Amber, and Striken, Julie. 2017. "Pimps, Bottoms, and the Nexus of Carin and Cash in a Harlem Sex Market". In *Third Party Sex Work and Pimps in the Age of Antitrafficking*, edited by Horning, Amber, and Marcus, Anthony. 71–88. Cham: Springer.

Houbre, Gabrielle (ed.). 2015. *Prostitutions. Des représentations aveuglantes* ["Prostitutions. Some blinding representations"]. Paris: Flammarion and Musée d'Orsay.

Hubbard, Philip. 1999. *Sex and the City. Geographies of Prostitution in the Urban West.* Aldershot: Ashgate.

Hubbard, Philip. 2004a. "Cleansing the Metropolis: Sex Work and the Politics of Zero Tolerance". *Urban Studies* 41 (9): 1687–1702.

Hubbard, Philip. 2004b. "Revenge and Injustice in the Neoliberal City: Uncovering the Masculinist Agendas". *Antipode* 36 (4): 665–686.

Hubbard, Philip, Matthews, Roger, and Scoular, Jane. 2008. "Regulating Sex Work in the EU: Prostitute Women and the New Spaces of Exclusion". *Gender, Place & Culture* 15 (2): 137–152.

Hughes, Everett. 1958. *Men and their Work*. Glencoe: Free Press.

Ingold, François-Rodolphe. 1993. *Le travail sexuel, la consommation des drogues et le HIV* ["Sex work, drug use and HIV"]. Paris: IREP.

Ingold, François-Rodolphe. 1994. *Les travailleurs sexuels et la consommation de crack* ["Sex workers and crack use"]. Paris: IREP.

Inspection générale des affaires sociales. 2019. *Évaluation de la loi du 13 avril 2016 visant à renforcer la lutte contre le système prostitutionnel et à accompagner les personnes prostituées* ["Evaluation of the law of April 13, 2016 aimed at reinforcing the fight against the prostitutional system and accompanying prostitutes"]. Paris: Report, Inspection générale des Affaires sociales [National Inspection of Social Affairs].

Jakšić, Milena. 2011. "Déconstruire pour dénoncer : la traite des êtres humains en débat" ["Deconstructing to denounce: human trafficking in debate"]. *Critique internationale*, 53: 169–182.

Jakšić, Milena. 2016. *La Traite des êtres humains en France* ["Human trafficking in France"]. Paris: Éditions du CNRS.

Jenness, Valerie. 1993. *Making It Work: The Prostitute's Rights Movement*. New York: Aldine de Gruyter.

Karady, Victor. 1994. "Bonnes à tout faire et prostituées" ["Maids and prostitutes"]. *Actes de la recherche en sciences sociales* 104: 3–17.

Katona, Noemi. 2017. "Loved or Seduced? Intimate Relationships Between Hungarian Sex Workers and Pimps in Berlin's Kurfürstenstrasse". In *Third Party Sex Work and Pimps in the Age of Anti-trafficking*, edited by Horning, Amber, and Marcus, Anthony. 49–69. Cham: Springer.

Kennedy, M. Alexis, Klein, Carolin, Bristowe, Jessica, T.K., Cooper, Barry S., and Yuille John C. 2007. "Routes of Recruitment. Pimps' Techniques and Other Circumstances That Lead to Prostitution". *Journal of Aggression, Maltreatment & Trauma* 15 (2): 1–19.

Krinsky, Charles. 2013. "Introduction: The Moral Panic Concept". *The Ashgate Research Companion to Moral Panics*. 1–14. Farnham: Ashgate.

Kulick, Don. 2003. "Sex in the New Europe. The Criminalization of Clients and Swedish Fear of Penetration". *Anthropological Theory* 3 (2): 199–218.

Latour, Bruno. 2009. *The Making of Law*. Cambridge: Polity Press.

Latour, Bruno. 2013. *An Inquiry into Modes of Existence. An Anthropology of the Moderns*. Cambridge: Harvard University Press.

Lavergne, Thomas, 2021. *Des hommes et des machines. Enquête sur la prostitution masculine entre hommes via internet* ["Men and machines. Investigation on male prostitution for men via the Internet"]. Doctoral thesis in sociology, Université Lumière-Lyon 2.

Lazaridis, Gabriella. 2001. "Trafficking and Prostitution. The Growing Exploitation of Women in Greece". *European Journal of Women's Studies* 8 (1): 67–102.

Lazerges, Christine, and Vidalies, Alain. 2001. *Rapport de la mission d'information commune sur les diverses formes de l'esclavage modern* ["Report of the joint information mission on the various forms of modern slavery"]. Paris: Assemblée nationale no. 3459.

Le Bail, Hélène, Giametta, Calogero, and Rassouw, Noémie. 2018. "Que pensent les travailleur.se.s du sexe de la loi prostitution ? Enquête sur l'impact de la loi du 13 avril 2016 contre le 'système prostitutionnel'" ["What do sex workers think of the prostitution law? Survey on the impact of the law of April 13, 2016 against the 'prostitutional system'"]. Paris: Report, Médecins du Monde.

Legardinier, Claudine. 1996. *La prostitution* ["Prostitution"]. Toulouse: Milan.

Legardinier, Claudine. 2000. "Prostitution". In *Dictionnaire critique du féminisme*, edited by Hirata, Helena, Laborie, Françoise, Le Doaré, Hélène and Senotier, Danièle. 61–166. Paris: PUF.

Legardinier, Claudine. 2011. "Prostitution : les 'clients' tremblent pour leurs petits privilèges" ["prostitution: 'clients' fear for their little privileges"] *Prostitution et société* ; http://www.prostitutionetsociete.fr/eclairage/point-de-vue/prostitution-les-clients-tremblent.

Legardinier, Claudine. 2012. "'Clients' : un droit de l'homme en question" ["'Clients': a human right in question"]. *Chronique féministe* 109: 49–53.

Lévy, Florence, Lieber, Marylène. 2009. "La sexualité comme ressource migratoire. Les Chinoises du Nord à Paris" ["Sexuality as a migratory resource. Northern Chinese women in Paris"]. *Revue française de sociologie* 50 (4): 719–746.

Ligue communiste révolutionnaire. 2006. "Prostitution : comment (s')en sortir" ["Prostitution: how to get out of it"]. Dossier Rouge, leaflet.

Louis, Marie-Victoire. 1991. "Prostitution et droit de la personne" ["Prostitution and human rights"]. *Cette violence dont nous ne voulons plus* 11–12: 3–10.

Louis, Marie-Victoire. 1992. "La conférence européenne sur le trafic des femmes: vers une reconnaissance légale du proxénétisme" ["The European conference on trafficking in women: towards a legal recognition of pimping"]. *Projets féministes* 1: 33–57.

Louis, Marie-Victoire. 1999. "Le corps humain mis sur le marché" ["The human body on the market"]. *Manières de voir* 44: 13–15.

Louis, Marie-Victoire. 2004. "Prostitution". in *Dictionnaire de sciences criminelles*, edited by Lopez, Gérard, Tzitzis, Stamasios. 759–761. Paris, Dalloz.

Mai, Nick. 2011. "Tampering with the Sex of 'Angels': Migrant Male Minors and Young Adults Selling Sex in the EU". *Journal of Ethnic and Migration Studies* 37 (8): 1237–1252.

Mai, Nick. 2012. "The Fractal Queerness of Non-Heteronormative Migrants Working in the UK Sex Industry". *Sexualities* 15 (5–6): 570–585.

Mainsant, Gwenaëlle. 2012. *L'État et les illégalismes sexuels. Ethnographie et sociohistoire du contrôle policier de la prostitution à Paris* ["The state and sexual illegalisms. Ethnography and sociohistory of police control of prostitution in Paris"]. Doctoral thesis in sociology: EHESS.

Mainsant, Gwenaëlle. 2021. *Sur le trottoir, l'État. La police face à la prostitution* ["The state on the sidewalk. Police and prostitution"]. Paris: Seuil.

Marcovich, Malka. 2002. *Le Système de la prostitution : une violence à l'encontre des femmes* ["The prostitution system. Violence against women"]. Paris: Commission nationale contre les violences envers les femmes.

Marcovich, Malka. 2006. "La traite des femmes dans le monde" ["World trafficking in women"]. In *Le Livre noir de la condition des femmes*, edited by Ockrent, Christine. 449–490. Paris: XO.

Marcus Antony, Horning Amber, Curtis, Ric, Sanson, Jo, and Thompson, Efram. 2014. "Conflict and Agency among Sex Workers and Pimps: A Closer Look at Domestic Minor Sex Trafficking". *The Annals of the American Academy of Political and Social Science* vol. 653: 225–246.

Mathieu, Lilian. 2000. *Prostitution et sida. Sociologie d'une épidémie et de sa prevention* ["Prostitution and AIDS. Sociology of an epidemic and of its prevention"]. Paris: L'Harmattan.

Mathieu, Lilian. 2001. *Mobilisations de prostituées* ["Mobilizations of prostitutes"]. Paris: Belin.

Mathieu, Lilian. 2002. "Rapport au politique, dimensions cognitives et perspectives pragmatiques dans l'analyse des mouvements sociaux" ["Relations to politics, cognitive dimensions and pragmatic perspectives in the analysis of social movements"]. *Revue française de science politique* 52 (1): 75–100.

Mathieu, Lilian. 2003. "The Emergence and Uncertain Outcomes of Prostitutes' Social Movements". *European Journal of Women's Studies* 10 (1): 29–50.

Mathieu, Lilian. 2012. "De l'objectivation à l'émotion. La mobilisation des chiffres dans le mouvement abolitionniste contemporain" ["From objectification to emotion. The mobilization of numbers in the contemporary abolitionist movement"]. *Mots. Les langages du politique* 100: 173–185.

Mathieu, Lilian. 2014a. *La Fin du tapin. Sociologie de la croisade pour l'abolition de la prostitution* ["The end of the trade. Sociology of the crusade for the abolition of prostitution"]. Paris: François Bourin.

Mathieu, Lilian. 2014b. "Prostitutes and Feminists in France in 1975 and 2002: the Impossible Renewal of an Alliance". *Travail, genre et société;* https://www.cairn-int .info/journal-travail-genre-et-societes-2003-2-page-31.htm.

Mathieu, Lilian. 2016. "Le mouvement abolitionniste français dans l'après-guerre. Recompositions et reconversions de la croisade contre la prostitution réglementée" ["The French abolitionist movement in the post-war period. Recompositions and reconversions of the crusade against regulated prostitution"]. *Déviance et société* 40 (1): 79–100.

Mathieu, Lilian. 2022. "Croisade morale et politique de statut. Quelques hypothèses à propos du mouvement abolitionniste" ["Moral crusade and status politics. Some assumptions about the abolitionist movement"]. In *Croisades privées et problèmes publics. L'héritage sociologique de Joseph Gusfield*, edited by Bernardin, Stève. 35–48. Rennes: PUR.

Mauger, Gérard. 1994. "Enquêter en milieu populaire" ["Investigating in popular milieus"]. *Genèses* 6:125–143.

Mauger, Gérard. 2006. *Les bandes, le milieu et la bohème Populaire* ["Gangs, underworlds, and popular bohemia"]. Paris: Belin.

Mauss, Marcel. 1973. "Techniques of the Body". *Economy and Society* 2: 70–88.

Mayer, Sibylla. 2012. *Lieux de prostitution : une analyse sociologique de la prostitution de rue à Luxembourg* ["Places of prostitution: a sociological analysis of street prostitution in Luxembourg"]. Doctoral thesis in sociology: Université Paris 10 and Université du Luxembourg.

Merleau-Ponty, Maurice. 2013. *Phenomenology of Perception*. London: Routledge.

Meunier, Micelle. 2014. *Rapport fait au nom de la commission spéciale sur la proposition de loi, adoptée par l'Assemblée nationale, renforçant la lutte contre le système prostitutionnel* ["Report made on behalf of the special committee on the law proposal adopted by the National Assembly to strengthen the fight against the prostitutional system"]. Paris: Sénat, no. 697.

Mignard, Annie. 1976. "Propos élémentaires sur la prostitution" ["Elementary remarks on prostitution"]. *Les Temps modernes* 356: 1526–1547.

Montreynaud, Florence. 1993. *Amours à vendre. Les dessous de la prostitution* ["Loves for sale. The underside of prostitution"]. Grenoble: Glénat.

Montreynaud, Florence. 1999. "La prostitution, un droit de l'homme ?" ["Prostitution, a human right?"]. *Manière de voir* 44: 19–21.

Montreynaud, Florence. 2002. "Table ronde. Prostitution et violence" ["Roundtable. Prostitution and violence"]. In *Collectif, De nouveaux défis pour le féminisme,* actes du Forum du Collectif national pour les droits des femmes. 195–198. Pantin: Le Temps des cerises.

Morin, Edgar. 1971. *Rumour in Orleans.* London: Blond.

Mossuz-Lavau, Janine. 2015. *La Prostitution.* Paris: Dalloz.

Mossuz-Lavau Janine, and Teixeira Maria. 2005. "Le vécu des femmes prostituées" ["The experience of women prostitutes"]. In *La prostitution à Paris,* edited by Handman, Marie-Elisabeth, and Mossuz-Lavau, Janine. 155–197. Paris: La Martinière.

Moujoud, Nasima. 2005. "Prostitution et migration de Maghrébines" ["Prostitution and migration of Maghrebi women"]. In *La prostitution à Paris,* edited by Handman, Marie-Elisabeth, and Mossuz-Lavau, Janine. 199–233. Paris: La Martinière.

Muel-Dreyfus, Francine. 1983. *Le Métier d'éducateur* ["The profession of educator"]. Paris: Minuit.

O'Connell Davidson, Julia. 1995. "The Anatomy of 'Free Choice' Prostitution". *Gender Work Organization* 2 (1):1–10.

Okland Jahnsen, Synnove, and Wagenaar, Hendrik (eds.). 2018 *Assessing Prostitution Policies in Europe.* London & New York: Routledge.

Olivier, Maud. 2013. *Rapport fait au nom de la Délégation aux droits des femmes et à l'égalité des chances entre les hommes et les femmes sur le renforcement de la lutte contre le système prostitutionnel* ["Report made on behalf of the Delegation for Women's Rights and Equal Opportunities between Men and Women on strengthening the fight against the prostitutional system"]. Paris: Assemblée nationale, no. 1360.

Olson, Mancur. 1965. *The Logic of Collective Action.* Cambridge: Harvard University Press.

Oso Casas, Laura. 2006. "Prostitution et immigration des femmes latino-américaines en Espagne" ["Prostitution and immigration of Latin American women in Spain"]. *Cahiers du genre* 40: 91–113.

Östergreen, Petra. 2017. "Sweden". In *Assessing Prostitution Policies in Europe,* edited by Okland Jahnsen, Synnove, and Wagenaar, Hendrik (eds.). 169–184. London & New York: Routledge.

Outshoorn, Joyce. 2004. "Pragmatism in the Polder: Changing Prostitution Policy in the Netherlands". *Journal of Contemporary European Studies* 12 (2): 165–176.

Pajinik, Mojca, Kambouri, Nelli, Renault, Matthieu, and Sori, Iztok. 2016. "Digitalising Sex Commerce and Sex Work: a Comparative Analysis of French, Greek and Slovenian Websites". *Gender, Place and Culture* 23 (3): 345–364.

Parent-Duchâtelet, Alexandre. 1981 . *La Prostitution à Paris au XIXe siècle* ["Prostitution in Paris in the 19th century"]. Paris: Seuil.

Passeron, Jean-Claude. 1991. *Le raisonnement sociologique* ["Sociological reasoning"].
     Paris: Nathan.

Pharo, Patrick. 2013. *Ethica erotica. Mariage et prostitution* ["Ethica erotica. Marriage
     and prostitution"]. Paris: Presses de Sciences Po.

Pheterson, Gail (ed.). 1989. *A Vindication for the Rights of Prostitutes*. Seattle: The
     Seal Press.

Philippon, Odette. 1958. *Un grave danger pour la jeunesse du monde : la traite des êtres
     humains* ["A serious danger for the world's youth: human trafficking"]. Paris: Tréqui.

Plumauzille, Clyde. 2016. *Prostitution et révolution. Les femmes publiques dans la cité
     républicaine (1789–1804)* ["Prostitution and revolution. Public women in the repub-
     lican city (1789–1804)"]. Ceyzérieu: Champ Vallon.

Pollak Michae. 1988. *Les homosexuels et le sida* ["Gay men and AIDS"]. Paris: Métailié.

Polletta, Francesca. 2006 *It Was Like a Fever. Storytelling in Protest and Politics*: Chicago,
     University of Chicago Press.

Pourette, Dolorès. 2005. "La prostitution masculine et la prostitution transgenre"
     ["Male prostitution and transgender prostitution"]. In *La prostitution à Paris*,
     edited by Handman, Marie-Elizabeth, and Mossuz-Lavau, Janine. 263–291. Paris, La
     Martinière.

Poulin, Richard. 2003. "Prostitution, crime organisé et marchandisation" ["Prostitution,
     organized crime and commodification"]. *Revue Tiers Monde* XLIV (176): 735–770.

Poulin, Richard. 2005. *La Mondialisation des industries du sexe* ["The Globalization of
     the Sex Industry"]. Paris: Imago.

Prieur, Annick. 1998. "Little boys in mother's wardrobe". *Actes de la recherche en sci-
     ences sociales* 125: 15–29.

Pryen, Stéphanie. 1999. *Stigmate et métier. Une approche sociologique de la prostitution
     de rue*. Rennes: PUR.

Ragaru, Nadège. 2007. "Du bon usage de la traite des êtres humains. Controverses
     autour d'un problème social et d'une qualification juridique" ["On the proper use
     of human trafficking. Controversies around a social problem and a legal qualifica-
     tion"]. *Genèses* 66: 69–89.

Redoutey, Emmanuel. 2005. "Trottoirs et territoires, les lieux de prostitution à Paris"
     ["Sidewalks and territories, places of prostitution in Paris"]. In *La prostitution à
     Paris*, edited by Handman, Marie-Elizabeth, and Mossuz-Lavau, Janine. 39–90.
     Paris: La Martinière.

Regard, Frédéric (ed). 2013. *Féminisme et prostitution dans l'Angleterre du XIXᵉ siè-
     cle : la croisade de Josephine Butler* ["Feminism and Prostitution in 19th Century
     England: Josephine Butler's Crusade"]. Lyon: ENS éditions.

Rénovation. Organe trimestriel du Cartel d'action morale et sociale, 1950. 11.

Rossiaud, Jacques. 1996. *Medieval Prostitution*. New York: Barnes & Noble.

Rozier, Janine. 2002. *Rapport d'information fait au nom de la Délégation au droit des femmes et à l'égalité des chances entre les hommes et les femmes sur le projet de loi n° 30 (2002–2003) pour la sécurité intérieure* ["Information report on behalf of the Delegation for Women's Rights and Equal Opportunities for Men and Women on the draft law n° 30 (2002–2003) for internal security"]. Paris: Sénat no. 34.

Rubio, Vincent. 2013. "Prostitution masculine sur internet. Le choix du client" ["Male prostitution on the internet. The choice of the client"]. *Ethnologie française* XLIII (3): 443–450.

Sacks, Harvey. 1972. "Notes on Police Assessment of Moral Character". In *Studies in Social Interaction*, edited by Sudnow, David. 280–293. New York: Free Press.

Safar, Pierre. 1973. "Psychologie des acteurs" ["Psychology of the actors"]. *Chronique sociale de France* 6: 22–26.

Sanselme, Franck. 2004. "Des riverains à l'épreuve de la prostitution" ["Residents facing prostitution"]. *Annales de la recherche urbaine* 95: 111–117.

Savoie-Gargiso, Isa and Morselli, Carlo. 2013. "Homme à femmes: le proxénète et sa place parmi les prostituées" ["Women's man: the pimp and his place among the prostitutes"]. *Criminologie* 46 (1): 243–268.

Silva Duarte, Marina. 2018. *Splendeurs et misères des travesties brésiliennes. Histoires croisées entre le Brésil et Paris (1960–2016)* ["Splendors and miseries of Brazilian transvestites. Crossed stories between Brazil and Paris (1960–2016)"]. Doctoral thesis in history: Université Sorbonne Paris-Cité and Université estatal paulista Julio de Mesquita Filhoune.

Scott, James C. 1990. *Domination and the Arts of Resistance: Hidden Transcripts*. New Haven: Yale University Press.

Scott Joan W. 1990. "L'ouvrière, mot impie, sordide" ["'The working woman, unholy word, sordid'"]. *Actes de la recherche en sciences sociales* 83: 2–15.

Scoular, Jane. 2010. "What's Law Got To Do With It? How and Why Law Matters in the Regulation of Sex Work". In *Regulating Sex/Work: From Crime Control to Neoliberalism?*, edited by Scoular, Jane, and Sanders, Teela. 2–39. Oxford: Wiley-Blackwell.

Scull, Andrew T. 1988. "Deviance and Social Control". In *Handbook of Sociology*, edited by Smelser, N.J. 667–693. Thousand Oaks: Sage.

Serre, Anne, Schutz-Samson, Martine, Cabral, Camille, Martin, Franck, Hardy, Raphaëlle, de Aquino, Olimpio, Vinsonneau, Paul, Arnaudies, Michèle, Fierro, François, Mathieu, Lilian, Pryen, Stéphanie, Welzer-Lang, Isabelle, and de Vincenzi, Isabelle. 1996. "Conditions de vie des personnes prostituées : conséquences sur la prévention de l'infection à VIH" ["Living conditions of sex workers: implications for HIV prevention"]. *Revue d'épidémiologie et de santé publique* 44: 328–336.

Signs. Journal of Women in Culture and Society. 1984. "Forum: The Feminist Sexuality Debate". 10 (1): 102–135.

Simoni, Vanessa. 2010. "Territoires et enjeux de pouvoir de la traite à des fins d'exploitation sexuelle : le cas de Paris" ["Territories and power issues in trafficking for sexual exploitation: the case of Paris"]. *Hérodote* 136: 134–149.

Solana Ruiz, José Luis and López Riopedre, José. 2012. *Trabajando en la prostitución: doce relatos de vida* ["Working in prostitution: twelve life stories"]. Granada: Comares.

Spector, Malcolm, and Kitsuse, John. 1977. *Constructing Social Problems*. New Brunswick, N.J.: Transaction Publishers.

Stead William T. 1885. "The Maiden Tribute to Modern Babylon". *Pall Mall Gazette*; https://attackingthedevil.co.uk/pmg/tribute/mt1.php.

Sudnow, David. 1965. "Normal Crimes: Sociological Features of the Penal Code in a Public Defender Office". *Social Problems* 12 (3): 255–276.

Sykes, Gresham M., and Matza, David. 1957. "Techniques of Neutralization. A Theory of Delinquency". *American Sociological Review* 22 (6): 664–670.

Ticktin, Miriam. 2008. "Sexual Violence as the Language of Border Control: Where French Feminist and Anti-Immigrant Rhetoric Meet". *Signs* 33 (4): 863–889.

Traïni, Christophe (ed.). 2009. *Émotions … Mobilisation !* ["Emotions … Mobilization!"]. Paris: Presses de Sciences-po.

Travers, Max. 2001. "Ethnométhodologie, analyse de conversation et droit" ["Ethnomethodology, conversation analysis and law"]. *Droit et société* 48: 349–369.

Trinquart, Judith. 2002. *La Décorporalisation dans la pratique prostitutionnelle : un obstacle majeur à l'accès aux soins* ["Debodification in prostitution: a major obstacle to access to care"], doctoral thesis in medicine.

Union française pour le relèvement de la moralité publique. 1936a. *Une Institution qui déshonore notre pays : la réglementation officielle de la prostitution* ["An institution that dishonors our country: the official regulation of prostitution"]. Paris: Union française pour le relèvement de la moralité publique.

Union française pour le relèvement de la moralité publique. 1936b. *Bulletin annuel de l'Union temporaire contre la prostitution réglementée et la traite des êtres humains 6.*

Union temporaire contre la prostitution réglementée et la traite des femmes. 1938. *Les Scandales de la prostitution réglementée* ["The Scandals of Regulated Prostitution"]. Union temporaire contre la prostitution réglementée et la traite des femmes.

Vance, Carole S (ed.). 1984. *Pleasure and Danger. Exploring Female Sexuality*. Boston: Routledge & Kegan Paul.

Van San, Marion, and Bovenkerk, Franck. 2013. "Secret Seducers. True Tales of Pimps in the Red Light District of Amsterdam". *Crime, Law and Social Change* 60 (1): 67–80.

Varela, Cecilia. 2015. "La campaña antitrata en la Argentina y la agenda supranacional" ["Argentina's anti-trafficking campaign and the supranational agenda"]. In *Género y violencia en el mercado del sexo*, edited by Daich, Deborah, and Sirimarco Mariana. 109–149. Buenos Aires: Biblos.

Vernier, Johanne. 2005. "La Loi sur la sécurité intérieure : punir les victimes du prox-énétisme pour mieux les protéger ?" ["The Internal Security Act: punishing the victims of pimping to better protect them?"›]. In *La Prostitution à Paris*, edited by Handman, Marie-Élisabeth, and Mossuz-Lavau Janine. 121–152. Paris: La Martinière.

Wacquant, Loïc. 1999. *Les prisons de la misère* ["The prisons of misery"]. Paris: Raisons d'agir.

Wacquant, Loïc. 2004. *Punir les pauvres. Le nouveau gouvernement de l'insécurité sociale* ["Punishing the poor. The new government of social insecurity"]. Marseille: Agone.

Walkowitz, Judith. 1980. *Prostitution and Victorian Society*. Cambridge: Cambridge University Press.

Walkowitz, Judith. 1992. *City of Dreadful Delight*. London: Virago.

Welzer-Lang, Daniel, Barbosa, Odette, and Mathieu, Lilian. 1994. *Prostitution : les uns, les unes et les autres* ["Prostitution: the female ones, the male ones, and the others"]. Paris: Métailié.

Weitzer, Ronald. 1991. "Prostitutes' Rights in the United States: The Failure of a Movement". *Sociological Quarterly* 32 (1): 23–41.

Weitzer, Ronald. 2007. "The Social Construction of Sex Trafficking: Ideology and Institutionalization of a Moral Crusade". *Politics & Society* 35 (3): 447–475.

Williamson, Kathleen S., and Marcus, Anthony. 2017. "Black Pimps Matter: Racially Selective Identification and Prosecition of Sex Trafficking in the United States". In *Third Party Sex Work and Pimps in the Age of Anti-trafficking*, edited by Horning, Amber, and Marcus, Anthony. 177–196. Cham: Springer.

Zimmermann, Marie-Jo. 2002. *Rapport d'information fait au nom de la Délégation au droit des femmes et à l'égalité des chances entre les hommes et les femmes sur le projet de loi adopté par le Sénat après déclaration d'urgence (n° 381) pour la sécurité intérieure* ["Information report on behalf of the Delegation for Women's Rights and Equal Opportunities for Men and Women on the bill adopted by the Senate after declaration of urgency (n° 381) for internal security"]. Paris: Assemblée nationale, no. 459.

Index